EARLY METHODIST LIFE
AND SPIRITUALITY

EARLY METHODIST LIFE AND SPIRITUALITY

A READER

LESTER RUTH

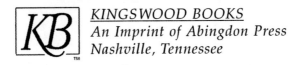

KINGSWOOD BOOKS
An Imprint of Abingdon Press
Nashville, Tennessee

EARLY METHODIST LIFE AND SPIRITUALITY
A READER

Library of Congress Cataloging-in-Publication Data

Early Methodist life and spirituality : a reader / edited, with an introduction by Lester Ruth.
    p. cm.
  Includes bibliographical references.
  ISBN 0-687-34274-0 (pbk. : alk. paper)
  1. Methodism—History—Sources.   2. Methodism—United States.   3. Methodist Church—Doctrines.   I. Ruth, Lester, 1959-
  BX8231.E37 2004
  287'.0973—dc22

2004018249

All scripture quotations unless noted otherwise are taken from the King James or Authorized Version of the Bible.

05 06 07 08 09 10 11 12 13 14—10 9 8 7 6 5 4 3 2 1

MANUFACTURED IN THE UNITED STATES OF AMERICA

CONTENTS

In memory of
James F. White
1932–2004

His dedicated service to Church
and Academy was
exemplary of God's Self-giving.

PREFACE

My intent in this book is to help modern readers become acquainted with early American Methodists by providing topical collections of writings from around sixty individuals in the first fifty years of American Methodism. Most of the material comes from never published sources or from materials long out of print.

In providing such hard-to-find material, this book follows a path blazed by earlier efforts, particularly Frederick A. Norwood's *Sourcebook of American Methodism* and *The Methodist Experience in America* edited by Russell Richey, Kenneth Rowe, and Jean Miller Schmidt.[1] These are fine collections of materials from the entire breadth of American Methodist history, and I encourage readers to know these books. The present volume differs from these collections by focusing on a narrower span of time. This allows me to provide many more—and a wider range of—sources from the first half-century of American Methodism. This collection also focuses more on the Methodist people and their spirituality than on Methodism as an institution. As a result, readers are provided a deeper sense of how everyday Methodists lived out their faith.

A couple of editorial decisions deserve mention at this point. First, I follow standard style of using short titles for published items after the first citation. When referring to manuscript items, I consistently identify only the essential details in the footnotes. Readers will find the full details for manuscript locations and for

---

1. Frederick A. Norwood, ed., *Sourcebook of American Methodism* (Nashville: Abingdon, 1982); and Russell E. Richey, Kenneth E. Rowe, and Jean Miller Schmidt, eds., *The Methodist Experience in America Volume II: Sourcebook* (Nashville: Abingdon, 2000).

short title citations in the Reference Bibliography. Finally, I have kept all biblical quotations in the version that these early Methodists used. Throughout the book I have used the King James Version whenever citing a biblical passage.

I wish to thank the people who have assisted this project. I thank Asbury Theological Seminary for granting a sabbatical that facilitated progress on the volume. Thank you to the student assistants whose help has been invaluable: Jeremy Sullivan, Scott Lees, Josh McKee, Rhonda Hartweg, and Ginny Deyo. I am grateful for the fine, cooperative staffs at the following archives and churches: Asbury Theological Seminary, Duke University, the University of North Carolina, Garrett-Evangelical Theological Seminary, College of William and Mary, Lovely Lane Chapel, Old St. George's, Barratt's Chapel, the Winterthur Museum, the Maryland Historical Society, the Delaware State Archives, and the General Commission on Archives and History at Drew University. The assistance and encouragement of several scholars has also been very helpful at crucial points: Richard Weiss, John Wigger, Karen Westerfield Tucker, Alan Rathe, Cindy Zirlott, and Russell Richey. The help of Randy Maddox is especially appreciated. Thanks, too, to the Worship and Spirituality working group of the 2002 Oxford Institute of Methodist Theological Studies for comments affecting chapter 5.

Finally, I wish to thank the Methodists who have most shaped me as a Christian scholar: Carmen Ruth, Dewey and Dora Ballenger, Lois Osborne, Carleton Dyer, Donald Boyd, Jerry Mercer, Don Saliers, James White, and Ed Robb, Jr.

> And are we yet alive,
> And see each other's face?
> Glory and thanks to Jesus give
> For his almighty grace![2]

---

2. *The United Methodist Hymnal* (Nashville: The United Methodist Publishing House, 1989), no. 553.

INTRODUCTION: EARLY AMERICAN METHODISTS IN CONTEXT

The goal of this book is straightforward: to give voice to average American Methodists within the first fifty years of the movement. These Methodists—black and white, men and women—are largely unknown, despite having a vibrant spirituality that won over a new nation. Those who have read church history will know a few as key figures. Present-day readers may even have seen some writings of such figures, particularly if they have been recently republished. The journal and correspondence of Francis Asbury are a case in point.[1] But beyond such figureheads as Asbury, Thomas Coke, Harry Hoosier, Thomas Rankin, Jesse Lee, Richard Allen, and Peter Cartwright, early American Methodism remains a sea of anonymous faces.[2]

Because of the desire to introduce other early American Methodists like Sarah Jones, Ezekiel Cooper, William Spencer,

---

1. Francis Asbury, *The Journal and Letters of Francis Asbury*, 3 vols., ed. Elmer T. Clark (London: Epworth; Nashville: Abingdon, 1958).

2. Fortunately, some recent works on early Methodism have begun to introduce these early Methodists. See, for example, the personal vignettes in John Wigger, *Taking Heaven by Storm: Methodism and the Rise of Popular Christianity in America* (New York: Oxford University Press, 1998); and Dee E. Andrews, *The Methodists and Revolutionary America, 1760–1800: The Shaping of an Evangelical Culture* (Princeton: Princeton University Press, 2000). See also Kenneth Cain Kinghorn, *The Heritage of American Methodism* (Nashville: Abingdon, 1999).

Nancy Welch, and George White, readers will not find much in what follows from the writings of the key figures usually associated with early Methodism. Instead, this collection consists mainly of the hopes and dreams, fears and tribulations of the people who stood in the pulpit, sat in the pews, and knelt on dusty floors to discover God in their midst. As a window into the spirituality of early American Methodists, this volume gathers hard-to-find passages from their diaries, sermon outline books, hymnals, letters, magazines, and even administrative records, among other sources. Here one can *read* the Methodists, rather than just read *about* the Methodists. The following pieces introduce these Methodists, giving readers access to documents that display the souls of these earlier Christians.

These excerpts focus specifically on the *spirituality* of early American Methodists. This needs to be clarified, because "spirituality" has become a vague, slippery word. I am using it in a sense akin to that of Gordon Wakefield and Geoffrey Wainwright. According to Wakefield, "spirituality concerns the way in which prayer influences conduct, our behaviour and manner of life, our attitudes to other people."[3] Wainwright suggests more simply that spirituality is "the combination of praying and living."[4] These definitions are helpful, as long as we bear in mind that prayer includes not only moments of conscious, intentional speaking to God but also more constant, internal give-and-take interaction with God. Accordingly, this volume surveys how early American Methodists interacted with God and the things of God, and how this interaction influenced their conduct, manner of life, and attitudes. There are accounts of their immediate experiences of God, but also accounts that reflect the outworking of their awareness of God in matters like disciplinary and ethical issues. We are introduced to the workings of their hearts, their mouths, and their hands—all in light of God.

In keeping with this focus, almost none of the excerpts come from formal theological treatises. To be sure, we will encounter

---

3. Gordon Wakefield, ed., *The Westminster Dictionary of Christian Spirituality* (Philadelphia: Westminster, 1983), v. Wakefield has also written a helpful introduction to the spirituality of British Methodists entitled *Methodist Spirituality* (Peterborough: Epworth, 1999).
4. Geoffrey Wainwright, "Types of Spirituality," in *The Study of Spirituality*, ed. Cheslyn Jones, et al. (New York: Oxford University Press, 1986), 592.

many of the theological convictions of early American Methodists, but in their integral connection to spirituality rather than in abstract summaries. As "embodied theology," the convictions that emerge in this collection are often robust, but rarely systematic. Moreover, much of the larger web of their beliefs remains implicit. While this poses a major challenge for any historical narrative of early American Methodist theology, such is not the goal of this book. The introduction to each chapter will provide context for discerning the theological convictions in the materials being considered. But there will be little concern to systematize or fill in the missing links. In the materials gathered in the chapter on Jesus Christ, for example, convictions about the Trinity come through only as hints and echoes. I have left them as such, allowing the sheer passion of these early Methodists for Jesus Christ to remain central, despite the unanswered questions their writings might raise for a systematic theologian.[5]

This volume is not intended as an exhaustive introduction to early Methodists, even with respect to their spirituality. The topics were suggested by their frequency in Methodist writings, not by some predetermined schema. While this means that some important issues of scholarly concern make only a peripheral appearance, it seemed appropriate to allow the themes of their own writings to set the agenda of this encounter with early American Methodists.

Given this goal, several principles guided selection of specific material. First, preference went to materials written from the mid-1770s to the mid-1810s, that crucial formative period staked out by Francis Asbury's ministry in America.[6] This guideline was stretched a little to include later-published material by women and African Americans, but even in these cases selection was made in

---

5. This approach seems consistent with the relative weight of the material available from early Methodists. They did little systematic theological writing for publication until the 1810s.

6. Francis Asbury arrived in America in 1771 and died in 1816. Soon after his arrival he became one of the more prominent itinerant preachers. He became bishop of the fledgling Methodist Episcopal Church in 1784 and was in many respects the public face of American Methodism. The time frame of his work in America provides a good bracket for the first phase of early American Methodism. Few writings are available from American Methodists prior to his arrival, and his death represented a significant corner turned for early Methodism.

terms of works displaying Methodist spirituality and life in the Asburian period. Second, preference among materials from this time period was given to those that had apparently never been published, or had been published only in this early period. Again the main deviation from this rule was to include some important representative material from women and African Americans that has been brought to light and published in the recent scholarly focus on these long-neglected groups.[7] Finally, preference went to materials that did not come from leaders and other well-known figures in early American Methodism. Thus Francis Asbury, for example, plays only a small role in this book. The goal was to give voice to rank-and-file Methodists as much as possible. Most of the authors included in this volume will not be familiar except to historians of early Methodism. Some of those included were significant figures in their time, but have faded into obscurity. Others bore no special significance then or now.

In order to give voice to these early Methodists, I have taken the liberty of updating the spelling, grammar, and punctuation found in their writings. This was necessary to achieve contemporary accessibility. Care was taken to keep the sense of the original. The most difficult situations were instances of phonetically spelled words written in a nearly indecipherable hand. Most of the time familiarity with the writings of early American Methodists allowed at least an educated guess. Where there was doubt, I have marked the spot with a question mark. Without updating, some passages (particularly those with phonetic spelling influenced by strong dialects) can be almost unintelligible.

WHO WERE THE EARLY METHODISTS?

Who were the American Methodist people in the late-eighteenth and early nineteenth centuries? They were the ones who launched a religious movement that expanded so rapidly that one historian has called it a "virtual miracle of growth."[8] In the early 1770s there

---

7. With a few exceptions, I have also stayed away from reproducing material from my earlier book, *A Little Heaven Below: Worship at Early Methodist Quarterly Meetings* (Nashville: Kingswood Books, 2000).

8. Wigger, *Taking Heaven by Storm*, 3.

were less than a thousand Methodists on the whole continent. An observant itinerant preacher[9] with a good memory for names could have known every single Methodist in those early years.[10] That situation did not last long. By 1780 there were around 8,500 Methodists; by 1785, after the movement had organized itself as a distinct church, there were around 18,000 members;[11] by 1790, over 57,000; by 1800, nearly 65,000; by 1810, over 174,000.[12] Perhaps the most amazing thing about this growth is not the numbers themselves but that they came in a time when American Methodists were notoriously rigorous in their religion, taking a sharp countercultural stance on many occasions. Some historians have pondered why Methodists succeeded to the extent they did, given the character of their religious life.[13] Even more explosive growth occurred as nineteenth-century Methodism became "domesticated" and in greater harmony with its surrounding culture.[14]

What kind of people made up these growing numbers? The most recent historical studies have sought to answer this question. John Wigger's summary is a good one: early American Methodists on the whole were "middling people on the make" such as "skilled artisans, shopkeepers, petty merchants, and ambitious small planters."[15] Initially most Methodists lived below the Mason-Dixon line, although by 1810 over one-third lived in the North.[16] In addition to the centrality of "middling people on the make," one should consider the diversity of Methodism in other ways. Not the least is

---

9. Methodist preachers were divided into two types: (1) itinerants who actively traveled and earned their living from preaching, and (2) local preachers who mainly resided in one place and worked another job.

10. American Methodism began with the spontaneous, uncoordinated efforts of members who had immigrated from England. Beginning in the latter half of the 1760s, these Americans began to organize themselves and call upon John Wesley, the founder of Methodism, for assistance. Wesley sent the first two itinerant preachers in 1769.

11. Prior to 1785 Methodism had existed as a kind of parachurch organization. In 1784, after several years of clamoring, John Wesley took the steps that allowed American Methodists to constitute themselves as a church. They did so at the famous Christmas Conference at the end of 1784. An account of this process can be found in any history of American Methodism.

12. The best source for statistics in this early period is *Minutes of the Methodist Conferences, annually held in America: from 1773–1813, inclusive* (New York: D. Hitt and T. Ware, 1813).

13. See, for instance, Christine Leigh Heyrman, *Southern Cross: The Beginnings of the Bible Belt* (New York: Alfred A. Knopf, 1998), 15-27.

14. Cf. A. Gregory Schneider, *The Way of the Cross Leads Home: The Domestication of American Methodism* (Bloomington: Indiana University Press, 1993).

15. Wigger, *Taking Heaven by Storm*, 5.

16. Ibid.

the presence of so many African Americans—both slave and free—in early Methodism, constituting nearly one in five Methodists during our period.[17] It is also easy to forget by using economic categories like "artisans" and "merchants" the strong presence of women in early Methodism. To forget Methodist women would be a deep mistake since they often made up a clear majority of the membership. In the eastern seaboard cities, for example, women usually comprised around 60 percent of the total.[18]

The identification of Methodism's core as "middling" in economic status should not obscure the diversity of its members in this regard. For example, people from a range of economic backgrounds were drawn to Methodism in the large cities on the East Coast.[19] In areas of Methodist concentration, like regions of Maryland and Delaware, it was also common to find members of the upper economic classes within the movement.[20]

Allowing this diversity, it remains true that most early Methodists came from certain social and economic backgrounds. Outsiders often noted such, sometimes in disparaging ways. For example, in 1789 Thomas Wallcut, a Massachusetts gentleman, wrote home alarmed at what he had discovered about the Methodists in Virginia and Maryland. In his estimation they were "short lived blazes of enthusiasm and intemperate zeal." Methodist influence, he wrote, was "principally felt among the Negroes and poorer and lower classes of the people."[21] Similarly, Episcopal priest Devereux Jarratt, a Methodist sympathizer early in his ministry, complained toward the end of his life about Methodist attempts at forming schools. How could any "considerate" person, Jarratt wrote, expect something good from a school controlled by "tinkers and tailors, weavers, shoemakers, and country mechanics of all kinds"?[22]

Such numerical and demographic information is important for us because it shows the compelling nature of Methodist spirituality.

---

17. Ibid., 127.

18. Andrews, *Methodists and Revolutionary America*, 112, 247-48.

19. Ibid., 112-17, 155.

20. Ibid., 160-61.

21. Thomas Wallcut to James Freeman, 31 October 1789. I am indebted for this quote to John Wigger who provides more of Wallcut's letter in *Taking Heaven by Storm*, 104-5.

22. Devereux Jarratt, *The Life of the Reverend Devereux Jarratt* (Baltimore: Warner & Hanna, 1806), 181.

It was the spirituality of a church initially on the margins of America but, bit by bit, along with other similar popular religious movements, a spirituality that captured the heart of a nation.

Who were these Methodists? Numbers and demographic labels only provide part of the picture. Focusing too intently on such things can keep us away from the names and faces of those who sought to encounter God in the Methodist way. The voices of more than sixty such Methodists fill this book. We cannot explore them all in depth, but brief biographical glimpses of three may help begin to convey how early American Methodists prayed and lived before God.

Consider first the spiritual journey of George White (1764–1836). In some ways White's life was the fulfillment of the scripture quoted on the first page of his autobiography: "God hath chosen the foolish things of the world to confound the wise … and base things of the world, and things that are despised, hath God chosen."[23] Over the course of his life White went from slavery to freedom, and from having little vital religion to being a licensed preacher in the Methodist Episcopal Church. White was born in Accomack County, Virginia, spending his first twenty-six years in slavery in Virginia and Maryland, having been sold by several masters. At age twenty-six White acquired his freedom when his master died and left him free. Even then he had to fight the heirs of the estate not to keep him in slavery.

Acquiring his freedom spurred White to contemplate God more fully in thanksgiving. Although previously he had often attended worship in the Church of England, he reported to have benefited little from it. Now, sparked by his freedom, White brought a new spiritual inquiry to his first encounter with Methodists at a quarterly meeting (a protracted gathering for worship and business). At this quarterly meeting White had opportunity to attend several preaching services. The result was a new alarm about his sinfulness.

---

23. See 1 Corinthians 1:27-28. White's autobiography, one of the few written by this period's African-American Methodist preachers, was printed as *A Brief Account of the Life, Experience, Travels and Gospel Labours of George White, An African* (New York: John C. Totten, 1810). The scripture citation is on pp. 9-10. White's narrative has been reprinted in Graham Russell Hodges, ed., *Black Itinerants of the Gospel: The Narratives of John Jea and George White* (Madison, Wis.: Madison House Publishers, 1993). Another short sketch of White's life can be found in Wigger, *Taking Heaven by Storm*, 131-32. The vignette that follows is dependent upon all these sources.

In 1791 White moved to New York City. There, at a special extended nighttime service called a "watch night," White's conviction of sin—his distress over seeing himself as a rebel before a righteous God—became acute. He soon found a degree of relief but not the clear, inward assurance of God's acceptance that Methodists considered normal for a salvation experience. Nonetheless, he formally joined the Methodists. (Joining before an experience of salvation was common for the period since Methodist polity required only a desire to be saved, not an actual experience of salvation.) On joining the Methodists White almost certainly began attending a weekly small group meeting for encouragement and accountability called a "class meeting." Such attendance was expected for all Methodists, though White did not specifically mention class meetings in his autobiography. What he does mention was a growing sense of love and unity with other Methodists as he struggled to resist what he understood to be the attacks of Satan on his soul. He continued to make spiritual progress.

At an 1804 camp meeting (another form of Methodist worship meeting lasting several days) White was given a major spiritual advancement, a much deeper sense of joy and internal witness of salvation than he had previously experienced. Soon after he had a dream of hell (see chapter 4) that included a call to begin speaking publicly. This dream was only the first of several extraordinary experiences. Notwithstanding the seemingly divine origins for his call, White had considerable trouble over the next several years gaining official license to speak publicly as an exhorter or preacher in the Methodist Episcopal Church (MEC). Such obstacles did not shut his mouth however. Continuing his job as an oysterman, White traveled and spoke throughout Long Island and New Jersey. Finally, in 1807, he obtained a license to preach.

The weight of speaking publicly for Christ stimulated additional spiritual growth for George White. He began to strive for a second experience of salvation known as sanctification (see chapter 3). After another worship experience—this time in his own home—that included a vision of heaven, White testified that God had given him a clean heart, leaving him feeling nothing but this purity. This deeper experience created a stir in his mind as well. Afterwards he had his sixteen-year-old daughter teach him how to read so that within a few months he could read the Scriptures for himself.

White continued in ministry in the MEC until 1820 when he joined the African Methodist Episcopal Church, which had been recently founded by another former MEC preacher, Richard Allen. White died on 12 January 1836.[24]

Sarah Jones (ca. 1753–1794) is another useful icon of early Methodist spirituality. Virtually unknown to current Methodists, she was in her day one of the better-known women within the MEC, "famous for her piety, her prose, and her assertive defense of Methodism," as one scholar has put it.[25] She was renowned at the time for the intensity of her encounter with God even in the midst of personal trials. She had, as Bishop Francis Asbury phrased it after staying at her home once, "waded through deep waters."[26] Similarly, after preaching her funeral in 1794, Asbury wrote, "She was doubtless a woman of sense, vivacity, and grace. She wrote to admiration—all in raptures. She would pray in any place, and before any people, she reproved with pointed severity, and sung with great sweetness."[27] In other words, she was the embodiment of Methodist spirituality.

Jones's life was an interesting, intense mix of difficulties with the most vivid spiritual experiences.[28] The trials came early as she, like many other women, became a Methodist over her husband's angry objections. Eventually Jones's husband and some of her children became Methodists too, although not showing the same level of zeal. Over the course of her life Jones continued to experience difficulties. The level of her zeal about Methodist commitments to simplicity of dress led to conflicts even with other Christians.

---

24. Hodges, *Black Itinerants of the Gospel*, 18.

25. Cynthia Lynn Lyerly, *Methodism and the Southern Mind, 1770–1810* (New York: Oxford University Press, 1998), 109. Among recent works on early Methodism, Lyerly's book has paid the closest attention to Jones, and I am indebted in my description here to her treatment.

26. Asbury, *Journal and Letters*, 1:456.

27. Ibid., 2:34.

28. There are several sources for information on Sarah Jones. Foremost is her manuscript diary located in the Manuscripts and Rare Books Department of Swem Library at the College of William and Mary. In 1804 Jeremiah Minter, a close acquaintance and Methodist preacher, published a collection of her letters as *Devout Letters: or, Letters Spiritual and Friendly. Written by Mrs. Sarah Jones* (Alexandria: Samuel Snowden, 1804). Minter reports that he also published a biography of Jones.

Likewise, others were not always comfortable with the gusto she exhibited in using opportunities for public speaking.[29] She must have been torn as well by the schism that split Virginia Methodism in the early 1790s. Jones, despite being a personal friend of James O'Kelly, the Methodist preacher responsible for the schism, and his wife, remained loyal to Francis Asbury and the MEC.[30] Jones was also hurt by the criticism and misunderstanding that was generated by her close (some thought too close) friendship with Methodist itinerant preacher Jeremiah Minter.[31] Finally, Jones suffered a debilitating terminal illness that sapped her life for more than a year before resulting in death. Perhaps it is no surprise that she selected for her funeral text Job 3:17: "There the wicked cease from troubling; and there the weary be at rest." She died at age 41 in 1794, in Mecklenburg County in southern Virginia, where she had been born.

In her life with God, Sarah Jones felt things deeply. This is seen in her written reactions to her outward trials as well as in reflection on her inward journey. The emphasis on affections was an important characteristic of all Methodist spirituality at the time, but Jones seemed to have carried it to a degree even more intense than most. This quality is most evident in her repeated episodes of rapturous ecstasy. These episodes were often triggered by such ordinary things as reading John Wesley's journal or contemplating the landscape.[32] The resulting ecstasy could be overwhelming. Poetry not prose, symbolic speech not rational description was what she needed to capture the experience. Not surprisingly, her diary slips in and out of verse form. If anything, Jones was so thoroughly and zealously Methodist in these spiritual qualities—so quintessentially Methodist—that she was beyond the experience of most. Even then, however, many appreciated her intensity and many looked to her as a positive model.

The rapturous quality of Jones's spirituality seems to be connected to certain practices she followed routinely. She fasted often.

---

29. Her efforts were also appreciated. See Lyerly, *Methodism and the Southern Mind*, 110.

30. For information on the schism see Wigger, *Taking Heaven by Storm*, 39-40.

31. See the introduction in Minter, ed., *Devout Letters*, iv. Although it is difficult to prove a direct causal relationship, one wonders about the connection of this "scandal" to Minter's decision to be castrated (see chapter 8).

32. Sarah Anderson Jones, Diary, 4 April 1792 and 14 June 1792.

Even when she did eat, she followed a restricted diet. She noted in 1792 that it had been eight years since she had eaten "flesh...fish or fowl."[33] She also spent extended time in solitary prayer, particularly early in the morning and late in the evening, offering hints of sleep deprivation.[34] She supplemented her individual prayer practices with several other spiritual disciplines: a steady stream of letters written and read for devotional purposes, regular partnering with others for prayer, and additional times of meeting with others before daybreak or late at night for prayer. In addition, she attended the regular rhythms of public Methodist worship.

For a good example of Methodist piety among the itinerant preachers, one can look at Ezekiel Cooper (1763–1847).[35] Cooper was born in eastern Maryland and grew up in the Church of England. Like many future Methodists, Cooper in retrospect was dissatisfied with the lack of vitality he found in his religious upbringing. Looking upon those years, Cooper's assessment of his family's religiosity was severe: "sorrowful to relate, we were all too great strangers to any thing truly spiritual. We had a name to live while we were dead; professing Christ, but in works denying him."[36] Such a reaction to one's religious upbringing was common among early Methodists. It was nearly universal for them to see their later religious experiences as having much more vitality than their nominal Christian upbringing. In his early teens Cooper heard Freeborn Garrettson, a Methodist itinerant preacher, speak in an outdoor meeting. Cooper began to feel the drawings of the Holy Spirit. His spiritual journey intensified over the next several years. In 1780, after a period of wavering, he again felt a deep conviction for sin. His anxiety increased. Like many, his distress became so acute that he could scarcely eat. Finally, while Cooper walked and prayed alone, he felt God access his heart:

---

33. Jones, Diary, 14 September 1792.
34. Minter, ed., *Devout Letters*, 58, 60.
35. For a brief biographical sketch, see James E. Kirby, Russell E. Richey, and Kenneth E. Rowe, *The Methodists* (Westport, Conn.: Greenwood, 1996), 284-85. Wigger, *Taking Heaven by Storm*; and Andrews, *Methodists and Revolutionary America*, also have useful information. Most of Cooper's papers are located at Garrett-Evangelical Theological Seminary in Evanston, Ill. Some are housed at Barratt's Chapel & Museum in Frederica, Del. The easiest way to access Cooper's writings is in George A. Phoebus, comp., *Beams of Light on Early Methodism in America* (New York: Phillips & Hunt, 1887).
36. Phoebus, comp., *Beams of Light*, 12.

> Presently I had an opening to my mind of the infinite fullness of Christ, and of the willingness of the Father, through his Son, to receive me into his favor. I had such confidence in the merits of Christ and the mercy of God that I laid hold of the promise, felt my burden remove, and a flood of peace, love, and joy break forth in my soul. I was now enabled to call Christ Lord, by the Holy Ghost sent down from heaven. I am assured, to the present moment, that at that time the Lord forgave me all my sins, and owned me for his adopted child.[37]

Such testimonies were the common spiritual language of early Methodists.

Ezekiel Cooper joined the Methodists in 1782, being placed in the mandatory class meeting, where he grew steadily as a Christian. It was in these class meetings and in prayer meetings that Cooper first began to exercise public ministry. With a soul "daily alive to God" and a zeal to reprove sinners, Cooper was called upon to pray and exhort often. Eventually Freeborn Garrettson, who was now the itinerant preacher on the circuit where Cooper resided, made him a class meeting leader. After a short time in this role, Cooper was called upon to become an itinerant preacher. He began this ministry in November 1784, immediately prior to the establishment of the Methodist Episcopal Church the next month. Cooper served a faithful ministry for the next several decades, serving Methodists from Boston to Charleston. Seemingly one of the more sophisticated Methodist preachers, Cooper was often placed in East Coast cities. He spent time as well as head of the Methodist Book Concern. Cooper died in 1847.

It is not just Cooper's journey from disaffected Church of England member to zealous Methodist preacher that makes him a window into early Methodist spirituality. Some form of this journey was repeated endless times in early Methodism. What also makes Cooper instructive is the tone of his spirituality: a combination of deep solemnity before God, rigorous ethics in the world, and exuberant rejoicing in the midst of religious revival.

The first element, solemnity, can be seen in Cooper's description of a funeral and wedding that were juxtaposed in a Methodist wor-

---

37. Ibid., 18.

ship service in 1787 New Jersey. The service began with a funeral. In Cooper's opinion, the arrival of the corpse was itself a useful proclamation for all to be ready to die and meet God. After the corpse was buried, a wedding followed. According to Cooper's approving opinion, it was "the most solemn wedding" he had ever seen.[38] There was little room for the trifling frivolity of the world here. With a single heart and eye, one must be attentive to the Savior and Judge of all.

Cooper brought that same intensity to his understanding of the Christian life, as can be seen in his writings on ethics included in chapter 7. Whether it was seemingly innocent recreational outlets like gaming and drinking, or the more serious matter of slavery (as it may seem to modern readers), Cooper was vehement about the diabolical sources of such evils. He was convinced that all such activity violated Scripture and was part of a complex of worldliness that should be equally attacked. Cooper's experience here is instructive for the varying degrees of success Methodists had in implementing their ethos. The record of early Methodism on slavery, for example, was an ambivalent one, as Cooper knew well. While he was instrumental in getting some slave owners to free their slaves, Cooper also served on a committee that failed to get the entire church to enact meaningful rules against slavery.[39]

We must be careful not to paint Cooper in too dour of tones. His spiritual experience also included episodes of great spiritual joy, even ecstasy, particularly in times of religious revival. Such a time came as he ministered in Baltimore in 1789. In February of that year Cooper noted that "the glorious work broke out like a fire which had a long time struggled for vent, and blazed forth in a flaming conflagration."[40] Such occasions were the deepest aspirations of Methodists. As people flocked to worship and many felt the passing over from the travails of distress of sin's guilt to the happiness of assurance of God's salvation, Cooper was nearly beside himself with joy. At times he could forget to which world he belonged: "In this my soul was ready to fly to the celestial world! How the love of heaven burned on the altars of our hearts! The place was truly

---

38. Ibid., 65.
39. Wigger, *Taking Heaven by Storm*, 149. The failure came at the 1804 General Conference, the quadrennial legislative meeting for the denomination.
40. Phoebus, comp., *Beams of Light*, 87.

awful because of God's presence! It appeared like the very suburbs of heaven."[41]

The joy transported him to sacred ground. Following a very common early Methodist practice, Cooper invoked an Old Testament image to describe his experience. He compared the effect of that revival to Moses viewing the promised land from the mountain: "We stood as on the top of Pisgah, and viewed the land of which the Lord had said, 'I will give it to you.' The love, joy, and power which we felt exceeds what human language can fully express."[42]

These sketches of George White, Sarah Jones, and Ezekiel Cooper give some hint as to the kinds of people and writings included in this book. These three represent early Methodism across gender, racial, and ministerial lines. George White was an African American man, unordained but with a local preacher's license. Sarah Jones was a white, southern woman, with neither ordination nor license to preach. But by a zealous piety and willingness to take advantage of opportunities, she influenced many, sometimes speaking in public settings. Then there is Ezekiel Cooper, who followed a very typical official path through the various levels of Methodist ministry, ordained and unordained.

These three Methodists' writings are typical of the material one will find in the following chapters. They span the range of early Methodist expression: hymns, poems, letters, diaries, outlines on important spiritual topics, autobiographies, and short essays. Obviously, only a small percentage of such items were intended for publication. But all allowed the early Methodist to speak deeply of his or her experiences of God. The selections gathered in the following chapters should help the reader feel the pulse of the spirituality that drove the Methodist movement.

THE CHARACTER OF METHODIST SPIRITUALITY

As suggested by these vignettes of George White, Sarah Jones, and Ezekiel Cooper, there were several common elements in early

---

41. Ezekiel Cooper to "Dear Brother," Baltimore, 14 August 1789, Ezekiel Cooper papers (vol. 16, ms. 8). See also chapter 6.
42. Phoebus, comp., *Beams of Light*, 95. For the biblical story, see Deuteronomy 34:1.

American Methodist spirituality. Among the most central of these shared traits are: emotionalism, ecstasy, rigorousness, exuberance, and evangelism.[43]

Emotionalism points to what the Methodists called "experimental religion" or what we might call "experiential religion." Methodists expected that the most important parts of religion—faith, salvation, God's grace, a sense of God's presence—were to be experienced inwardly. These aspects were to be felt. A primarily rational spirituality was not satisfactory. One's sins were forgiven, for example, when one felt it inwardly. Such feelings were not mere emotional states, although deep emotions were typically expected, but were analogous to the sense of touch.[44] Inward feeling was an experience of real spiritual realms. Accompanying this inward emphasis was a suspicion of any Christianity that seemed to consist only of cognitive ideas and outward practices done from a sense of obligation. In their estimation such Christianity was "formal" or "cold." In contrast, one of the favorite Methodist words to describe powerful experiences of God was "melting."

A second trait of early Methodist spirituality was its ecstasy. They insisted on a place for immediacy in their experience of God. Without repudiating the importance of outward forms like Scripture, organization, and the means of grace, early Methodists gave privilege as well to dreams, visions, and signs. To borrow a phrase from Gordon Wakefield's description of early British Methodists, Methodist spirituality was a combination of "rapture and order."[45] The frequency of such phenomena and the amount of

---

43. Compare the discussion of Methodist "style" in Lyerly, *Methodism and the Southern Mind*, 34-46 (using the terms "emotionalism, mysticism, asceticism, enthusiasm, and evangelism"). Although Lyerly focuses on Southern Methodism, her description is appropriate for all American Methodism. While adopting her fivefold characterization, I am opting for different terms in several cases. I use the term "ecstatic" rather than "mystical" to speak of those dimensions of Methodist spirituality that involved heightened states of awareness or interaction with the supernatural, in order to avoid entangling early Methodists with Roman Catholic mysticism and out of awareness of current academic debate about the usefulness of the latter term (cf. Leigh Eric Schmidt, "The Making of Modern 'Mysticism,'" *Journal of the American Academy of Religion* 71 [2003]: 273-302). Likewise, to avoid confusion with earlier Eastern and Western forms of monasticism, I prefer "rigorousness" over "asceticism." Finally, I will use "exuberance" rather than "enthusiasm" since the latter was a technical term in the eighteenth century to describe a Christian approach that early Methodists often desired to avoid (see chapter 6 for more information).

44. Frank Whaling, ed., *John and Charles Wesley: Selected Writings and Hymns* (Mahwah, N.J.: Paulist, 1981), 44.

45. Wakefield, *Methodist Spirituality*, 10.

reliance Methodists placed on them can be shocking to modern readers. It was as well to many of early American Methodists' peers, who considered such experiences of common, uneducated Christians to pose a danger to long-held religious institutions.

If emotionalism and ecstasy might be considered the sweetness of early Methodist spirituality, its third characteristic—rigorousness—will likely be viewed as its sour edge. Early Methodists were rigorous in their self-appraisal and rigorous in their lifestyle. In many respects, they did not trust the things of this world, including themselves. In self-appraisal, this attitude could lead to despair and self-loathing.[46] The accounts of their religious experiences often show a growing conviction of their unworthiness as they prostrated inwardly before a holy God (though this God ultimately proved to be abundantly gracious as well). Methodists were equally rigorous in lifestyle, rejecting many of the cultural practices associated with leisure, pleasure, position, and honor. Fasting was common, as was simplicity of dress. Methodists also rejected such diversions of masses as dancing, racing, drinking, cultural holidays, and even basic frivolity. The goal, as historian Cynthia Lyerly points out, was to master the self[47] and to provide countercultural witness of an alternative world of true, "experimental" religion.

Perhaps the most distinctive aspect of Methodist style was its exuberance. The decibel level of Methodist activity—especially worship—was one of the most common ways that Methodists were identified. Methodist spirituality was expressive. It was often boisterous. It could be infectious. Sometimes it was just overwhelming. Remember Thomas Wallcut describing Maryland and Virginia Methodists in the 1780s. In the same letter Wallcut spoke of "that confusion, violence and distortion of the body, voice & gestures that characterizes such a boiling hot religion" as early American Methodism.[48] This exuberance was something that even British Methodists found initially distasteful. As Bishop Thomas Coke described his experience, "the shouts in the congregation, which at first I reluctantly entered into met with my full approbation in a little time. I saw in them the hand of God, and the signal and numer-

---

46. Lyerly, *Methodism and the Southern Mind*, 37.
47. Ibid., 40.
48. Thomas Wallcut to James Freeman, 31 October 1789.

ous convictions and conversions which took place at those times, were demonstrative proofs of the approbation of the Most High."[49] To be sure, there were degrees of exuberance among American Methodists, varying by region, gender, and race; but expressive piety was a generally recognized trait of the group as a whole in the period under consideration.

The final common trait of Methodist spirituality was aggressive evangelism. It is fair to say that Methodists' main preoccupation was salvation. All other concerns orbited around this center of gravity. They were so intent on exploring the nature of salvation, on being saved, on adoring the God who saves, and on offering this salvation to others, that their concern can seem obsessive. Through the structure inherited from their British roots, early Methodists embodied missionary enterprise in nearly every aspect of their common life and energy. Their goal was to orchestrate experiences of justification—the initial experience of salvation including forgiveness of sins and the new birth—and sanctification—a subsequent experience that dealt with God inwardly cleansing by love the remaining vestige of sin's power.

With respect to justification, early Methodists considered that this initial experience of salvation normally took the form of a crisis event. They did not, however, require such an experience as a prerequisite to membership. Thus many Methodists joined as "seekers" and experienced saving grace within the communal structures and rhythms of circuit life. This setting helped ensure that experiences of salvation, while deeply personal, were usually not excessively individualistic. Indeed, Methodists conceived of their ultimate destiny in God's grace in striking, communal terms.

The backdrop for the evangelistic emphasis was a doctrine of universal atonement. Methodists never tired of saying that Christ died for all people, and that all people could benefit from experiencing God's grace. This message created a deep sense of spiritual opportunity that fit well with post-Revolutionary optimism. In the competitive arenas where Methodists preached and testified, the opponent was a form of Calvinism that denied such a broad scope to Christ's saving work. Thus, the evangelistic emphasis in Methodist

---

49. Thomas Coke to Ezekiel Cooper, 7 July 1789, Ezekiel Cooper papers (vol. 17, ms. 6).

spirituality took the form, as others have labeled it, of a "crusade against Calvinist orthodoxy and control."[50]

Another useful window for gaining perspective on early American Methodist spirituality is by paying attention to its style of discourse. In an insightful study Russell Richey has argued that four overlapping styles of discourse, each with its own vocabulary, can be discerned in early American Methodism. He calls these the four "languages" of American Methodism.[51] Richey designates the four styles of discourse as: (1) popular or evangelical, (2) Wesleyan, (3) episcopal or Anglican, and (4) republican. While each brought something to strengthen early Methodism, they also created tensions among themselves. For any one topic or issue, Methodists might use terms derived from any of the languages. Consider the example of the church. In popular settings early Methodists often used the common (for the time) term "Zion" to refer to the church, embracing the implications of this biblical image of the church as a kind of New Jerusalem. For more formal purposes Methodists turned to the definition of the church found in its Articles of Religion, derived directly from the Church of England and framed in theological categories familiar since at least the Reformation. Early Methodists also had a third language for church, the terms inherited from John Wesley's organization of the movement in the eighteenth century. In this discourse the focus of church life was its expression in societies, circuits, and conferences.[52]

Richey's model of the four languages of early American Methodism provides further insight into the Methodist voices gathered in this volume. In many of these voices we hear clear resonance with certain strands of "evangelical" or pietistic Christianity in the late-eighteenth century. They readily adopt the language of love, fear, and hope, mixed with striking religious experience, biblical allusions and types, and a tangible sense that God is present to save. But this shared language is spoken with a distinctive Methodist accent; their "Wesleyan" heritage also shines through, providing several terms that serve to define Methodists *as Methodists* within the larger evangelical setting. In comparison with

---

50. Wigger, *Taking Heaven by Storm*, 17.

51. Russell E. Richey, "The Four Languages of Early American Methodism," in *Early American Methodism* (Bloomington: Indiana University Press, 1991), 82-97.

52. Ibid., 94-95.

these first two, the "episcopal/Anglican" and "republican" languages of early American Methodism emerge less frequently in the spiritual writings that we are considering.

The intertwined languages of early Methodist spirituality are just one expression of its overall hybrid nature. For example, many of the Anglican notions about salvation and God came into early Methodism, but with the important difference that Methodists consistently internalized these notions and sought them through affective experience. A case in point is the Collect for Purity, one of the classic prayers from the Anglican tradition, which asks God to "cleanse the thoughts of our hearts by the inspiration of thy Holy Spirit, that we may perfectly love thee and worthily magnify thy holy name." For early Methodists this prayer became connected with the experience of sanctification. Surely, they argued, we expect God to answer the prayer at a particular time, effecting an inner renewal that enables us to love God perfectly and thoroughly.

Several authors have recognized this hybrid nature to early Methodism and its spirituality and tried to capture it with creative descriptions. One of the most illuminating is the suggestion that "[early] Methodism is Church of Englandism *felt*."[53] Russell Richey speaks in similar terms of early Methodism as "an evangelical Anglicanism...an Episcopal church defined by conversion."[54] While the specific connection to Anglicanism faded in later American Methodism, this hybrid character remained in place for some time.

American Methodists derived the hybrid quality to their religious life from John and Charles Wesley, the movement's founders. These two men, both Church of England priests, were in many respects the embodiment of "Church of Englandism felt." They devoted their mature ministry to developing a movement, supplemental to parish life in the Church of England, in which an "experimental" gospel could be proclaimed. This Methodist movement soon evolved its own system of lay preaching, discipleship, and

---

53. Leslie F. Church, *The Early Methodist People* (London: Epworth, 1948), 97. While Church uses this definition to describe early British Methodism, it could apply to American Methodism as well.

54. Russell E. Richey, "The Formation of American Methodism: The Chesapeake Refraction of Wesleyanism," in *Methodism and the Shaping of American Culture*, ed. Nathan O. Hatch and John H. Wigger (Nashville: Kingswood Books, 2001), 210.

21

worship. Both the structures and spirituality of the British movement were exported to America.

The mixing of classic Christianity with a concern for affective experience, connecting the result to both heart and head, was not unique to the Wesleys. It was actually a common agenda in the seventeenth and eighteenth centuries, particularly among those Protestants known as Pietists. The Wesleys are best seen as an Anglican example of this larger phenomenon. As Ted Campbell expressed the connection:

> Just as Reformed and Lutheran Pietists had reinterpreted their own doctrines concerning salvation, placing the stress on the personal apprehension of faith, so [John] Wesley reinterpreted the teaching of the Anglican tradition in the light of his new-found experience of the assurance of pardon.[55]

In other words, American Methodists inherited through the Wesleys a spirituality with roots in the Church of England and in the broader Pietist movement.

The Pietist influences on early American Methodist spirituality deserve more attention than they have usually received. These influences came not only through Wesleyan mediation but through their own interaction with Pietist strands of Baptists, Presbyterians, German-speaking fellowships (like the United Brethren), and even some Quakers. What these groups shared in common was an emphasis on the "religion of the heart." As Ted Campbell has summarized this emphasis:

> The religion of the heart movements maintained that this separation [from God] is overcome in affective ("heartfelt") experience: typically, in experiences of repentance (sorrow over sin) and faith (personal trust in God), but sometimes in more vivid experiences of personal illumination. The key element in their understanding of religious life, then, was their insistence that the "heart," denoting the will and affections (or "dispositions"), is the central point of contact between God and human kind.[56]

---

55. Ted A. Campbell, *The Religion of the Heart: A Study of European Religious Life in the Seventeenth and Eighteenth Centuries* (Columbia: University of South Carolina Press, 1991), 120.

56. Ibid., 2-3.

The context for Pietism's concern in this respect was a desire to supplement doctrinal correctness with proper interior experience and external practice. The goal was congruence between a person's head, heart, and life, all rightly touched by the grace of God in Christ. For Pietists, salvation could not be seen simply as God's work *for* us, something external to us. Being saved was not just assent to right doctrine and acknowledgment of what God had done. Salvation was also God's work *in* us.[57]

What came to the foreground in this type of spirituality was an emphasis on the heart, the human will, and the affections.[58] With this strong interior gaze also came concern with intent, with inward assurance, and with a perceived inward change of nature, most often going under the name of "regeneration" or "new birth." The shorthand way of emphasizing this aspect of inward religion was to speak of "experimental religion," that is, religion that had been inwardly experienced, particularly in the heart as the primary meeting ground between God and the human person.

Original Wesleyan spirituality, at its best, "combined inward faith with outward works, individual interiority with communal fellowship, the grace of God with the response of men (sic), spiritual experience with social involvement, ascetic intent with a purpose to actively love all men (sic)."[59] The dynamic tensions of this "Wesleyan" spirituality were transported to America with the early Methodist immigrants.

American Methodism did not arise independently as an indigenous movement; it shows its British Wesleyan roots in several places. The introduction of Methodism to America was neither planned nor coordinated. In the 1760s some Methodists who had immigrated to America simply began to gather for support and fellowship in places like Maryland and New York City. Eventually they issued a call for John Wesley to provide for them traveling preachers (known as "itinerants"). Wesley sent the first itinerant

---

57. John Weborg, "Pietism: 'The Fire of God which . . . Flames in the Heart of Germany,' " in *Protestant Spiritual Traditions*, ed. Frank C. Senn (Mahwah, N.J.: Paulist, 1986), 190.

58. Campbell, *Religion of the Heart*, 177. For a useful grid showing how Methodist spirituality would compare to other pietists and other Christians, see Urban T. Holmes III, *A History of Christian Spirituality: An Analytical Introduction* (New York: Seabury Press, 1980), 3-5 and 140-42.

59. Whaling, ed., *John and Charles Wesley*, 44.

preachers in 1769, and they served to solidify the distinctive corporate rhythms and structures of Methodist spirituality.

The fact that most of the early members and all of the initial itinerant preachers were immigrants from Britain helps account for the Wesleyan flavor of early American Methodist spirituality. But other factors were also important. For the first decade or so, John Wesley attempted a very directive hand in American Methodism, particularly in his choice of chief itinerants to serve as his proxy. He was also the source of most of the literature that shaped the American Methodist church through its first generation, providing them with devotional reading as well as doctrinal, homiletical, musical, and administrative material.

The administrative material should not be underestimated. Methodist organization was not simply for institutional administration. Rather, as others have noted, the organization created an environment in which the spirituality was brought to birth, nurtured, and deepened into the fullest enjoyment of God.[60] A large part of what made Methodist spirituality distinctive in relation to other pietistic and evangelical Christians were the structures and rhythms that guided the Methodists' experience of God. They were called "Methodists" for a reason. Early Methodism was not only "Church of Englandism felt," it was also these feelings organized.

EARLY METHODIST STRUCTURES AND DISTINCTIVES

A look at some of these structures would be helpful, not only to see how they guided Methodist spirituality but also to enable a modern reader to go past his or her experience of current forms of Methodism. Early Methodism worked on a much different basis than contemporary Methodism.

The backbone of early Methodist life were circuits with their itinerant preachers. These preachers, the chief ministers for Methodism, traveled around a somewhat fixed, somewhat fluid schedule of preaching appointments. The typical circuit was a "four-weeks" cir-

---

60. See Russell Richey, *The Methodist Conference in America: A History* (Nashville: Kingswood Books, 1996).

cuit, meaning that it took about a month to travel around.[61] The itinerants preached most days every month. In cities with several congregations (called "stations"), several itinerant preachers shared responsibility. They rotated among the congregations from worship service to worship service.[62] Placement of the itinerant preachers was the responsibility of the "General Assistant" before the creation of the Methodist Episcopal Church in 1784, and afterward the responsibility of a bishop. In the Asburian period, only whites *officially* served as itinerant preachers. A few itinerants became so popular that they functioned as roving evangelists with regional or even international appeal.

The numerous local preachers supplemented the work of itinerants. It appears that there were about three or four local preachers for every itinerant, whether on a circuit or in a station. Local preachers did not earn their living by preaching, in contrast to itinerant preachers. Local preachers received their authority to speak from the four-times-a-year business sessions for the circuit called "quarterly meetings" or "quarterly meeting conferences." For some, being a local preacher was a stepping stone on the way to itinerancy. For others, it was a place for continued ministry after itinerancy. For many, it was a long-term means for service in its own right. Both black and white men served officially as local preachers.

Other leaders shared the ministry with both kinds of preachers. Every circuit and station usually had "exhorters," who had received a license to publicly speak in worship but without seeking to expound a biblical text.[63] Stewards handled the financial matters. Trustees maintained what buildings there might be. Class leaders conducted the weekly class meetings required for all members. If the circuits and itinerant preachers were the basic skeleton for early Methodism, then class meetings were the central nervous system that brought life to the whole. In these weekly meetings, Methodists held each other accountable for growing in grace. Here they rehearsed their experiences of God's salvation and deepened

---

61. Wigger, *Taking Heaven by Storm*, 35.
62. For more information, see Lester Ruth, "Urban Itinerancy: 'Stational' Liturgy in Early American Methodism," *Studia Liturgica* 32 (2002): 222-39.
63. Wigger, *Taking Heaven by Storm*, 29.

their desire for the next step of grace. In some locales bands also existed. These band meetings, which were not required for membership, were a more intensive form of small groups where those who had already experienced the first aspect of salvation (justification) could join with others to plunge the depths of salvation, including the seeking of sanctification. Given the nature of itinerancy, class and band leaders provided much of the pastoral care for rank-and-file Methodists.

Beyond all these official categories, there were a variety of types of informal leadership within early American Methodism. This was where many women and children, black and white, had opportunity. As worship became intense, for example, it was common for anyone (and everyone!) who had felt the power of God to begin to exhort their neighbors. No one was concerned about official licenses at that point. Well-respected women and men also carried influence as models/mentors or "mothers" and "fathers of Israel."

It was noted earlier that the threshold for membership in the Methodist society was not an interior experience of salvation but the earnest desire for such an experience. As Wesley had put it, the threshold was a desire to "flee from the wrath to come, and to be saved from their sins." This phrase comes from the General Rules, which outline Methodist spirituality in terms of detailed expectations for moral behavior and for regular use of the "means of grace." Those desiring membership were admitted for an initial probationary period. Membership continued on a continual probationary status, since membership tickets were to be renewed every quarter by the chief itinerant for a circuit. Theoretically, failure to live methodically could lead to the chief itinerant denying the renewal of one's ticket.

The "means of grace" were central to Methodist spirituality. This phrase designated the normal channels in which continued progress in a life of grace was nurtured. These were also the settings where the climactic experiences of salvation—justification (forgiveness of sins) and sanctification (the cleansing of sin)—were normally experienced. This was not a passive piety. Methodists were expected to cooperate with the grace of God by using the means of grace.

There were two general kinds of means of grace: instituted and prudential.[64] Instituted means were those commanded of all Christians, generally those found specified in the Bible. Prudential, on the other hand, were those means Methodists considered to have been given by God specifically to nurture Methodist growth and identity. In this latter category were some of the most dearly loved aspects of Methodist life like love feasts, covenant services (an opportunity to renew one's covenant with God), and class and band meetings.

The contemporary reader, particularly a Methodist one, may have to give up many presumptions to understand early Methodism's nature. Some deal with ministry issues. The reader today must put away any thought about Methodism operating like parishes. Early Methodists had no pastor in residence, for instance. This made ministry a shared responsibility. Whether in circuits or stations, multiple itinerant and local preachers shared responsibilities for multiple congregations. Virtually none had formal theological training.

Readers should also avoid projecting back other common features of contemporary church life. Do not assume that Methodists in every locale had a building. By 1785, for instance, Methodists had built or purchased only sixty chapels—at a time when there were more than eight hundred recognized preaching places.[65] Most Methodist meetings in this period took place in a variety of domestic and public buildings.

Perhaps the most important presumption which should be set aside is to link the word "Methodist" with some sort of middle-class, sedate, religious respectability. Such domestication of Methodism came largely in the nineteenth century, though the first inklings emerge toward the end of the period we are considering.[66] Though despised and even mimicked for their exuberant worship behavior, early Methodists often relished how a marginal social position allowed them to maintain a countercultural witness. Being on the periphery of respectable society, however, made becoming a Methodist a difficult choice for many. Attracted by the gospel

---

64. Henry H. Knight III, *The Presence of God in the Christian Life: John Wesley and the Means of Grace* (Metuchen, N.J.: Scarecrow, 1992), 2-5.

65. Wigger, *Taking Heaven by Storm*, 36.

66. To document this transition, see Schneider, *Way of the Cross*.

Methodists preached, some knew they would lose status, even family connections, by joining this movement. Early Methodism was not mainstream initially, and family members worried about their kin who joined.

CONCLUDING CAUTIONS

With all of the attention that has been given to its "Wesleyan" roots, it is important to close with a counterpoint about early American Methodist spirituality: it was never an exact replica of the Wesleys' spirituality, even while the two men were alive. For one thing, American Methodists were not nearly as well read as the founders of the movement. There is still input from patristic, Puritan, and other sources, but the amount and breadth of material did not match what influenced the Wesleys. On top of this, the Americans had a marked tendency to emphasize—perhaps even exaggerate—the interior, subjective aspect of religious experience and the strong emotions that often accompanied such experiences.[67] One result was a growing expectation for an emotional crisis experience of salvation in a public worship setting.

The very setting of America also helped shift Methodist spirituality from its Wesleyan roots. For one thing, Anglicanism did not provide the pervasive context here that it did in England. As Methodism expanded into New England and into new settlements west of the Appalachians and in the deep South, there was little, if any, Anglican backdrop against which to place Methodism. Even in the middle Atlantic states, where Anglican presence was strongest, the period of Methodist growth after the Revolution came as Anglicanism was struggling to survive in the region.[68] Increasingly Methodists did not come from Anglican backgrounds and were not used to interacting with Anglicanism as the dominant religious partner.

---

67. Robert E. Chiles, *Theological Transition in American Methodism 1790–1935* (New York: Abingdon, 1935), 43. See too Randy Maddox's suggestion that, although Americans adopted the doctrines of John Wesley, they changed the method of doing theology: Randy L. Maddox, "Respected Founder/Neglected Guide: The Role of Wesley in American Methodist Theology," *Methodist History* 37 (1999): 74.

68. For a comparison of Methodism to Anglicanism in this region, see Richey, "Formation of American Methodism," 210-11.

The distinctive American context also provided other shifts in Methodist spirituality. One important factor was the presence of so many African Americans within Methodism. In many circuits their numbers rivaled those of Methodists from European descent. They influenced the character of American Methodism in its exuberance, its ecstasy, and its manner of preaching, making music, and behaving in public worship, among other things. This influence might have been even stronger, but for the resistance of some white Methodists and the growing tensions over slavery and black/white relations.

The American Revolution, and the changes it brought to American society, also influenced Methodist religious life. The emerging democratic and free-market environment of the early republic brought increased opportunity for grassroots religious movements like Methodism.[69] The displacement of established churches and waning of long-respected venues for bestowing ministerial authority opened room for popular religious movements like Methodism, with its marginally educated preaching corps, to flourish. This fostered increased pragmatism. American Methodists became much more attentive to religious means that "worked" evangelistically. These means then were promoted aggressively. Increased consciousness about counting numbers and institutionalizing successful innovations were the results. The history of the emergence of camp meetings as a staple of Methodist spiritual life is a prime example of this process.[70]

In such a setting, just as early American Methodists differed from the Wesleys, they could differ from one another. While more uniform in spirituality than contemporary Methodism, the ethnic and regional variations among the earlier generation should not be overlooked. I will draw attention to several examples of this variation in the thematic survey that follows of this vibrant spirituality that swept a new nation.

---

69. See Wigger, *Taking Heaven by Storm*; and Nathan O. Hatch, *The Democratization of American Christianity* (New Haven: Yale University Press, 1989).
70. Cf. Lester Ruth, "Reconsidering the Emergence of the Second Great Awakening and Camp Meetings among Early Methodists," *Worship* 75 (2001): 334-55.

CHAPTER 1

JESUS CHRIST

Early American Methodists were obsessed with salvation. If there was one concern around which all other convictions orbited, it was salvation. Among theological categories, salvation predominated. Among spiritual desires, salvation was central. Among topics for preaching and singing, salvation held sway. Among motivations for ministry, salvation provided the impulse for all others.

This preoccupation came to Methodism from its roots in John Wesley. He had structured his movement as one large missionary enterprise. Wesley's rhetoric was quite clear. "You have nothing to do," as he put it in instructions to his traveling preachers, "but to save souls."[1] If the writings of rank-and-file Methodists are any indication, this charge was taken seriously. Nothing concerned Methodists more than salvation.

And so, not surprisingly, American Methodists were obsessed with the savior, Jesus Christ. They understood salvation not as some generic or abstract experience, but as something intimately linked to a particular person, Jesus Christ. Salvation and the savior, both gifts of God, were inseparably joined in their spirituality. In particular, he was the key mediator in God's offering of human salvation. As Leland Scott has suggested, the central biblical text for early Methodism could well have been 1 Corinthians 1:30, which

---

1. See "Large Minutes," Q. 26, a. 11, *The Works of John Wesley*, ed. Thomas Jackson (London, 1872; Grand Rapids: Zondervan, 1958), 8:310.

speaks of Christ as humanity's "wisdom, and righteousness, and sanctification, and redemption."[2]

Why were early Methodists so enamored of Jesus Christ? The first thing that contributed to their loving devotion was their conviction about the scope and breadth of the salvation he had won for humanity. They were staggered by contemplating someone who could be a savior for *all*. The salvation God had wrought in Jesus Christ extended over all God's creation. Most striking in this realization were the claims that Christ had died for all people and that all could benefit from his death. In their religious context—one in which widespread, popular forms of Calvinism spoke of a limited scope to Christ's saving work—such claims sparked adoring awe.

Consequently, one of the recurring themes in their contemplating Christ was that of fullness. They dwelled on the One who was a savior for all. As the breadth of his grace covers the whole world—even the whole cosmos—so should his praises ring from "ev'ry nation, ev'ry tongue," from "worlds on worlds with all their throng," and from "pole to pole."[3] The Methodists were staggered by the scope of the savior's love, and they were zealous to call everyone to loving praise of this savior.

Another reason that early Methodists were so enamored of Christ was the deeply personal understanding they accepted about salvation. It was not only that Christ was savior of all; he was the savior *for me*. Their testimonies speak repeatedly about the moment this realization dawned on them. Experienced by faith, this awareness was their deepest spiritual treasure.

It was not simply this personal awareness that enamored them to the savior. The sheer graciousness or largesse of the love they found in Christ also overwhelmed them. What they saw in their savior intrigued them. Christ represented both the transcendence and immanence of God. God's vastness and the opportunity to be intimate with God were wrapped up in the same person, Jesus Christ, whose basic disposition was a love that exceeded human description. This dual quality sparked a range of spiritual response from intimidation to intimacy. Reflecting this complexity, they called

---

2. Leland Howard Scott, "The Message of Early American Methodism," in *The History of American Methodism*, ed. Emory Stevens Bucke (Nashville: Abingdon, 1964), 1:296.

3. See the first excerpt of this chapter, a hymn by Methodist preacher John Adam Granade.

Jesus Christ both "Lord" and "dearest friend,"[4] and they loved him for the full spectrum.

The reader should not underestimate that it was a *person* with which they were enamored. In the eighteenth century there were theological forces like Deism at work that reduced God's nature and work to that comprehensible to human reason. On these terms there was no need for special revelation.[5] Nor was one likely to adore Christ as the special revealer of God. But, in Methodist estimation, there was no one who could compare to Jesus Christ. All other claimants for the heart were pretenders. This led to claims that there was no other way to God than Christ, but it was more characteristically expressed in the awe of exclusive devotion: absolutely no one could compare to the breadth and depth and height of grace shown in him!

Their consuming passion for salvation, and the incessant impulse to be actively engaged in evangelism, meant that there was little abstract or theoretical thought given to Jesus Christ in early American Methodism. There is again a parallel to John Wesley in this regard. Speaking of his understanding of the incarnation of Christ, John Deschner suggests that Wesley was much more intrigued by the *fact* of the incarnation as a knowledge "useful for plain people" than by debates over the *manner* of the incarnation (that is, exactly how it was that the Son of God could assume human nature).[6] Similarly, most American Methodists valued contemplation of Christ primarily as it issued forth in worship and in offering to others the salvation he brought. This salvation became the lens for organizing almost all thought about Christ. Indeed, it became the main interpretative lens for reading Scriptures and for reflecting on all theological topics.

This orientation is reflected in the kinds of writings that American Methodists produced about Jesus Christ. In their early decades there was little energy given to formal theology. They produced no scholastic survey texts. Even short treatises were late in

---

4. Lyerly, *Methodism and the Southern Mind*, 30.

5. For more detailed analysis of this aspect of Methodism's theological context, see Mark A. Noll, *America's God: From Jonathan Edwards to Abraham Lincoln* (New York: Oxford University Press, 2002), 138-57.

6. John Deschner, *Wesley's Christology: An Interpretation*, rev. ed. (Grand Rapids: Francis Asbury Press, 1985), 14.

coming. There was virtually no attention given to providing a systematic exploration of Jesus Christ or of the Trinity. This is not to suggest that early Methodist theology wandered freely among heterodox understandings. With their roots in Wesleyan theology, and the guidance of their Anglican-derived Articles of Religion, Methodists' understandings of Christ and of the Trinity generally fell within orthodox boundaries. And American Methodists were concerned enough to exercise disciplinary measures if they found someone advocating a position outside these boundaries.[7]

While Methodists were concerned with classic theological definitions for Christ, they did not spend much time in the early decades writing new explications of these. Their energy was spent instead in evangelistic effort and in communal discipleship. Accordingly, their efforts concerning Christ were turned upward as adoring prayer or outward as an exhorting offer to the world. When put in writing, these efforts took the form of hymns, sermons, and edifying letters and diaries. As Mark Noll has aptly stated it, "The literature of an experiential religious movement was experiential literature."[8]

If pressed to detail their understandings of Christ, most early Methodists would have sounded rather routinely—even simply—orthodox and Wesleyan. With respect to the Trinity, they would affirm the unity of the Godhead, with three equal Persons (the Father, Son, and Holy Spirit) making up the same. Jesus Christ, the second Person of the Trinity, was both fully human and fully divine, having been truly born to a human mother. His ministry, life, death, and resurrection occurred within human history with a fully human body. The pinnacle of his saving actions came in his death as an atonement for human sin and his resurrection that conquered death. Having ascended to heaven after the resurrection, Christ continues his saving work at God's right hand. There he is creating a place for his people for eternal enjoyment. The early Methodists awaited Christ's coming again to fulfill God's saving purposes.

---

7. See Ruth, *A Little Heaven Below*, 128; Richard P. Heitzenrater, "At Full Liberty: Doctrinal Standards in Early American Methodism," in *Perspectives on American Methodism*, ed. Richey, et al., 67-68; and *Doctrines and Discipline of the MEC* (1798), 113.

8. Noll, *America's God*, 336. The experiential nature of Methodism is explored more fully in chapter 2.

Even when early Methodists showed a range of opinions about some aspect of Christ-related doctrine, both the range and the predominant opinion tended to replicate that found among contemporary Pietistic Protestants. Consider the doctrine of the atonement. Although all four of the classic views of the atonement existed among eighteenth century Protestants, the penal substitution view (by his death, Christ fulfills the requirements of God's righteousness; in his death, Christ receives the just penalty for humanity's sin and forestalls the wrath of God falling upon humans) predominated.[9] Not surprisingly, that seems to be true for early American Methodists too, although other opinions were also held, as will be seen below.

Only in a few critical points does the typical early Methodist understanding of Christ stand out from that of their Protestant contemporaries in America. As noted earlier, one point was in their emphasis on the global scope of Christ's atonement. Regardless of the particular theory adopted, American Methodists insisted that the atonement benefited all people. Against a widespread Calvinist background, this was by no means a universally accepted idea. The other place where Methodists would have stood out was in their spirituality's emphasis on the affective encounter of an atoning Christ. Atonement was first of all something to be inwardly experienced. To adjust a phrase from the introduction, the goal for Methodist contemplation of Christ was not just theological orthodoxy but "orthodoxy felt."

Early American Methodists did not champion a new idea about Jesus Christ; they reveled in a new experience of Christ. They embraced Christ, feeling him and contemplating him in the deepest regions of their hearts. As Bishop Asbury described it, the true knowledge of Christ was "saving knowledge," it was "a spiritual and experimental knowledge of repentance, faith, regeneration, and sanctification, producing a holy life, a triumphant death, a joyful resurrection, and a crown of eternal glory."[10] In other words, we come to know Christ truly in the experience of salvation. Bare assent to doctrinal statements falls far short of such true knowledge.[11]

---

9. Ibid., 267-68.
10. Asbury, *Journal and Letters*, 2:597.
11. Compare John Wesley's statements about the type of knowledge demons have of Christ; Sermon 1, "Salvation by Faith," §I.2, *The Works of John Wesley*, ed. Frank Baker (Nashville: Abingdon, 1984), 1:119-20.

The transcendence of bare assent to doctrine in early Methodist writings is perhaps best seen in the passages that speak of Jesus Christ as intimate friend or lover. Christ was the One with whom their hearts could share deep communion.

Such intimate spirituality is a recurring strand in Christianity, though I have found no evidence of direct influence of earlier classic examples upon American Methodists. More significant was surely the latent potential for such affection in the Wesleyan hymnody that they inherited.[12] This hymnody presented God as divine love in highly personified terms. It also encouraged them to expect the thresholds of their relationship with Christ—the rhythms of conversion and sanctification—to be characterized by deep experience of fulfillment. In the American setting it became common for these thresholds to be intense episodes of resolving great desire. This fostered a spirituality that conceived of relationship with God in intimate terms.

Perhaps the most striking example was Sarah Jones, the Virginian Methodist from the late-eighteenth century. There is an explicitly erotic quality in her relationship with Christ. The images she used were some of the most vivid and sensual in the early American Methodist material. On one occasion, for instance, she described Christ as a mother at whose breast Jones and a prayer partner nursed.[13] More typical were images of Christ as a male lover, often based on the biblical book known as Song of Songs or Song of Solomon. For example, Jones could speak of Christ as a perfumed lover with whom she enjoyed the delight of kissing.

It is difficult to know how exceptional other Methodists considered such imagery.[14] There are indications in Jones's writings that some Methodists were uncomfortable with her, though the specific reasons are unclear. On the other hand, Francis Asbury spoke

---

12. Perhaps the harshest judgment on this hymnody in this respect is E. P. Thompson's description of it as a "ritualized form of psychic masturbation" (cited in Andrews, *Methodists and Revolutionary America*, 78). Andrews suggests that Thompson's critique is overstated.

13. Minter, ed., *Devout Letters*, 34. See also Lyerly, *Methodism and the Southern Mind*, 30.

14. For evidence that some other Methodist women shared such erotic imagery, see Cynthia Lyerly, "Passion, Desire, and Ecstasy: The Experiential Religion of Southern Methodist Women, 1770–1810," in *The Devil's Lane: Sex and Race in the Early South*, ed. Catherine Clinton & Michelle Gillespie (New York: Oxford University Press, 1997), 168-86. Such imagery has been a recurring element in broader Christian spirituality as well. For American Puritans, see Richard Godbeer, "'Love Raptures': Marital, Romantic, and Erotic Images of Jesus Christ in Puritan New England, 1670–1730," *New England Quarterly* 68 (1995): 355-84. Even the image of Christ as nursing mother has roots as far back as the early patristic period; cf. Caroline Walker Bynum, *Holy Feast and Holy Fast: The Religious Significance of Food to Medieval Women* (Berkeley: University of California Press, 1987), 270-71. For discussion of the interpretation of the Song of Songs as a basis for such spirituality, see Carey Ellen Walsh, *Exquisite Desire: Religion, the Erotic, and the Song of Songs* (Minneapolis: Fortress Press, 2000), 196-201.

approvingly of her piety and ability to pray,[15] and numerous itin-erant preachers collected and reproduced her material. This sug-gests that Jones's spirituality was not too far removed from the center of Methodism. It might best be characterized as a more intense form of something inherent in Methodist piety. In like man-ner, Jones's ascetic practices like restricted diet, extended fasting, sleep deprivation, and extended times in prayer—all reasons for the intensely intimate nature of her spirituality—were not unknown to other Methodists, even if practiced less zealously. Whether or not they reached the erotic intensity of Jones's expres-sions, other Methodists would recognize—and they all deeply shared—the same devotion of love for Jesus Christ. Such devotion was the common inheritance of all early Methodists.

Most of the twenty-three selections below, offering early Methodist reflections on Christ, come from the mainstays of Methodist experiential literature: sermons, letter, diaries, journals, and, especially, hymns. The material comes from fifteen distinct sources, although the specific number of Methodists involved is impossible to tell since some of the hymns were recorded without naming an author. The reflections are gathered around topics sug-gested by their frequency (or intensity) within Methodist writings. The first two sets focus on Jesus as Lord and Savior, which was surely the core of Methodist conviction about Christ. The last set of excerpts focuses on Jesus as Lover, reflecting the passion of the love Methodists had for Jesus Christ.

JESUS, LORD

Popular Appalachian preacher John Adam Granade is the author of the following hymn entitled "The Glories of Immanuel." Using the word "Immanuel" (meaning God with us) as the ending note for each stanza, Granade builds a hymn that glorifies Christ in all his different attributes and in various aspects of his saving work.

>1. Hail, God the Father, glorious light;
>Hail, God the Son, my soul's delight;

---

15. Asbury, *Journal and Letters*, 2:34.

Hail, Holy Ghost, all one in three,
My anthem through eternity.

2. The glitt'ring orbs all round the skies,
But speak his glory in disguise;
Their silent notes too weak to tell
The wisdom of Immanuel.

3. Those wretched souls who dwell in fire,
Quite sunk beneath his dreadful ire,[16]
Their dismal groans would fail to tell
The justice of Immanuel.

4. Tall mountains that becloud the skies,
With all the hills that round them rise,
While time endures you ne'er can tell
The power of Immanuel.

5. Ye tumbling seas with dismal roar,
Whose numbers sound from shore to shore,
Your thund'ring language ne'er can tell
The grandeur of Immanuel.

6. Could ev'ry nation, ev'ry tongue
Join in one universal song,
Their stamm'ring tongues could never tell
The love of King Immanuel.

7. Let worlds on worlds with all their throng
Through ev'ry chime extend the song,
A guilty world preserved from Hell
By Christ, the King Immanuel.

8. Behold him leave his Father's throne.
Behold him bleed and hear him groan.

---

16. Impenitent sinners suffering in hell.

Death's iron chains would fail to tell
The strength of King Immanuel.

9. Behold him take his ancient seat
And millions bowing at his feet.
He's conquered Satan, Death, and Hell
And wears the crown, Immanuel.

10. His fame shall sound from pole to pole,
While glory flows from soul to soul.
The gospel now goes forth to tell
The myst'ries of Immanuel.

11. While I am singing of his name,
My soul begins to feel the flame.
I'm full, I'm full, yet cannot tell
The goodness of Immanuel.

12. I long to hear his trumpet sound
And see his glory blaze around.
I then will shout and sing and tell
Salvation to Immanuel.[17]

13. The thousand thousand in the throng,
The thousand thousand join the song;
He saved us from a gaping Hell.
All glory to Immanuel.

14. Meanwhile the shining angels try
In flaming notes each to out vie.
They tune their harps each to excel
In praising of Immanuel.

15. My soul's transported with those charms.
I long to lie in Jesus' arms.

17. Meaning salvation belongs to or comes from Immanuel.

Through countless ages there to tell
How dear I love Immanuel.[18]

In this letter passage, Virginia Methodist Sarah Jones piles up biblical names and allusions for Jesus Christ to create a sense of awe in Christ's greatness. For Jones, the breadth and number of names for Jesus reveals the wonder of his glory. Jesus Christ is obviously all in all to her.

Let us learn his name: what is it? The Scripture says his name is a well of living water, a well of life, a wedding garment, Shiloh, a heart, a stone cut out of the mountain, the Paschal Lamb, rain and showers, an apple tree, a bundle of myrrh, a cluster of camphire, fuller's soap, a purging fire, a ladder, a rose, a lily, the desire of nations, the door of the sheep, the ancient of days, God's beloved, the bread of life, a branch, the law, the end of the law, a light, a great light, etc., etc. He is the finisher of faith. This makes my heart glad. He is the head of all power, the head of the church, the lion of Judah, and the Amen. O, how am I buried in wonder, swallowed up in ecstatic joy and gladness to think his name is ointment for every sore, for every complaint, [and] for all my infirmities. For he bears my sickness, and weakness, and the iniquities of my holiest things, or I could not see God, that composition of bright holiness.[19]

Based on Colossians 3:11, this hymn entitled "Christ Is All" extols the fullness of the Lord Jesus Christ.

1. O Christ, the God of love,
Teach me the holy art,
In love to rise, and walk above,
And give thee all my heart!

2. Though I could span the earth,
Its honors, wealth, and ease,

---

18. Thomas S. Hinde, ed., *The Pilgrim Songster* (Chillicothe, Ohio: 1815), 74-75. See also Richard A. Humphrey, comp., *History and Hymns of John Adam Granade: Holston's Pilgrim-Preacher-Poet* (Commission on Archives and History, Holston Annual Conference, The United Methodist Church: 1991).

19. Minter, ed., *Devout Letters*, 40.

All mine, and all the heavens hath,
'Twere naught to Jesus' grace.

3. All strength to strength in thee,
All loveliness to thine,
Are weakness and deformity;
O make thy fullness mine!

4. What are the seas, and isles,
The mountains, clouds, and skies,
To Jesus' fullness, love, and smiles,
In life that never dies?

5. What is the human form,
To his majestic grace,
But as a poor decaying stream,
To streams of endless bliss?

6. Ah, what is human love,
That mortals count so dear,
To Jesus' favor from above,
And love that brings us there?

7. Thus all that's good agree
In Christ, as all in all;
For time, and to eternity,
Adore him, O my soul!

8. O mortals hear, and learn,
See also, and be wise,
Christ to embrace as all, and shun
The loss that he supplies![20]

---

20. Jeremiah Minter, *Hymns and Spiritual Songs, For the Use of All Christians* (Baltimore: G. Dobbin and Murphy, 1809), 44-47.

In this 1813 sermon, a preacher named Graber expounds the greatness of Christ by a typological comparison to Moses. As great as Moses was as a man of God, Christ excels over him.

Deuteronomy 18:15: A Prophet shall the Lord, etc.[21]

1. Christ alone was like Moses as a prophet (Deuteronomy 34:10, 11, 12; Acts 2:22).

2. Christ was like Moses as a mediator (Deuteronomy 5:5; 1 Timothy 2:5) but [was] greater than Moses as he was mediator of a better covenant or testament (Hebrews 7:6).[22]

3. Christ was like unto Moses in excellency for Moses excelled all the prophets in speaking to God mouth to mouth (Numbers 12:6, 7, 8), but Christ excelled him and all men in that, being in the bosom of the Father, he has come down from heaven and declared Him unto us (John 1:18, 3:13).

4. Christ was like unto Moses in faithfulness but therein also excelling [Moses] for Moses was faithful in God's house as a servant but Christ as a Son over his own house (Hebrews 3:2, 3, 4, 5).

5. Christ was like unto Moses in signs and wonders, wherein also he excelled Moses as the Gospels show (Luke 24:11; Acts 2:22)[23] for he did among them the works which none [other person did] (John 15:24)....

6. As Moses was king among his people, in this respect Christ is like unto Him, but infinitely greater for he is King of kings and Lord of lords (Revelation 19:16; 1 Timothy 5:15). And

7. He was like [un]to Moses as legislator. Moses gave laws to Israel by the authority and commandment of God, which the Jews have ever acknowledged as coming from the immediate inspiration of the Almighty. Christ gave a new law, the Gospel, contained in the 4 evangelists and Acts of the Apostles[24] on which the Christian Church is founded and governed both in heart and life.

---

21. Deuteronomy 18:15 actually reads like this: "The LORD thy God will raise up unto thee a Prophet from the midst of thee, of thy brethren, like unto me; unto him ye shall hearken."

22. The preacher actually means Hebrews 8:6: "But now hath he obtained a more excellent ministry, by how much also he is the mediator of a better covenant, which was established upon better promises."

23. It is not clear what passage in Luke is actually in mind.

24. Meaning the first five books of the New Testament: Matthew, Mark, Luke, John (the four evangelists), and Acts.

To which may be added

8. That God never commissioned any human being to give laws to mankind but Moses and Christ. For to the present hour none but themselves have given laws to mankind in the name of God, ratified and confirmed by such undebatable and infallible signs, proofs, and miracles.[25]

Using the word "wonderful" as a kind of refrain, Maryland itinerant preacher Daniel Fidler builds a sermon that praises Christ for his role for God's way of salvation. In the sermon, Fidler shows how he understands the reason for Christ's passion in "the plan of redemption."

Isaiah 9:7.[26] Give my sentiments on the wonderful counselor.

1. He was wonderful in the plan of man's redemption.

1. Justice cries for satisfaction.

2. Love interposed on behalf of the offender.

3. Truth joins justice.

4. Mercy joins love.

5. Righteousness joins justice and truth.

6. Peace sound [?] the voice with love and mercy.

7. Divine wisdom points [to] a way [so] that all the attributes of God may be glorified, and [that] God be just and the justifier of the ungodly race of Adam.[27]

2. He was wonderful in his incarnation.

3. He was wonderful in his humiliation.

4. He was wonderful in his sufferings and death.

5. He was wonderful in his resurrection.

6. He [has] exaltation as a prophet, priest, and king.

7. He [will have exaltation] when he shall sit on his throne of glory, yea, when he judges the godly.

8. [He is] Wonderful to all eternity.

Conclusion.[28]

---

25. Nathaniel Mills, Journal, 19 August 1813.

26. Fidler must mean Isaiah 9:6: "For unto us a child is born, unto us a son is given: and the government shall be upon his shoulder: and his name shall be called Wonderful, Counselor, The mighty God, The everlasting Father, The Prince of Peace."

27. Fidler seems to be saying that God's just character required sacrificial satisfaction for humanity's sins. The death of God Incarnate, Jesus Christ, allows God to provide that satisfaction, thus being both "just and the justifier."

28. Daniel Fidler, Sermon Notebook, 2.

JESUS, SAVIOR

Henry Bradford includes the following hymn in his hymnal handwritten in the early nineteenth century. Written as a song of praise to Jesus Christ, it rehearses the basic elements of Christ's saving actions.

1. Salvation to Jesus,[29] he's Zion's[30] bright King.
Oh! God with thy praises let all the earth ring.
We hear from the east, from the west, north, and south
To conquer the nations the Lord's going forth.

2. Salvation to Jesus, let all the world know
He died to redeem us from sorrow and woe.
He arose to declare our justified[31] state.
Come, seek your salvation before it's too late.

3. Salvation to Jesus, he's now gone above
Where he will prepare for us mansions of love.
He has sent down the Comforter into the world[32]
And causes salvation from Zion to roll.

4. Salvation to Jesus, his mercy abounds
And sinners take shelter in his precious wounds.
They're crying and turning and coming to God
And finding redemption in Jesus' blood.

5. Salvation to Jesus, my soul is alive.
This word is now spreading, his work does revive.
O! God, shake the nations until they submit
And bow down with pleasure at Jesus' feet.

---

29. Compare Revelation 7:10. An unusual phrase for modern ears, it probably means salvation belongs to or comes from Jesus.

30. Zion was often used as a typological term for the church. See Richey, *Early American Methodism*, 95.

31. For early Methodists, justification would refer to the first experience of salvation.

32. See John 14:2, 16.

6. Salvation to Jesus, my soul's in a flame.
My heart does rejoice at the sound of his name.
Shout all the creation below and above
Ascribing salvation to Jesus' love.

7. Salvation to Jesus, my soul's all on fire
I feel I am rising but I want to rise higher.
O! Angels O! Angels, come lend me your wings
To fly to my Jesus, the King of all kings.

8. Salvation to Jesus, we'll quickly appear
In bright flaming glory, he's now drawing near.
I am going, my brethren, to meet him above
Where I shall eternally feast on his love.

9. "Salvation to Jesus" shall then be my song
When I meet my dear brethren around the bright throne.
With loud hallelujahs all heaven shall ring
Salvation, salvation to Jesus, my king."[33]

Here is another hymn from the Bradford collection extolling Christ for being savior. Unlike the previous hymn, this one is signed by Henry Bradford and dated 10 May 1804. The images for salvation are more exotic and sensual. The hymn includes many common early Methodist themes, particularly its emphasis on experiencing heaven as the climax of salvation. Notice, however, this hope is a communal one centered in fellowship with Christ and others who adore him. Thus Bradford's hope for heaven is neither individualistic nor primarily concerned with individual enrichment.

1. The Lord into his garden comes.
The spices yield a sweet perfume.
The lily grows and thrives.
Refreshing showers of grace divine
From Jesus flows on every vine
And makes the dead alive.

---

33. Henry Bradford, Hymnbook, 13.

2. O that the dry and barren ground
In springs of water may abound.
O fruitful soil become.
The desert blossoms as the rose[34]
Till Jesus conquers all his foes
And makes his people one.

3. That gracious time is rolling on.
The glorious work is now begun.
My soul a witness is.
I taste and see that grace is free
And all mankind as well as me
May come to Christ and live.

4. The worst of sinners here may find
A Savior pitiful and kind
Who will them all receive.
None are too bad who will repent
Out of one sinner legion[35] went
The Lord did him relieve.

5. Come, brethren, you that know the Lord,
That taste the sweets of Jesus' word,
In Jesus' ways go on.
Our troubles and our trials here
Will only make us richer there
When we arrive at home.

6. We feel that heaven is now begun.
It issues from the sprinkled throne,[36]
From Jesus' throne on high.
It comes like [a] flood we can't contain.
We drink and drink and drink again,
And yet we still are dry.

---

34. Isaiah 35:1.

35. The line refers to Jesus commanding the demons to leave a man. See Mark 5:1-13 and Luke 8:27-33.

36. Probably a reference to the throne of God, which the hymn writer assumes has been sprinkled with the blood of Christ.

7. But when we come to reign above,
And all around the throne of love,
We'll drink a fresh supply.
Jesus will lead his armies forth
To [a] living fountain pure and fresh
That never will run dry.[37]

8. 'Tis there we'll sing and shout and sing
And make the upper regions ring
When all the saints get home.
Come on, come on, my brethren dear,
We soon shall meet together there
For Jesus bids us come.

9. "Amen, Amen," my soul replies.
I'm bound to meet you in the skies
The Savior to adore.
Now here's my heart and here's my hand
To meet you in that heavenly land
Where we shall part no more.[38]

The various aspects of Jesus Christ's life and ministry could be objects for Methodist devotion and contemplation. In the following passage, Lucy Watson reflects on the humility she sees in Christ's birth, a humility that accomplishes our salvation.

The rain confines me to the house but reading the nativity of our Savior has been blest to my soul. I find that pride was the first sin that made havoc of God's creation, but humility was the first grace that appeared in our blessed Savior's life and, from the first to the last, this [humility] was manifest by [his] example and precept.

---

37. Compare Song of Solomon 4:15 and Jeremiah 2:13.
38. Henry Bradford, Hymnbook, 10.

Surely this is the "new and living way"[39] wherein we ought to follow him. By this, we may gain the top of the ladder that scales the mount of God.

By humility he raised our fallen nature. By suffering he was made perfect.[40] By submission he overcame. O the wonderful plan of redemption![41]

Christ's birth is also the subject of the following hymn. The piece places the reader in the perspective of the shepherds who receive the angelic announcement of the birth in Luke 2. The second stanza marks the saving significance of Christ's birth as a reversal of the effects of Adam's original rebellion.

On the Nativity of Christ
   1. As shepherds in Jewry were grazing their sheep
   Promiscuously seated, estranged to sleep,
   An angel from heaven presented to view
   And thus he accosted the trembling few:
   "Dispel all your sorrow and banish your fears
   For Jesus your Savior in Jewry appears."

   2. Though Adam the first in rebellion was found,
   Forbidden to tarry on hallowed ground,
   Yet Adam the second appears to retrieve
   The loss we sustained by the devil and Eve.
   Then shepherds, be tranquil, this moment arise.
   Go, visit your Savior and see where he lies.

   3. A token I give whereby you may find
   This heavenly stranger, this friend to mankind:
   A manger his cradle, a stall his abode,
   The oxen are near him and low on your God.
   Then shepherds, be humble, be meek and lie low
   For Jesus your Savior's abundantly so.

---

39. Hebrews 10:20.
40. See Hebrews 2:10.
41. Lucy Fanning Watson, Experiences, 54.

4. This wondrous story scarce cooled on their ear
When thousands of angels in glory appeared.
They joined in the concert and this was the theme:
"All glory to God and good will towards men."
Then shepherds strike in, join your voice to the choir
And catch a few sparkles of celestial fire.

5. "Hosanna," the angels in ecstasy cry.
"Hosanna," the wondering shepherds reply.
Salvation, redemption are centered in one.
All glory to God for the birth of his Son.
Then shepherds adieu, we commend you to God.
Go, visit the Son in his humble abode.

6. To Bethlehem city the shepherds repaired
For full confirmation of what they had heard.
They entered the stable with aspect so mild
And there they beheld the mother and child.
Then make proclamation divulge it abroad
That gentle and simple may hear of the Lord.[42]

The following hymn, entitled "Christ Our Salvation," praises the saving effect of the death of Christ. It uses several images to describe the various aspects of Christ's atonement, including the important notion that Christ's crucifixion is a substitutionary atonement that diminishes the wrath of God the Father toward humankind.

1. When man was fallen far from God,
Exposed to condemnation,
The Lord of glory interposed
And purchased our salvation.
He laid his richest glory by
And groveled in the garden.[43]
'Twas love divine did him incline
To purchase for us pardon.

---

42. Spiritual Songs (Edward Dromgoole papers), 3.
43. The Garden of Gethsemane.

2. None could atone but Christ alone,
His Father's wrath diminish.
To make us kings and priests to God[44]
Jesus has cried, "'Tis finished!"[45]
The work of man's salvation's wrought,
The sacrifice accepted.
Now man may live for Christ hath died.
His pardon is contracted.

3. Come, Lord, and bring us to the pool
Was opened for uncleanness.
Bid us step in and be made whole
And cry no more our leanness.
For to bring fire on earth he came,
O burn my vile desires,
And then my mind shall be inclined
To join celestial choirs.

4. Like Moses' bush[46] then may we burn
Without receiving harm.
And then thou dost to earth return
To sound the great alarm.
Then may our souls with thee arise
 Whatever may oppose us,
With angels mount above the skies
And sing the song of Moses.[47]

5. So be it, Lord, thy will be done.
Appear and be victorious.
The Spirit and the bride say, "Come
And make us with thee glorious."[48]
Then shall we walk with thee in white

---

44. Revelation 1:6.
45. John 19:30.
46. See Exodus 3:2.
47. Revelation 15:3.
48. See Revelation 22:17.

And cast our crowns before thee.
With Abr'am sing, our glorious king,
And evermore adore thee.[49]

William Colbert, an itinerant preacher, discusses his discomfort with some explanations of Christ's death as a substitutionary sacrifice in this 18 April 1796 journal entry. Without fully explaining his understanding, Colbert would rather emphasize the death of Christ as an expression of God's love. Colbert's emphasis was a common one for early Methodists, although it is likely that most Methodists held the two explanations simultaneously.

And I fear that the disciples of Paine[50] will triumph as long as the advocates of Christianity hold up the idea of God the Father being so angry with the world of mankind as not to be pacified toward them until he had punished his Son in their [i.e., humankind's] stead. And the idea of God punishing the innocent in the place and stead of the guilty, the Deists[51] say they cannot receive. How I firmly believe that Christ has suffered and died for us, and that it is only by the merits of his death that salvation is made possible, but that God punished him in our stead I have been in doubt. I have been more inclined to believe that God the Father in love to a guilty world freely gave his Son to submit to all the indignities and sufferings he endured, and that the Son patiently submitted to bear our sins in his own body on the tree [i.e., the cross], and that the suffering and death of Christ was more the effect of the Father's love toward man than [of] appeasing his wrath. May the Lord stop the progress of Deism.[52]

In contrast to Colbert's understanding, the following hymn holds in tension the ideas of Christ's death as an appeasement of God's wrath and as an

---

49. Spiritual Songs (Edward Dromgoole papers), 11.

50. Thomas Paine, an influential writer and thinker of the late-eighteenth century, who championed a type of Enlightenment Deism.

51. Deists sought to conform religious belief to the principles of reason. This led to a downplaying of God's active intervention in the world, and—as Colbert suggests—questions about the appropriateness of any substitutionary notion of atonement.

52. William Colbert, Journal, 2:88-89.

*expression of God's graciousness. It is found in the little book Lucy
Watson compiled of her favorite hymns. It is an abbreviation of one of the
eucharistic hymns (#21) written by Charles Wesley, one of the founders
of Methodism.*[53]

To the tune of Springfield
1. Jesus drinks the bitter cup
The winepress treads alone,
Tears the graves and mountains up
By his expiring groan.
Lo, the powers of heaven he shakes.
Nature in convulsion lies.
The earth's profoundest center quakes.
The great redeemer dies.

2. Dies the glorious cause of all
The true eternal Pan,[54]
Falls to raise us from our fall
To ransom sinful man.
Well may Sol[55] withdraw his light
With the sufferer sympathize,
Leave the world in sudden night
While his creator dies.

3. Well may heaven be clothed in black
And solemn sackcloth wear,
Jesus' agony partake,
The hour of darkness share.
Mourn the astonished hosts above,
Silence saddens all the skies,
Kindler of seraphic love,
The God of angels dies.

---

53. Watson omits stanzas 1-3 from the original. For the complete hymn, see J. Ernest
Rattenbury, *The Eucharistic Hymns of John and Charles Wesley*, ed. Timothy J. Crouch (Akron,
Ohio: OSL Publications, 1996), 166. This hymn is additional evidence that Wesleyan
eucharistic hymns were known and appreciated on this continent.

54. An allusion to the Pan of Greek mythology. The point is that Christ, as God, is the true
Creator of all things.

55. The sun.

4. O my God, he dies for me
I feel the mortal smart,
See him hanging on the tree
A sight that breaks my heart.
O that all to thee might turn.
Sinners ye may love him, too.
Look on him ye pierced and mourn
For one who bled for you.

5. Weep over your desire and hope
With tears of humblest love.
Sing for Jesus is gone up
And reigns enthroned above.
'Twas our head to die no more.
Power is all to Jesus given,
Worshiped as he was before
The immortal king of Heaven.

6. Lord, we bless thee for the grace
And truth which never fail.
Hast'ning to behold thy face
Without a dimming veil,
We shall see our heavenly king,
All his glorious love proclaim,
Help the angels' choirs to sing
Our dear redeemer's name.[56]

Peggy Dow, wife of the popular and eccentric preacher Lorenzo Dow, reflects on the meaning of Christ's resurrection. In her emphasis on the broad universal effects of the resurrection, Dow is almost reflective of ancient, patristic ways of speaking about Christ's resurrection. The rest of the passage, however, reflects typical evangelical rhetoric of the early nineteenth century.

This is the day that our all conquering Savior burst the bands of death, and led captivity captive, [and] opened the door of mercy to

---

56. Lucy Watson, Hymns and Poems (1786).

the enslaved sons and daughters of Adam, that they may profit by the rich sacrifice which has been offered for their redemption! What matter of sorrow it is, that the offers of such unbounded mercy should be neglected by those who are so deeply interested in it, to prepare them for the day of adversity and death; which must assuredly overtake them, whether they will or not—there is no escape! Moments fly on without control and will shortly bring us to the place appointed for all living! O that it may rest with ponderous weight on the hearts of all concerned in it! And you, O my soul! Look well to yourself, that you may meet your Judge in peace, when he shall come in the clouds of heaven, attended with his glorious retinue of saints and angels, to set in judgment on the descendants of the first man and woman, who have all had the offers of life and salvation made to them! It will be a joyful day to those who have improved their time "and have washed their robes, and made them white in the blood of the Lamb"[57] but O what horror will seize the guilty soul that squandered away his precious time and slighted the overtures of mercy, who did despite to the Spirit of grace and the Son, who took upon him[self] the form of a servant, spent many years of toil and pain, and at last gave his life a ransom for our salvation! O what unbounded mercy! O unexampled love! Why are not our souls lost in wonder, love, and praise? May I ever tremble at his word! My departure may be at hand—time is short at the longest. O that I may improve my precious moments as they pass to the glory of my God and the good of my own immortal soul![58]

The following hymn describes the scene envisioned at Jesus Christ's Second Coming. The hymn hopes for the resurrection Christians, who rise shouting and flying from their "dusty beds." The hymn has a holistic scope as it connects Christ's future work to his birth and crucifixion.

Yonder comes the Lord descending.
Hark his chariot's drawing nigh.

---

57. Revelation 7:14.
58. Lorenzo Dow, *Vicissitudes in the Wilderness; Exemplified in the Journal of Peggy Down*, 5th ed. (Norwich, Conn.: William Faulkner, 1833), 115-16.

The starry vaults before him rending,
Flaming troops descend from on high.

Heaven's shaking, Earth is quaking,
Mountains fly before his face.
The dead their dusty tombs forsaking,[59]
Nature sinking in a blaze.

"Hallelujah, Hallelujah,"
Hark the herald angels sing,
"Hail him, Christians, hail him, Christians,
Yonder is your Glorious king."

Now behold each shining Christian,
Shouting from their dusty beds,[60]
Fly to meet their blessed Savior,
Glittering crowns upon their heads.

Hear them tell the pleasing story
To their smiling, lovely King.
Glory, glory, glory, glory,
Glory is the song they sing.

"Hallelujah, Hallelujah,"
Hark the Christian army sings.
"Join us, angels, join us, angels,
Help us praise our conquering King."

Once an infant in a manger
There the Lord of glory lay.
No place to lay the newborn stranger
But among the oxen's hay.
Now he's crowned with the rainbow
Brighter than the sardine stone.[61]

---

59. This refers to a general resurrection of the dead.
60. Again, a reference to the resurrection of the dead at the return of Christ.
61. Revelation 4:3.

He comes, he comes, the Christian's hero
Seated on his great white throne.[62]

"Hallelujah, Hallelujah,"
Hark the Christian army sings.
"Join us, angels, join us, angels,
Help us praise our conquering king."

Jesus saves us from temptation,
Sin and Satan, death and hell
And he's brought our great salvation.
Glory to Emanuel.

Once was bleeding on the mountain,[63]
There his precious blood did run.
Now he's brought us to the fountain
Springing from his Father's throne.[64]

"Give him glory, give him glory,"
Let all heaven begin to sing.
Glory, glory, glory, glory
Through eternal ages ring.[65]

This next hymn takes the idea that Christ is Savior and places it within a relational motif. Jesus Christ—the one who died, is risen, and will return to take his people to heaven—is also friend and brother.

1. Ye travelers to paradise, that happy, happy place
Whose works and way and spirits a wicked world doth hate,
Your highway lies before you and upward does ascend
And leads you on to glory to see your dearest friend.

2. A friend that's nearer to you than any brother here,
Your Lord and only Savior, your great Redeemer dear,

---

62. Revelation 20:11.
63. His crucifixion on Calvary.
64. Compare Revelation 22:1.
65. Henry Bradford, Hymnbook, 21.

Who once a human body upon himself did take,
Us sinners heirs of glory eternally to make.

3. He suffered groaned and bled and died upon the Roman
   cross
To make atonement for our sin and to retrieve our loss.
He gained our pardon when he died and so removed the
   curse[66]
And then ascended up on high to intercede for us.

4. Exalted there at God's right hand, the lovely lamb does set
And shows his wounded body, his head, his hands, and feet.
He pleads his matchless merits before his Father's throne
And sends us down his Spirit and holds us out a crown.

5. The crown of life of endless life, the sovereign gift of God,
In which you have a title through faith in Jesus' blood.
If you your title still would hold, you still by faith must view
The lamb once slain but lives again to intercede for you.

6. Do not grow faint and weary as many a one hath done
But finish well your journey as you have well begun.
You're on a state of trial but that will shortly end
And you'll ascend to glory to see your dearest friend.

7. Not transiently to view him and from him then remove
But dwell forever near him and ever taste his love.
Then sin will cease to trouble, your temptations all be o'er.
O brethren, keep a closer walk, and love your Jesus more.[67]

As expression of the love of God, Christ's saving work calls for a response of human love. The following hymn explores how reflecting on the depth of Christ's passion causes love to swell in the heart.

1. When on the cross my Lord I see,
Bleeding to death for wicked me,

---

66. Compare Galatians 3:13.
67. Henry Bradford, Hymnbook, 9.

Satan or sin no more can move
For I am all dissolved in love.

2. His thorns and nails pierced through my heart,
In every groan I bear a part.
I view his wounds with streaming eyes,
But see he bows his head and dies.

3. Come, sinners, view the Lamb of God
Wounded and dead and bathed in blood.
Behold his side and center near.
The well of endless life is there.

4. There I forget my cares and pain.
I drink yet still my thirst remains.
Only the fountainhead above
Can satisfy [my] thirst of love.

5. Oh! that I thus could always feel.
Lord, more and more thy love reveal.
Then my glad tongue shall loud proclaim
The grace and glory of thy name.

6. Thy name dispels my guilt and fears,
Revives my heart and charms my ears,
Affords a balm for every wound,
A cordial for my fears.[68] (alternate reading: And Satan trembles
at the sound.)[69]

JESUS, LOVER

*Continuing the line of piety in the previous hymn, the following piece
from Lucy Watson's hymnal deepens the notion of reciprocal love between*

---

68. Ibid., 23.

69. A version of this hymn with this alternate reading is found in Stith Mead, *A General
Selection of the Newest and Most Admired Hymns and Spiritual Songs Now in Use,* 2nd ed.
(Lynchburg, Va.: Jacob Haas, 1811), 161.

Jesus Christ and his believer. The intensity of emotion seems even deeper in this hymn than in the previous.

1. I'm tired with visits, modes, and forms
And flatteries paid to fellow worms,
Their conversation cloys,
Their vain amours[70] and empty stuff.
But I can ne'er enjoy enough
Of thy blest company, my Lord,
Thou life of all my joys.

2. When he begins to tell his love,
Through every vein my passions move,
The captives of his tongue;
In midnight shades, on frosty ground,
Nor would I feel December cold
Nor think the darkness long.

3. There, while I hear my Savior God
Count o'er the sins (a heavy load)
He bore upon the tree,[71]
Inward I blush with secret shame,
And weep, and love, and bless the name,
That knew not guilt nor grief his own,
But bore it all for me.

4. Next he describes the thorns he wore,
And talks his bloody passion o'er,
Till I am drown in tears.
Yet with the sympathetic smart
There's a strange joy beats round my heart.
The cursed tree has blessing in it,
My sweetest balm it bears.

5. I hear the glorious sufferer tell
How on his cross he vanquished hell
And all the powers beneath.

---

70. Vain loves.
71. The tree is the cross upon which Christ was crucified.

Transported and inspired my tongue
Attempts his triumphs in a song:
How has the serpent lost his sting,
And where's thy victory, O death?[72]

6. But when he shows his hands and heart,
With those dear prints of dying smart,
He sets my soul on fire.
Not the beloved John could rest
With more delight upon that breast,
Nor Thomas pry into those wounds
With more intense desire.[73]

7. Kindly he opens me his ear,
And bids me pour my sorrows there
And tell him all my pains.
Thus while I ease my burdened heart
In every woe he bears a part,
His arms embrace me, and his hand
My drooping head sustains.

8. Fly from my thoughts all human things
And sporting swains and fighting kings
And tales of wanton love.
My soul disdains that little snare
The tangles of Amira's hair
Thine arms, my God, are sweeter bands
Nor can my heart remove.[74]

In 1792 itinerant preacher George Wells preached on the reasons Christ is to be loved. His sermon has a strong exhortatory character as he discusses the danger of not loving Jesus Christ.

We had the sacrament at 9 o'clock after which we added 5 to our church. At 12 preaching began. Bro[ther]. B.[75] and myself spoke in

---

72. See 1 Corinthians 15:55.
73. See John 13:23 and 20:27.
74. Lucy Watson, Hymns and Poems (1786).
75. Wells is following the popular convention of identifying a person in his journal by initial only.

the house and Bro[ther]. Scott and Bro[ther]. Lyell outdoors. It was a good time. I hope great good was done. At night I preached again from 1 Corinthians 16:22.[76]

1. I delineated on the three characters or names in the text.

2. [I] proved that the Lord Jesus Christ should be the object of every man's love.

3. I laid down some marks whereby they might know whether they loved him or not.

4. [I spoke on] the greatness of the curse that would come upon those who loved him not.

5. I made some observations upon the Lord's coming quickly to execute the curse.

There was a great many people who appeared to be all attention.[77]

Most discussions of Christ's love had a softer tone. In the following passage, itinerant preacher William Ormond makes a passing—but revealing—statement about his love for Christ. The scene is the conclusion of a multiple day worship occasion. Although Ormond must part with his other preachers, he will remain with his closest companion, the "lovely Jesus."

I've set out anew for heaven. We came to N. Moore's and had the Lord's Supper.[78] Then [we] went to the chapel. Bro[ther] Merit and Bro[ther] Ellis preached and several exhorted. This has been a precious quarterly meeting. I hope great good has been done. I now part with the preachers but not with lovely Jesus....[79]

Expressions by early Methodists of love with Christ could be quite intense, even erotic. The following passages are from the diary of Virginian Methodist, Sarah Jones, in 1792. Jones has one of the most intense spiritualities among early American Methodists.

---

76. "If any man love not the Lord Jesus Christ, let him be Anathema [cursed]." "Maranatha" Jan is an Aramaic word meaning "Lord, come."

77. George Wells, Journal, 14 October 1792.

78. Having the Lord's Supper on the second morning of a quarterly meeting (the extended business and worship sessions for a circuit) was a common occurrence. Because early Methodists restricted access to the Lord's Supper, it appears on this occasion that the Lord's Supper was held in a private home before the public preaching service in the chapel.

79. William Ormond, Journal, 13 October 1791.

Oh, what a fair One! What a lovely One! What an only One is my Beloved. If all the worlds of Paradise like the garden of Eden was all in One—trees and flowers and smells and colors, all tastes, all joys, all sweetness, all loveliness therein—what would that be when the wonder of heaven and my soul, my matchless, almighty-to-save Jesus, my lovely friend is only spoken of.... His beauty and glory has almost killed me this day as well as for several [days] of late. Oh, could I, oh, could I![80] Let my heart be seen. Oh, believe me, my love to Jesus and his burning flaming nearness truly keeps my feeble trembling body on the bounds of Eternity. I can just bear the insufferable weight of crushing glory. I am chained and fettered with love.

> My breath is flame at Jesus' name,
> Today as yesterday the same.[81]
> Almighty glories through me fly
> While Earth is far and heaven nigh.
> I run with all my powers to meet
> The band of angels in the street.
> They wait in smiles and beckon me
> While Jesus calls, "Oh, come away."
> My life is hid with Christ in God.[82]
> Although I am an earthen clod,
> I soon shall mingle with the dust
> And rise triumphant with the just.[83]

Jones's diary entry on the following day continues the erotic images of communion with Christ. The idea that Christ kisses comes from a particular interpretation of the biblical book called Song of Songs or Song of Solomon.

I am now after breakfast in a silent chamber trembling with the infinite weight of falling glory. As by ten thousand bullets shot at

---

80. The ecstasy of the moment seems to keep Jones from forming complete thoughts.
81. Hebrews 13:8.
82. Colossians 3:3.
83. Sarah Anderson Jones, Diary, 6 March 1792. Compare the spirituality of Catherine Livingston Garrettson in Diane Lobody, "Lost in the Ocean of Love: The Mystical Writings of Catherine Livingston Garrettson" (Ph.D. diss., Drew University, 1990).

once, they meet my heart from Jesus' bow.... How overwhelmed I am in the sea of Jesus' love. I really do not feel as I can bear much more without bursting my chains and hurling them aside and seeing Jesus as he is. A river of God's untold love from bank to bank has flowed over my soul. How do you think Christ's breathing is just as he pronounces you his fair one and kisses you with the kisses of his mouth.[84] His love, I see, is so kingly he will not abide a rival but must have a throne all alone in the soul.[85]

The images Jones uses to describe her desire for and communion with Jesus Christ are very sensual. The intensity of these prayer experiences is hard for her to capture if the disjointed nature of her writing is any indication. The following diary passage describes a morning prayer time.

I arose up this morning to open the door to my beloved. And my hands dropped[86] with myrrh and my fingers with sweet smelling myrrh upon the handles of the lock. I opened [the door] to my beloved and he was not gone. But [he] smiled with beauty. His cheeks were as bows of jewels. His neck with chains of gold appeared while solidly charmed I sprang into his arms and his Name poured out as ointment and his lips dropped as the honeycomb. Honey and milk was under his tongue and the smell of his garments were as the flowery field. I felt my body made his temple and springing wonders rolled anew. I found the sacred path of holiness still narrow and an absolute necessity for fortitude to run in God's commandments, [to] keep on [in] resignation, and to bear every repeated temptation to discouragement.[87] This is a season of conflict [and] the hour of temptation, but I find Jesus the new room which at 12 o'clock I entered through faith and agony and dressed all in the needlework of patience shining with brilliant tears. And Love drove my sorrows away and showed me the gates of the city where the King and his people were waiting. I poured out my soul in begging to be ready to go with the Lamb to the marriage.[88] Oh, what sobs and flowing reasons run through my swimming eyes and cut a

---

84. Compare Song of Solomon 1:2.
85. Sarah Anderson Jones, Diary, 7 March 1792.
86. Jones means that myrrh dropped off of her hands because it was so thick.
87. That is, for fortitude to keep God's commandments, to keep on living in resignation to God's will, and to bear every repeated temptation to be discouraged.
88. See Matthew 22:4 and Revelation 19:7.

certain passage above the azure skies. I lodged [with] my spirit crying close by the ear of God and pointing him to Jesus who showed his streaming blood. Great things I saw and believed. Oh, there is a temple in the tabernacle of my testimony[89] where I hope Jesus is seated and keeps the door without a rival. I have got the morning star.[90] Therefore it is always morning and never night with me. He shines with unspeakable brightness upon me, and I have a peaceable dominion in his favor.... Oh, may a sense of these inestimable blessings produce an increasing conformity to all [of] God's will and a steady attachment to the precepts [of God].[91]

Jones expressed her devotion to Christ, her lover, in poetic form, too. The rapturous quality of Jones's experience of Christ is captured in the repetitive nature of the lyrics of the following hymn.

1. O Jesus, my Savior, to thee I submit,
With love and thanksgiving fall down at thy feet!
The sacrifice offer, my soul, flesh and blood;
Thou art my Redeemer, my Lord and my God.

2. I love thee, I love Thee, I love thee my Love!
I love thee my Savior, I love thee my Dove!
I love thee, I love thee, and that thou dost know
But how much I love thee, I never shall show.

3. All human expressions are empty and vain.
They cannot unriddle the heavenly flame!
I'm sure if the tongue of an angel I had,
I could not the myst'ry completely describe.

4. I'm happy, I'm happy, O wond'rous account!
My days are immortal, I stand on the mount!
I gaze on my treasure, I long to be there,
With angels my kindred and Jesus my dear.

89. See Exodus 30:26, Numbers 1:50, and Revelation 15:5.
90. Revelation 22:16.
91. Sarah Anderson Jones, Diary, 5 July 1792.

5. O Jesus my Savior, in thee I am blest:
My life and my treasure, my joy and my rest,
Thy grace be my theme, and thy name be my song,
Thy love doth inspire my heart and my tongue!

6. Thy fullness reveal, thy promise fulfill,
O take and direct me to the heavenly hill.
There wrapped in thy love, to be lost in thy charms,
With angels transported, and freed from all harms.

7. O who is like Jesus? He's Salem's bright king,
He smiles and he loves me, he learns me to sing.
I'll praise him, I'll praise him, with notes loud and shrill,
While rivers of pleasure my spirit doth fill.[92]

---

92. See Richard Allen, *A Collection of Spiritual Songs and Hymns, selected from various Authors* (Philadelphia: John Ormrod, 1801), 4-5; or Spiritual Songs (Edward Dromgoole papers), 6. The attribution to Jones is based on the observation of the editor of the reprint edition of Allen's hymnal (Nashville: A.M.E.C. Sunday School Union, 1987).

CHAPTER 2

CONVERSION AND "EXPERIMENTAL RELIGION"

Just as early American Methodists were enamored with the Savior Jesus Christ, they were obsessed with salvation. Few topics drew more of their attention. Even other spiritual topics often appear as little more than footnotes in Methodist accounts of their lives before God. Salvation through Christ, by contrast, was the organizing principle and the central theme of these accounts. This chapter and the next will explore early Methodist accounts of the experience of salvation, beginning with conversion.

In early Methodism, "conversion" was an event that marked a definite turn in a person's experience of God. Most typically, it involved coming to some deep awareness of God forgiving one's sins for Christ's sake. The technical name for this aspect of salvation, derived from Protestant roots through John Wesley, was justification.[1] The earth-shattering nature of conversion reflected the common Methodist sense of being under God's condemnation prior to this event. The transition from judgment to forgiveness was inwardly revolutionary. Forgiveness, free and unmerited, stood in stark contrast to the wrath they had felt so heavily in their hearts before.

---

1. For explication of this understanding of salvation in Wesley, see Kenneth J. Collins, *The Scripture Way of Salvation: The Heart of John Wesley's Theology* (Nashville: Abingdon, 1997), 86-92.

The themes of God's judgment of sinners and unmerited for-giveness of those who repent were obviously not unique to Methodists. What was distinctive of early Methodist spirituality is the way they incorporated these classic themes into what they called "experimental religion." Put very simply, early Methodists were never satisfied with a mere affirmation of rational belief that one understood Christ saved sinners; they sought to lead a person into an inward experience of assurance that Christ had saved *her* or *him*. This was *experimental* religion, and anything less fell short of true Christianity in their opinion.[2]

The Methodist experience of conversion was propelled by a view of God as powerful in justice, righteousness, and mercy. A convic-tion of God's justice lay behind their typical sense of dread for the coming of God's wrath. The assumption of God's righteousness made the work of Christ in establishing and fulfilling the law cen-tral to their approach to conversion. But most important, a deep trust in God's mercy encouraged them to seek the Holy Spirit's wit-ness of the pronouncement of forgiveness in their hearts.

There were usually dual aspects to the testimonies of the newly converted.[3] One aspect was a deep sense of what God had done *for me*. This was often connected to affirmation of the gracious activity of Jesus Christ in securing God's forgiveness. The other aspect highlighted the beginnings of what God was doing *in me*. In this case the emphasis lay on the exercise of God's power within a per-son. Methodists spoke not only of an inner witness to forgiveness, but of spiritual regeneration or new birth accompanying their awareness of forgiveness.

The Methodist experience of conversion touched the depths of a human person. Gregory Schneider aptly captures the character of these experiences:

> Conversion, then, started in the awakening of an uneasy awareness of sin and judgment that led to the terror and despair of conviction. By its very intensity, this negative condition of feel-

---

2. For background of these sensibilities in Wesley, see Collins, *Scripture Way of Salvation*, 131-52. The emphasis on "experimental religion" was not limited to Methodists. Pietists and certain Puritans also held this emphasis.

3. Again, compare the Wesleyan roots in ibid., 90-91.

ing cried out for a transformation into a condition in which an ecstasy of joy led to peace, hope, and love. Metaphors of depths leading to heights, heaviness to lightness, and especially darkness to light fill accounts of the change the believers felt.[4]

Not surprisingly, Methodist conversions sometimes exhibited physical and emotional intensity. As the great inward tension created by a sense of one's conviction was resolved with a new awareness of God's grace, new converts often burst with emotion and physical demonstrations. Joy, jumping, and shouting were common.

There is a significant degree of overlap in early Methodist conversion accounts. They tend to describe progressing through similar spiritual stages. In fact, a semitechnical vocabulary emerged to identify different people in these stages. The journey began when an "unawakened" person was awakened to his or her sinfulness and became a "seeker." As the sense of conviction for sin grew, one became a "mourner." When conversion was experienced, one became a "believer" or "professor" (that is, one who could profess experimental religion). As Methodists testified to their spiritual experiences in these terms, they created the expectations that shaped the salvation experiences of others in their circles.

Yet Methodist conversions were not exact clones of each other. For one thing, levels of Christian background varied—ranging from the actively churched, to disenfranchised church members, to those who were truly unchurched. Likewise, settings for the conversion varied. Many occurred in private, but conversions were common as well in small groups and in large worship settings. The frequency of the latter setting increased significantly with the rise of camp meetings in the early-nineteenth century. Another element that varied was the immediate catalyst for the conversion. Contemplation, visions or dreams, prayer, hearing testimonies, or hearing a public speaker were all common possibilities.

Although Methodist conversions were deeply personal, it would be wrong to consider them individualistic. For one thing, many occurred in social settings, most often worship settings. Christian

---

4. Schneider, *Way of the Cross*, 45.

fellowship was considered the normal arena for progressing in God's grace.[5]

Methodists also typically understood conversion within the grand scope of God's activity of judgment and redemption. Behind the immediate intensity of one's personal experience was the backdrop of a cosmic drama of wrath, satisfaction, and redemption. One of the most common expressions of this interplay was how early Methodists connected their saving experiences to expectations for hell and heaven. Neither of these were individual destinations in the Methodist view. They were contrasting final states for whole classes of people (see chapter 4). Conversion shifted one's affiliation and created the hope for a destiny with fellow heavenly "pilgrims."[6]

One major way in which Methodists affirmed a broader view of God's saving work was in their constant harping against Calvinist theology. Methodists found totally unacceptable any suggestion that there was some limit—particularly a God-determined limit—to the scope of God's saving work in Christ. In the face of this suggestion that they discerned in widespread Calvinism, Methodists insisted that all persons could benefit from Christ's atoning death.

Early Methodists in America were equally concerned to challenge the merely "formal" religion that they discerned in most other churches. Their personal experience of the influence of "experimental religion" made them zealous to offer this benefit to others. It often also led them to lament their upbringing in non-Methodist settings. The reflections of Philip Gatch on his upstanding Anglican parents and neighbors in mid-eighteenth-century Maryland are typical:

> My parents belonged to the Episcopal Church; and though destitute of experimental religion, they paid some attention to its restraints and forms.... All was dark and dreary around me, and there was no one in the neighborhood who possessed religion. Priests and people in this respect were alike.[7]

---

5. See Ruth, *A Little Heaven Below*, 164-80 for a more detailed exploration of fellowship as context for grace. See also chapter 8 below.

6. For the most part, early Methodists held the personal and cosmic dimensions of salvation together, though they continually verged on unraveling.

7. John M'Lean, *Sketch of Rev. Philip Gatch* (Cincinnati: Swormstedt & Poe, 1854), 7.

Gregory Schneider has aptly described this emphasis on experimental religion as "the center of Methodist identity and the mainspring of the Methodist salvation machine."[8] Its roots can be traced to John Wesley, with his emphasis on an inward assurance of God's pardoning love. In the American setting this emphasis often took the form not only of assuming that a person *could* have inward assurance of God's saving work, but also of insisting that a person *must* have inward knowledge of God's forgiveness of their sins to be considered truly saved.[9]

Methodists linked intimately the inward knowing of forgiveness to the new birth (also called regeneration or being "born again"). This meant that in their initial experience of salvation Methodists expected not only an inward assurance of God's forgiveness, they also anticipated that the saving power of God would begin to transform their heart.[10] They firmly believed that, as a result of this conversion experience, one would be a different person inside.

In these expectations we see again the early Methodist preoccupation with interiority and the affections. But the discerning eye will also catch the assumption of divine initiative and agency. These Methodists were not emphasizing their inherent ability but their reception of God's empowering affect, which they believed enabled them to overcome any problem created by sin. As one scholar has put it, "to *experience* the living God in all his fullness . . . [was] the essential theme in early American Methodism."[11]

In the context of the late-eighteenth and early-nineteenth centuries, American Methodists shared much of what they understood about conversion and "experimental religion" with other Christians.

---

8. Schneider, *Way of the Cross*, 43.

9. Whether John Wesley held to this more strident belief, particularly in his later life, is a matter of much scholarly discussion. Cf. Collins, *Scripture Way of Salvation*, 131-52; Randy L. Maddox, *Responsible Grace: John Wesley's Practical Theology* (Nashville: Kingswood Books, 1994), 124-27; and John H. Tyson, "John Wesley's Conversion at Aldersgate," in *Conversion in the Wesleyan Tradition*, eds. Kenneth J. Collins and John H. Tyson (Nashville: Abingdon, 2001), 34-37.

10. For the parallel in John Wesley's expectations, see Henry H. Knight III, "The Transformation of the Human Heart: The Place of Conversion in Wesley's Theology," in *Conversion in the Wesleyan Tradition*, eds. Collins and Tyson, 46-55.

11. Scott, "Message of Early American Methodism," 358. The emphasis on interior feelings and the divine enabling of a new way of sensing grace meant that Methodist conversion stories usually did not highlight a "decisionistic" view of conversion. The term is Knight's, in reference to the parallel emphasis in John Wesley. See Knight, "Transformation of the Human Heart," 45.

They were, for instance, neither the originators nor the exclusive users of the term "experimental religion." Puritans, including Jonathan Edwards, a leader in the religious revival earlier in the eighteenth century, had long been using the phrase.[12] Likewise American Methodist conversion narratives read much like those from their British counterparts[13] and from like-spirited Christians in other denominations.

The excerpts that follow have been selected to exhibit the essential features of American Methodist spirituality on conversion and "experimental religion." Several conversion testimonies, which reflect the experiential quality of salvation and the concern for "experimental religion," come first. Next is a group of excerpts that illustrate central images associated with the various aspects of conversion and initial salvation. The collection then moves to material that shows sides to Methodist contemplation of salvation beyond individual feelings and inward states. The final set of entries reflect the tensions between Methodists and Calvinists over their respective emphases on salvation.

CONVERSION TESTIMONIES

Rebecca Ridgely, a well-to-do Methodist from Maryland, describes her conversion in the 1770s under one of the first Methodist preachers in America. Influenced by her mother's Quaker background (Quakers would have emphasized an inward spiritual baptism rather than an outward, water baptism), Ridgely uses the biblical image of "baptism with the Holy Ghost and fire" to describe what she experienced.

It so happened in the year 1774 that Mr. Webb[14] came to town to speak. I was then with my sister Goodwin [who was] with her first child. Some lady being there asked me if I would go to preaching. I asked, "Who was to preach?" They said, "Captain Webb." "No,"

---

12. Ann Taves, *Fits, Trances, & Visions: Experiencing Religion and Explaining Religion from Wesley to James* (Princeton: Princeton University Press, 1999), 48.

13. See D. Bruce Hindmarsh, "'My chains fell off, my heart was free': Early Methodist Conversion Narratives in England," *Church History* 68 (1999): 910-29.

14. Captain Thomas Webb, a Methodist preacher and British army officer who was instrumental in helping fledgling American Methodism in the 1760s and 1770s.

I said. "I had heard him about 3 years before and got so displeased that I went away before his sermon was done." "Well," said one, "Do go. It is as good as a play to hear him." "Well," [I] said, "I'll go then." She said she would go and [would] get ready and call for me. [But] She did not return, and Pleasy Goodwin and Mr. Chimene then [went] with me.... [Webb] began [and] preached on the text "Now is the appointed time; now is the day of salvation"[15] and made it out that the Spirit of God would not strive with man always, and that the day of visitation might be past. And [he] spoke so plain of the spiritual baptism and how we might through prayer come to receive that blessing and through neglect might lose it.

O, how I began to weep. I saw I was the very person who had neglected the call of God: a lost, poor, undone creature. O, how I fell on my knees and prayed to the Lord to call me once more and how I would run [to God]. It then was a shame to kneel before the people, but, O I thought, what is all the world to me if I must lose my soul? Mr. Chimene and Mrs. Goodwin were both convinced[16] that same night and wept but [were] not so struck as I was. Well, we went to my lodging and Doctor Goodwin was with me at meeting and took notice that I knelt and soon told Mrs. Goodwin of it. He then said [that] if he was in my husband's place he would not let me go again. But I, then knowing it was the truth Mr. Webb had spoke, I jumped up, being of a gay disposition, and danced and clapped my hands and said [that] it was the truth he had spoke that night, and that, if I had that peace that he spoke of, [I] would give all the world, and that I would go to hear him every night as Captain Ridgely[17] was gone to Annapolis [Maryland]. And so I did and wept much and prayed much but found no peace all the time I was in town.

At length [I] came home [with] no peace [and] still in great distress. No one knew it but myself. [I was] agonizing in prayer that night. And, one morning after I had been at praying [and] found no relief, I was meditating as I was dressing myself on what I had lost and that it was just and what I deserved, and [I] seemed to give myself up as lost. I [then] felt something come as an arrow out of a

---

15. Probably 2 Corinthians 6:2.
16. Ridgely means that they were convicted of sin, an initial stage toward salvation.
17. Her husband.

bow into my heart. "O," said I, "what is this?" I had scarcely said this then I found it was the holy baptism. I was then baptized with the Holy Ghost and with fire.[18] ... I opened the Bible. I found then [that] I had got ... the love of God and my neighbor [and] that I was born again [as] a child of God and an heir.[19] O, glory, glory be to God.[20]

Freeborn Garrettson, who eventually became a prominent Methodist preacher, offers another example of conversion in the 1770s. Like many early Methodists, his conversion was not from a completely unchurched background but from a kind of religiosity that failed to satisfy. The long nature of Garrettson's conversion, with its many significant milestones and a climactic experience in private, was also common.

I was born in the year of our Lord 1752. My parents were of the Church of England and brought up their children in that way. My father was a very moral man and thought by his neighbors to be a very good Christian, and my mother was a woman who feared the Lord. I was from infancy prone to pride, self-will, and stubbornness, which I afterward felt to the sorrow of my heart. Very early I was taught the Lord's Prayer, Creed, Ten Commandments, and the Catechism and was restrained by my tender parents from open sin....

We lived in a very gloomy day [with] no preached Gospel, only a moral sermon read in the Church on the Lord's day, and very little of the new birth known or spoken of in the parish. One day when I was about nine years of age, as I was walking all alone in the field, it was as sensibly pressed on my sensitive powers, as if I had heard a voice saying, "Ask and it shall be given you, etc."[21] I was immediately drawn out in thought to know what it meant, and it was pressed on my mind that it was a token for good, and a spirit of joy sprang up within me.

Shortly after, I was by myself, and there seemed to be a question asked me, "Do you know what a saint is?" I paused awhile and then answered to myself, "There are no saints on earth in this our

---

18. See Matthew 3:11 and Luke 3:16.
19. Compare John 3:3, John 1:12-13, and Galatians 4:7.
20. Rebecca Ridgely, Reminiscences.
21. Matthew 7:7.

day." The same voice seemed to reply, "A saint is one that is wholly given up to God." Immediately in idea, I saw such a person, the most beautiful, I thought, that ever my eyes beheld. I was much affected and wished to be a saint, and it was pressed on my mind that I should be one. And a spirit of joy sprang up within me, but I had no one to open the way of salvation to me.

Sometime after this a great affliction came on my father's family: a sister, then my mother, [and] after them, two servants were removed from time to eternity. The ninth day of my sister's illness she asked for some victuals [i.e., food] and, after she had eaten a little, desired to be raised up in the bed. "I am going," said she, "to leave the world and wish to bid you all farewell." The family was soon gathered in the room, and all were bathed in tears. "Weep not," said she, "for me for I am going to Jesus, who will do far more for me than any of you can." She spoke as one from the dead, and I believe the exhortation will never be forgotten. When almost spent, she desired to be laid down and, within a few minutes, left the world with a smiling countenance. I do believe [that] according to her knowledge she feared the Lord from her youth up, and it was in the nineteenth year of her age when she was taken away. O! what I felt! A melancholy gloom hung over me for a long time. I frequently withdrew into secret places, and wept bitterly but knew not what I wanted. Had gospel light shone in that day as it does now, I might [have] had a better chance to have known the way of salvation....

In my eighteenth year I now particularly began to think of living in the world. [It was a] Melancholy consideration [since] I was dead to God and my own eternal welfare. I did by no means run into scandalous company or crimes, but I was a pleasure taker and a lover of this world more than God. O! What a reason I have to be thankful to God for his restraining grace which gave me a dislike to many of the practices which were prevalent among many of the youth of my age.

About this time it was, that there was a great talk of the people called Methodists in Baltimore County where I lived. Many went out to hear them, and among the Methodists I went to hear Mr. Strawbridge and Mr. Williams,[22] but the place was so crowded that

---

22. Robert Strawbridge, a Methodist preacher in Maryland instrumental in promoting Methodism there in the 1760s and 1770s, and Robert Williams, one of the first itinerants from England.

I could not hear with any satisfaction. But from what I could understand I thought they preached the truth, and I did not dare join with the multitude to speak evil of them but thought that I would let them alone and keep close to my own church. O! Those soul damning sins, pride, and unbelief, kept me from God and his people....

As my good and gracious God did not will my damnation, his Spirit still strove with me. One day as I past over a rapid stream, the log on which I had frequently past gave way, and I stood a near chance of being swept down the stream. After struggling a while, I got out much wounded among the rocks. It came to me with power: "what would have become of your soul had you been drowned?" I wept bitterly and prayed to the Lord and made many promises. But O! My stubborn heart was unwilling to submit....

I had heard as yet but two or three Methodist sermons, and the devil strove to keep me away. I heard Mr. Pilmore[23] and thought he preached the truth and had a smooth pleasant voice, but it seemed to have no effect on my mind. Again, I went to Richard Webster's to hear my (since) well-tried friend and brother, [Francis] Asbury.[24] He began his sermon about sunset, and I can truly say that his doctrine was a salve to a festering wound. I sat by the door bathed in tears the whole time and heard the sermon with great delight. As night came on I was convinced that he did not read his sermon and was much surprised to hear such fluency of speech in an extempore [i.e., extemporaneous] way.[25] I suppose hundreds of thoughts past my mind but I returned home with gladness of heart, fully satisfied that he was a servant of God....

About this time [mid-1770s] it was that I became more particularly acquainted with our new parish minister, who was a very upright man in his outward deportment, and must set by in the parish [i.e., he was well regarded by the parish], and he had a great zeal for the truth in his preaching as far as he had knowledge. I believe he was instrumental in keeping me for God and his people for I was a constant attendant on his ministry and began to think

---

23. Joseph Pilmore, one of the first two itinerant preachers sent by John Wesley to America.

24. Francis Asbury, another itinerant sent in the early 1770s and eventual founding bishop of the Methodist Episcopal Church.

25. From his Church of England background, Garrettson was more used to preachers reading aloud their written sermons.

that the doctrine which he inculcated would do very well. And the more I fell in with his plan for salvation the less I thought of the Methodists. Having an opportunity of several conversations with him on the subject, he told me that the Methodists carried the matter too far [and] that there was no such thing as for a man to know his sins forgiven and that all we could expect in this world was a hope, and that this hope was from an upright life and a trust in God. Those advices were as kindling to my nature, and it was not long before I corroborated with him in sentiment, concluding that I was a Christian and pled that it was impossible for any man to know his sins forgiven.

I became so bigotly [i.e., as a bigot] attached to the church that I thought it sinful to go by it to hear the Methodists, although I frequently went to hear them after the service of the church was over and likewise on weekdays.[26] At the former we had a smooth, moral sermon read, which did not disturb the consciences of any; at the latter the law was thundered down on the hearers and the plan of salvation pointed out. During the time of my self-secure state, I had the form of godliness and would not willingly or knowingly do anything which I thought to be sinful and was very strict with respect to private prayer, fasting, [and] keeping the Sabbath. And I read much and for a considerable time was under consideration about a literary qualification for the ministry in the church way and frequently consulted my new counselor. I thought that I was a good Christian but at times I had doubts, especially under the preaching of the Methodists. Many are the times that my poor foundation has shaken under the preaching of Brother Shadford[27] in so much that it would be a considerable time before I could get all things to go on clearly with me again. And then I would be ready to conclude that I would hear the Methodists no more. But still I was drawn to hear again. I stood as it were between the people of God and the world and at times had hard struggles.

One day, being a distance from home, I met with a zealous Methodist exhorter. He asked me if I was born again. I told that I had a hope that I was. "Do you," said he, "know that your sins are

---

26. The earliest Methodist instructions for preachers informed them not to hold services at the same time as those in the neighboring Church of England parish.

27. George Shadford, another itinerant preacher sent by John Wesley to America in the early 1770s.

forgiven?" "I do not," said I, "neither do I believe that there is such a knowledge to be had in this world." "I perceive," said he, "that you are in the way to hell, and be ye well assured, that if you die in that state, you will be damned." Said I, "our blessed Lord says, 'Judge not, etc.'[28] What did you ever see, or know of my life," said I, "to cause you to denounce me in that manner?" I pitied and turned my back on him. The words of that zealous young man did not soon leave me, for the Spirit of the Lord strove with me, and something within frequently told me "all is not well with you."

On this self-righteous way I continued until June 1775. O! My dear Lord, I never shall forget the blessed morning.... Just as I awoke I was alarmed by an awful voice. It was as powerfully impressed on my eternal powers as if it had been a human voice in thunder: "You are not prepared to die." Conviction was thundered down upon my poor, guilty soul, and all my fig leaves were torn away.[29] Immediately I started from my pillow and cried out, "Lord, have mercy on my soul." As it was about the commencement of the late, unhappy war,[30] and as there was to be a general review that day near my house, I had promised myself much happiness at it, as I was a professed friend to the American cause. But, instead of giving my attendance there, I past away the day in solitude and in the evening I went to hear Brother Ruff[31] preach. In deep distress I went, and in deep distress I returned but let no one know my case. I was sorely tempted of the devil and was ready to conclude that I had withstood so many calls that the Lord would not be gracious to my soul. I fasted, prayed and cried to God in secret places but received no answer. I carried my burden day after day but opened my case to none but the Lord.

On Whitmonday[32] 1775 in the evening I went to hear Br. Ruff preach again, and it was in my return home that I lost my burden. After preaching was over, I called in at Mr. G—n's[33] where I stayed

---

28. Matthew 7:1.

29. Garrettson is alluding to the story of Adam and Eve (Genesis 3), who were clothed in fig leaves after their sin. He is saying that all his sin-related guilt and shame were exposed.

30. The American Revolution.

31. Perhaps Daniel Ruff, an itinerant preacher.

32. The Monday after Pentecost, called at the time Whitsunday.

33. Garrettson is following a convention for the day of identifying a person by his initial or abbreviation.

until near 9 o'clock and then set out on my way home. I had not rode a mile until I was so oppressed that I was constrained to light from my horse and humble myself on my knees before the Lord in a solitary wood, where no mortal eye could see or ear hear me. And my poor distressed soul was in an agony. I cannot convey to anyone the tenth part of what I felt. While I was on my knees before the Lord, I sensibly felt two spirits with me: the blessed spirit on the right and the evil spirit on the left. The good spirit set forth to my inmost mind, the beauties of religion so that it appeared as if I was almost ready to lay hold on Christ by faith. O! Unbelief, that damning sin, kept me from my dear Savior. The devil on the other hand would rise up and dress religion in as deformed a part as possible, telling me, that if I did not forsake that way, I could not carry on my business, and that I should be ruined, etc. The temptations of the devil were so powerful that they might with propriety be compared to a sweeping rain. I was a long time in this posture and in deep exercises until at length I began to reason with the devil and he overpowered me, and my tears and groans were soon gone. But I continued on my knees looking towards heaven in a kind of meditating way and sensibly felt the two spirits with me.

After waiting on my knees a considerable time, very powerfully tempted, I broke out thus, "Lord, spare me one year more and let me live as I have done, and then I will serve thee." The answer was "Now is the accepted time."[34] I then pled for six months but it was not granted. Three months, [but] the answer was no. One month, [but] I was denied. Two weeks, still the answer was no. The carnal[35] knows nothing of this, but it was as perceptible as if I had been conversing with a person face to face. O! How high the carnal mind did rise. The enemy[36] of my soul broke in upon me in a powerful manner. "You see," said he, "that the God whom you have been attempting to serve is a hard master. I would have you give up his service and pray to him no more." O! Wretch, wretch that I was. I immediately arose from my knees with these thoughts in my heart. I know not but that I uttered [these] words: "I will take my own time for it, and when it suits me, then I will be religious." O! What

---

34. See 2 Corinthians 6:2. Compare, too, the Ridgely account above.

35. Garrettson means that people who have not been born again are unfamiliar with what he describes.

36. The devil.

a good God I had to deal with. Had he sent me to [be] killed it would have been just what I deserved. I got on my horse and was making towards home with a heart as hard as a stone. But I had not rode a quarter of a mile before the Lord met me with these words, "These three years I have come seeking fruit on this fig tree[37] and find none." Then the following words were added: "I have come once more to make you an offer of salvation and it is the last time. Choose or refuse."

I verily did believe that, if I rejected that offer, mercy would be clean gone forever. Heaven and hell were disclosed to my interior eye, and life and death were set before me. I was surrounded as it were by a divine power and shaken over hell. I saw clearly that pride and unbelief had kept me from God. It was like giving up the ghost. I was perfectly reconciled with the justice of God for I never could before now be reconciled to that attribute. I threw down my bridle on my horse's neck and lifted my hands and eyes to heaven and cried out, "Lord, I submit, make me as thou wouldest have me to be." I know the moment when every false prop was taken away, and I reconciled to the plan of salvation by Jesus Christ. I could look up and see by an eye of faith the great Jehovah reconciled through Jesus Christ to my poor soul. This power was attended with peace and joy in so much that I seemed to be all taken up with Jesus, and although all alone in a solitary wood, in the dead time of night, I could but lift up my voice and praise God aloud so that I might have been heard a far off. Now it was that I saw the way of salvation and knew that my sins were forgiven.[38]

Massachusetts Methodist Nancy Welch tells about her 1788 conversion in poetic form. Blind from infancy, Welch uses enlightenment images to discuss how God brought her to an awareness of her sin and to seeing Christ as the remedy. After her conversion, Welch also talks about how God brought a desire for sanctification, a second saving experience (discussed more fully in the next chapter).

---

37. Compare Matthew 21:19 and Luke 13:7. Preaching on the barren fig tree was a common occurrence for early Methodist preachers.

38. Freeborn Garrettson, "A Short Account of my Life till I was Justified by Faith," Garrettson Family papers. For more information on Garrettson, see Robert Drew Simpson, ed., *American Methodist Pioneer: The Life and Journals of The Rev. Freeborn Garrettson* (Rutland, Vt.: Academy Books, 1984).

I, Nancy Welch, in Essex bred,
Was born and raised in Marblehead.
But while I was an infant quite
The Lord deprived me of my sight.

Though still his love and guardian care
Protected me through every snare,
And safely led me up to youth,
Although I disobeyed his truth.

Soon as to speak I did begin
My infant heart was prone to sin,
Which as I grew to riper age
Made me in Satan's cause engage.

With speed I ran the downward road,
Slighting the mercy of a God
Who kept me, though I did rebel,
'Tis mercy all, I'm out of hell.

When fifteen years I lived to see,
God by his Spirit strove with me.
But still I grieved the holy dove[39]
And sought me out some other love.

I constantly did go astray
Nor loved nor sought the better way,
My heart depraved on folly bent
My days in sanity I spent.

But in the year of eighty eight,[40]
The Lord made known my fallen state.
I saw myself a wretch undone
And felt I had a heart of stone.

39. The holy dove is the Holy Spirit.
40. 1788.

Then did I sigh and mourn and pray
Expecting to be cast away.
What then I felt no tongue can tell
With fears of dropping into hell.

I think it was the month of March
God's lighted candle thus did search,
Emitting light into my heart
And showed in Christ I had no part.

While on the brink of deep despair,
All filled with horror and with fear,
Of sinners I appeared the worst
And most deserving to be cursed.

But O the goodness of a God
Who pointed me to Jesus' blood.
In depth of my extremity
I saw that Jesus died for me.

I saw O happy, happy day!
It was the seventeenth of May.
My soul was filled with light and love
And raptures raised to things above.

When Jesus granted this release
And filled me with such heavenly peace,
My sins I knew were blotted out
And ever since I cannot doubt.

The Lord is still my constant friend
On whom for succor I depend.
Though I confess and that with shame
Too little I revere his name.[41]

---

41. Nancy Welch, Poem, Ezekiel Cooper papers (vol. 7, ms. 56).

IMAGES FOR SALVATION, EXPERIMENTAL RELIGION, AND BACKSLIDING

Early Methodists use various terms to highlight the various aspects of a conversion experience. One of the most common is to be "born again." Preacher John Price outlines what it means to be born again in this sermon on John 3:3. Price emphasizes the necessity of a real, inward change of the heart.

John 3:3 Ye must be born again.

Introduce by explaining the context.

I. The necessity of the new birth or a change of heart.

1. The necessity appears from man's depravity, consisting in a loss of the image of God and the evil propensities dwelling in the mind.
2. The necessity of a change appears from a want of happiness in the mind.
3. [The necessity of the new birth appears] From its being impossible to please God in an unconverted state.
4. We cannot see the Kingdom of God without our hearts are changed.

II. Show what the new birth implies, together with the fruits and effects [of the new birth].

1. [It implies] The light in the mind: a man must see and feel the need of Jesus Christ.
2. It implies a changed heart, and it is not a partial but a real change.
3. It is attended with obedience of heart and life.
4. It brings joy and peace, etc.
5. Finally, [it brings] heavenly glory.[42]

New York Methodist William Keith remembers such a strong assurance of grace in his conversion that all doubt is pushed aside.

I soon fell into darkness by reason of unbelief. I found, however, that a change was wrought in me for I sensibly felt no happiness but in God. His character and his works appeared excellent in my

---

42. John Price, Sermon Book.

view. I could meditate on death, judgment, and eternity, with a degree of pleasure, when formerly they filled me with a sense of guilt and horror. I lived between hope and fear until the July following. I had then joined the Methodist society and, one day in class meeting,[43] I obtained such an assurance of God's love that I could no longer doubt. I could truly say, "My Jesus is mine and I am his" or, like Thomas, "My Lord and my God."[44] I lived three weeks in the full enjoyment of religion. No darkness of trials in that time ever disturbed my peace, which flowed like a river.[45]

In 1796, James Watts describes multiple, related aspects in his saving experience: a strong inward sense of acceptance, redemption, and the forgiveness of sins.

I was at a prayer meeting one night when my mind was in deep distress. I prayed or strove to pray, but my heart felt very hard, and the meeting closed and I went away in distress. It was near the time of the full moon. One of my sisters, another friend, and myself were walking on our way home, and I cast my eyes toward the moon. And all of a sudden my mind was relieved, and all my sorrows were removed, and an indescribable joy filled my poor heart. I did not know what name to give the blessing which I then received because I was young and inexperienced, but I had walked but a very few steps until I received the evidence of my acceptance with God through my adorable Redeemer, Jesus Christ. I then knew that I had redemption in his blood, even the forgiveness of my sins. My heart was so full I could scarce contain, although I said nothing to any one that night about the matter.

But all night my heart was so full that I could scarce contain [myself] but kept inwardly whispering in my heart and easily with my tongue, saying, "Glory to God. Glory to God."[46]

As the previous accounts make clear, early Methodists greatly emphasized the inward dimension of a saving experience. Their shorthand term

---

43. "Society" is the typical Methodist term for a local congregation. A class meeting was the required weekly small group meeting for nurture and accountability.

44. John 20:28.

45. William Keith, *The Experience of William Keith. [Written by Himself.] Together with Some Observations Conclusive of Divine Influence on the Mind of Man* (Utica, N.Y.: Seward, 1806), 12.

46. James Watts, Journal, 3-4.

for this emphasis was "experimental religion," meaning that one would inwardly experience salvation if one had truly been saved. In the following passages, Methodist preacher Benjamin Abbott shows how critical having an inward experience is to being saved. He highlights how closely Methodists linked inward, experiential knowledge and conversion. In the first passage Abbott describes his own journey to conversion; the second shows what he considered lacking in a Presbyterian elder.

... as yet I never had heard the nature of conviction or conversion. It was a dark time respecting religion, and little or nothing [was] ever said about experimental religion. And to my knowledge I never had heard either man or woman say that they had the pardoning love of God in their souls or knew their sins were forgiven. My wife was a member of the Presbyterian Church, and a praying woman; yet at that time she knew nothing about a heart work.[47]

A few days after, an elder of the Presbyterian meeting [came] to talk with me, to whom I told my experience and that I knew that God for Christ's sake had forgiven my sins. He replied that he had been a member of the church twenty-five years, and never before heard any one say that he knew his sins were forgiven, and for any one to say that he knew his sins were forgiven he ought to be burned for he made himself as perfect as an angel in heaven. "Nay," said he, "I would help to burn such a man myself." I told him [that,] if he never had felt a conviction for sin to make him cry to God to save him a poor sinner, and [if he] had not felt the blood of Christ applied to the washing away of his sins, his religion was still no better than the devil's.[48]

Describing the sermon of another preacher, Nathaniel Mills uses the term "experimental" to describe the kind of knowledge of Christ that is saving.

Bro. Wells preached from Philippians 3:8.[49] He showed that knowledge of Christ which is the privilege of mortals to obtain. [It

---

47. John Ffirth, *Experience and Gospel Labors of the Rev. Benjamin Abbott; to which is annexed a Narrative of his Life and Death* (New York: Carlton & Phillips, 1853), 6-7.

48. Ibid., 27.

49. "Yea doubtless, and I count all things *but* loss for the excellency of the knowledge of Christ Jesus my Lord: for whom I have suffered the loss of all things, and do count them *but* dung, that I may win Christ."

is] Not the knowledge that was in Christ. [It is] not a literal or historical knowledge but a saving and experimental [knowledge] of Him as our Savior.[50]

In a wonderfully honest diary passage, itinerant preacher William Spencer discusses the inner turmoil he felt after his conversion. By showing how an inward feeling (Spencer's being "happy") can be too closely linked to whether one considers himself to be saved, Spencer demonstrates the potential problem with overemphasizing "experimental religion."

I believe for fifteen months after my soul was converted I would at times doubt my conversion. I could not believe that I really was converted [at] no other times but when I was happy.[51] [And] so, soon as I would lose my happy frames [of mind], I would begin to doubt my conversion and pray for conviction. And so I went on, judging of my state by my frames, until at last, I began to see that this was losing time, etc. and that, if I was to pray my heart out, I could not get conviction again for my former sins.... How I would at times grieve because I could not grieve and mourn because I could not mourn. And the devil would tell me that it would be daring presumption in me (so vile and unworthy as I was) to expect mercy from God. I believe the old serpent [i.e., the devil] keeps many dear souls a long time in this condition so that they do not thrive in religion.[52]

The concern for inward experience as a necessary part of salvation made early Methodists quite concerned about affections and feelings. The following journal passages of itinerant preacher Nathaniel Mills are typical expressions of this concern.

[We] held a love feast.[53] I preached. B[rother] Hutchinson exhorted. Then [we] gave the love feast. A few spoke feeling and simple [i.e., feelingly and simply] their experience.[54]

---

50. Nathaniel Mills, Journal, 9 February 1812.

51. "Happy" is the word early Methodists use to describe a joyful sense of God's presence and graciousness.

52. William Spencer, Diary, 13 May 1790.

53. Methodists shared water, bread, and testimonies of Christian experience in a love feast. See chapter 6.

54. Nathaniel Mills, Journal, 17 April 1788.

I had a large congregation, chiefly attentive. But [the people were] not much affected, nor [was] the society.[55] But some spoke feeling [i.e., feelingly].[56]

Kentucky itinerant Benjamin Lakin connects feelings, affections, and the power of God to save in an 1803 service.

At watch night[57] the powers of darkness were most sensibly felt. Preaching and exhortation seemed of no effect. We sang a hymn, and then I called on the people to present their prayers to God in secret. We fell on our knees. I instantly felt the power of God. The people began to pray. And we soon had a time of power and sinners crying for mercy and some converted.[58]

Henry Boehm, another itinerant preacher, would rather feel God's saving power than explain it as early Methodists worship.

They had their love feast. The power of the Lord was among the people. One was converted. Many were amazed at the sight. So it is. The work of God seems to be foolishness in the eyes of the unconverted. Glory to God. It is better felt than explained.[59]

The power of salvation released in affections can be electric. Itinerant Ezekiel Cooper describes a representative response to his preaching.

In my last proposition before I quite closed, the people being generally much affected, it appeared like as if fire had been applied to power, there went of such an explosion, as is seldom seen or known. I don't know when if ever I saw a more general shout through all the congregation. Before the shout began, I believe nine out of ten were affected less or more and some very powerfully so that they were ripe for it, like a vial well charged with the electrical fluid discharged and gives a shock to all around.[60]

---

55. Mills is probably referring to the practice of meeting the Methodist members in that place (the "society") separately after the public preaching service.
56. Nathaniel Mills, Journal, 22 April 1810 (Easter Sunday).
57. A watch night was a kind of preaching service lasting several hours; cf. chapter 6.
58. Benjamin Lakin, Journal, 16 September 1803.
59. Henry Boehm, Journal, 8 June 1800.
60. Ezekiel Cooper, Journal, 12 June 1796.

In such an "electric" time, the emotional tumult from those seeking conversion and from those who had passed over to salvation can be great, as is evident in this account by Stith Mead of his ministry, sent to Thomas Coke.

. . . the Lord showed himself in majesty and power. I labored incessantly for four days together, and often until the sun went down. A great number of awakened sinners lay across the benches and on the floor in agonies of distress for their souls. Their groans and cries seemed to pierce the very heavens. Some of their expressions were as follows: "O Lord, be merciful to me a sinner, and save my soul from hell! Lord, remove this hardness from my heart. No mercy for me! I am lost! I shall be undone forever. My aged father and mother and the preachers have so long and often prayed for me, and I have never prayed for myself before today. Thank God, I am not dead and damned. Glory to God, I am out of hell and upon pleading ground. O that I could find but one crumb of mercy! The Lord has long strove with me, but I have barred the door of my heart against him. O that I could clasp him in my arms! O that he would convert my soul! Lord, heal my backslidings! O my hard heart. What shall I do to be saved? Where are my father and mother that they don't come and pray for me? I shall be damned if Jesus doesn't save me! It was but last night I was laughing and making game of religion. Lord, forgive my sins! etc., etc."

Now hear the expressions of joy which flowed from the hearts and lips of those that found peace with God through faith in Christ Jesus: "I feel lighter. I love my sweet Jesus. I love you all. Glory to God, I am happy! O how happy I am! O that I had known how good he was before, I would have sought him sooner. Come, father and mother. Come, brothers and sisters. Come, relations and neighbors. Come and go with me to heaven! Glory to God, he has pardoned my sins and has had mercy on my soul! I have felt more happiness in these few minutes, than in all my life before, etc." In six days, forty persons professed to be converted.[61]

For early Methodists, one could not stand still in a conversion experience. Once saved, we will either be progressing in grace or backsliding.

---

61. "Stith Mead letter to Thomas Coke, Georgia, 11 May 1802," *Methodist Magazine* (London) 25 (November 1802): 522-23.

Popular Appalachian poet and preacher John Adam Granade details in his hymn "Recovery from Despair" what a person experiences when realizing that he or she has backslid.

Ye happy souls, whose peaceful minds,
Are free from pain and fear,
Ye object which kind Heav'n designs
To make its constant care.
To you I'll vent my mournful sighs,
Pressed by my dismal fate.
O! Can you with me sympathize,
While I my case relate?

I once was happy in the Lord.
My soul was in a flame.
I did delight to hear his word
And praise his holy name.
His children were my heart's delight.
I loved their company.
I lived by faith, both day and night,
That Jesus died for me.

But woe is me, those joys are past.
Those blissful scenes are o'er.
I'm like a city quite laid waste
To be rebuilt no more.
In vain I cry, in vain I mourn,
In vain I seek for rest.
I fear the dove[62] will ne'er return
To my poor, troubled breast.

Alas! Alas! Where shall I go?
Jesus from me has gone,
A child of sorrow, grief, and woe,
Forevermore undone.

---

62. The Holy Spirit.

The gospel too, is hid from me
Though often I do hear.
The law denounces death on me
And thunders out despair.

My hope is fled, and faith I've none.
God's word I cannot bear.
My sense and reason almost gone,
Filled with tormenting fear:
What next to do, I cannot tell,
So keen my sorrows are.
Without relief I sink to hell
To howl in long despair.

The devil waiting me around
To make my soul a prey.
I wait to hear the trumpet sound,
"Take, take the wretch away."
I linger, pine, I groan and sigh.
Sleep now has left mine eyes.
And ghastly death seems drawing nigh
And that without disguise.

O! that I was some bird or beast,
Was I a stork or owl,
Some lofty tree should bear my nest,
Or through the desert prowl.
But I have an immortal soul,
Within this house of clay,
That either must with devils howl,
Or dwell in endless day.

One ev'ning pensive as I lay,
Alone upon the ground,
As I to God began to pray,
A light shone all around.
These words with power went through my heart,
"I've come to set you free;

Death, hell or grave shall never part
My love, (my son) from thee."

My dungeon shook, my chains flew off.
"Glory to God," I cried.
My soul was filled, I cried, "Enough,
For me the Savior died."
The winter's past, the rain is gone,
Sweet flowers do appear.
The morning's brought a glorious sun,
That's banished every fear.

Hail, brightest Prince, eternal Lord,
That left the blazing throne.
Eternal truth attends thy words;
Thou art the Father's son.
When on the brink of hell I lay,
Enclosed in blackest night,
Thou, Lord, didst hear the sinner pray,
And brought my soul to light.

All you that's groaning in your chains,
Without one spark of hope,
Though inexpressible your pains,
O! still be looking up
The winds may blow, and storms arise,
A dark and gloomy night;
The morning sun will clear the skies,
With sweet prevailing light.[63]

COSMIC SALVATION

Early Methodist conversion is an intensely personal experience, but Methodists do not think of it as an isolated experience. In this hymn

---

63. Hinde, *Pilgrim Songster*, 54-57.

entitled "Scriptures Fulfilling," John Adam Granade places an appeal to unconverted sinners within a larger framework of God fulfilling the Scriptures with the return of Christ and a general judgment of all humankind.

1. See how the Scriptures are fulfilling!
Poor sinners are returning home.
The time that prophets were foretelling
With signs and wonders now has come.
The gospel trumpets are a-roaring,
From sea to sea, from land to land.
God's Holy Spirit is down pouring,
And Christians joining heart and hand.

2. Ten thousands fall before Jehovah.
For mercy, mercy loud they cry.
They raise a shouting "Hallelujah,
All glory be to God on high."
But many cry, "'Tis all disorder,"
And disbelieve God's holy word.
This makes them cry and shout the louder,
"All glory, glory to the Lord."

3. O! sinners hear our invitation:
"You are but feeble, dying worms.
O! fly to Jesus for salvation,
Or you will meet God's awful storms."
We charge you all in the name of Jesus,
The awful judge of quick and dead.
But if you should refuse to hear us,
Your blood shall be upon your head.

4. Now God is calling ev'ry nation,
The bond and free, the rich and poor.
These are the days of visitation.
Sweet gospel grace will soon be o'er.
The Lord shall come, all clothed in thunder

And lightning streaming from his eyes.
O! then he'll cut his foes asunder,
And lay them where the damned lies.

5. The sun affrighted from his center,
Enveloped in a western cloud.
The stars to shine now dare not venture.
Pale Phoebus[64] clothed in scarlet shroud.
The sea and land together burning,
The flames ascend the melting sky.
All nature now to naught returning.
"Hark! Hark!" the herald angels cry.

6. Rise, Zion, rise in brilliant glory,
And mark toward the judgment seat.
Now hearken to the pleasant story,
When Jesus and his bride shall meet,
With smiling looks of approbation,
Invites her to his lovely arms;
And she is filled with transportation,
Dissolved in his heav'nly charms.

7. There lovely spirits harmonizing,
In all the sweets of perfect love.
Meanwhile a gloomy cloud arising,
And seemed toward the bar to move.
See millions of poor wretched creatures,
Compelled by justice to appear.
Deep horror painted all their features
And colored them with black despair.

8. Hideous cries and lamentations,
But no relief can there be found.
The judge pronounces condemnation,
And seven thunders echo round.

---

64. In mythology, the god of the sun.

"Down the lake of burning fire,
And never more my face to see.
You're bound to bear my dreadful ire
And blow the flames eternally."

9. Now devils drag them down the center
Into the gulf of burning woe.
Poor wretches! How they dread to enter,
But, forced by vengeance, down they go.
Now they are paid to persecuting
And opposing the work of God,
For all the time they spent disputing
And trampling on a Savior's blood.

10. O! Christians double your diligence.
With courage march the heav'nly road.
Remember this: that double vengeance
Will fall on those that turn from God.
Your children all must be converted,
Or they can never rest with you.
God's word cannot be controverted.
God bless you all. Amen. Adieu.[65]

Similarly, in his hymn entitled "Invitation and Terror," New York Methodist Ebenezer Hills calls for sinners to repent in light of Christ's second coming and the cosmic dimensions of God's pending judgment.

Sinners, arise, repent, return,
Come, hear the Gospel call.
And for your sinful practice mourn
For Jesus died for all.

Jesus his precious life did give.
He died for all our race.

---

65. Hinde, *Pilgrim Songster*, 28-30.

He died that sinful man might live
To see his smiling face.

Repent before it be too late,
When mercy's door is shut,
When awful, dreadful is your fate
By fiends of hell beset.

Pale death erupts the feeble clay.
The soul must take its flight.
And devils drag that soul away
To everlasting night.

When Jesus shall in clouds descend,
With trumpets solemn sound,
Those angel bands their God attend,
Their Lord encircle round.

In flaming fire, vengeance to take
On those that know not God.
"Arise to judgment," hear him speak.
Earth trembles at his nod.

The earth shall melt with fervent heat.
The raging seas retire.
All must appear before his feet
And leave the world on fire.

Sinners in vain on mountains call.
Nor will the rocks attend
The flinty rocks tremble and fall.
The solid marbles rend.[66]

Some Methodists think that God's saving purposes ultimately include more than just humans. In this humorous passage, itinerant preacher

---

66. Ebenezer Hills, Hymnal, hymn 6.

William Ormond speaks of his desire to reunite with his horse in the general resurrection. Ormond is moving from a circuit where he needs his horse to a city station where he does not.

I have agreed for bro[ther].[67] J. Moody to take my horse and sell him for me as I am going to stay in town. I rode him to bro[ther]. Charles Murphrey's [and] then to bro[ther]. Cowling's. Now I am to part with the good slave that has carried me more than four years. From Maryland to the frontier part of Georgia my faithful horse has borne me safe. Now bro[ther]. Cowling's Negro man takes him and is to deliver him to Charles Murphrey and bro[ther]. Joseph Moody is to send for him on Monday next and keep him till Southamton Court[68] and then and there sell him on credit for me. I now, about four o'clock in the evening, this 12th day of March, 1803, take the last look on my horse until the G[eneral]. Resurrection. Then I shall (I believe) see him in an immortal state never more to suffer.[69]

ARMINIAN, NOT CALVINIST

Within the different schools of thought in the eighteenth century, Methodists were very self-consciously Arminian, not Calvinist. In this essay for publication in the **Virginia Gazette,** *itinerant preacher Ezekiel Cooper describes the differences between the two approaches to grace and salvation. Cooper speaks of Calvinists as "Predestinarians."*

They (Arminians) do not believe absolute predestination. The difference is here [that] Predestinarians say "God has absolutely decreed from all eternity, to save such and such persons, and no others, and that Christ died for these and none else." The Arminians hold God has decreed … all who have the word "He that believeth not shall be damned."[70] And, in order to [accomplish] this, Christ died for all, all that were dead in trespasses and

---

67. Brother is the term used for a Methodist man.
68. Probably referring to the quarterly session of a judicial court, around which, it seems, people gathered to conduct other business.
69. William Ormond, Journal, 12 March 1803.
70. Compare John 3:18.

sins, that is, for every child of Adam since in Adam all died.[71] Hence they may be saved provided they live not in unbelief.

Predestinarians say the grace of God is absolutely irresistible. The Arminians hold that although there may be some moments wherein the grace of God acts irresistibly, yet in general many may resist— and that to his [or her] eternal ruin—the grace whereby it was the will of God [that] he [or she] might have been eternally saved.

The Predestinarians say that a believer in Christ cannot possibly fall from grace. The Arminians hold that a believer may make shipwreck of faith and a good conscience. That he may fall, not only foully, but finally, so as to perish forever, if he dies in his apostasy.

The Arminians hold that irresistible grace and infallible perseverance are the natural consequences of unconditional decree or absolute predestination. For if God has absolutely decreed to save such and such persons, it follows both that they cannot resist his saving grace (else they might be lost) and that they cannot fall from that grace which they cannot resist. So that in effect the three questions come into one: "Is predestination absolute or conditional?" The Arminians believe it conditional; the Calvinists that it is absolute or unconditional.

Many Calvinists are pious, learned, sensible men. And so are many Arminians. Only the former hold absolute predestination, the latter conditional. Arminians have as much right to be angry at Calvinists as Calvinists have to be angry at Arminians. To be more fully acquainted with what Arminius held, let his own, and not the writings of his enemies, be consulted.

One word more. Is it not the duty of every Arminian preacher, first, never in private or in public to use the word "Calvinist" as a term of reproach, seeing it is neither better nor worse than calling names? [Calling names is] A practice no more consistent with good sense or good manners than with Christianity. Secondly [is it not the preacher's duty] to do all he can to prevent this among his hearers? And should not a Calvinist preacher in his turn do the same, with respect to the Arminians?[72]

A 1784 diary writer complains about one of the effects of people believing in popular Calvinistic doctrines: it often makes them less zealous

---

71. See 2 Corinthians 5:14, Ephesians 2:1, and 1 Corinthians 15:22.

72. Undated ms. essay entitled "A Lover of Free Grace," written as a letter from Ezekiel Cooper to Messrs. Hanson and Bon (Printers, *Virginia Gazette*, Alexandria, Va.), Ezekiel Cooper papers (vol. 20, ms. 16).

about a methodical use of the means of grace. These means included such practices as fasting, prayer, the reading of Scripture, and public worship. In Methodist understanding, using the means was the way to progress in God's grace.

I was greatly mortified in class meeting to find such a deadness among the members. I spoke of it again and again and I found afterwards that they frequently neglect their own meetings and go to hear Dissenters[73] which seldom fails to make Christians doubtful and no wonder when they hear such doctrines of predestination, final perseverance, and believers' baptism, which have a tendency to make people careless as to earnestly and constantly using the means of grace.[74]

In this final excerpt, itinerant preacher William Colbert contends with several Calvinists in 1792. The Calvinists, seemingly eager to get preaching of any kind, remain unconvinced by Colbert's logic and somewhat sarcastic comments. In the second episode, Colbert states another problem Methodists saw in Calvinist sentiment: it undercut a desire to pursue sanctification (Christian perfection) beyond conversion. Colbert is traveling a circuit in mountainous Pennsylvania and New York.

I preached at Guy Well's on Hebrews 2:3, "How shall we escape, if we neglect so great salvation." Here I was attacked by two Calvinists. The debate was on falling from grace. I asked them if David[75] was not a child of God. They said, "He was." I then asked them, "What would have become of him had he died in the bed of adultery?" One of them said he would have gone to heaven, but another said he could not die there [in the bed of adultery]. I then observed to them that, according to their doctrine, David might have remained alive by continuing in sin. They said they were in a remote part of the world and ought to have the truth preached to them for (they said) they had been used to preaching. I told them if God had foreordained that I should come and preach to them [then] I could not help it. It is surprisingly strange that the Calvinists

---

73. In Britain, and the Anglican-chartered colonies, "dissenters" were those who refused to attend the Church of England. This would include Baptists, whom he seems to have in mind.

74. [Author?], Diary fragment for 10 July 1784, Edward Dromgoole papers.

75. David, the Jewish king, once caught in adultery.

are not ashamed of their Doctrines. At night I preached at Mr. Price's ... with liberty on Matthew 5:6.[76] Here we had much talk about final perseverance and [Christian] perfection,[77] which the Calvinists abhor. Mrs. Price gives a very satisfactory account of her conversion. It is well if she does not trust too much in what has been done for her in time past instead of striving to advance in the divine. She is much opposed to Christian perfection. I told her she must be perfect in the scripture sense of the word or she could never enter the Kingdom of Heaven.[78]

---

76. "Blessed are they which do hunger and thirst after righteousness: for they shall be filled."
77. The distinctive Methodist doctrine of Christian perfection is the focus of chapter 3.
78. Compare Matthew 5:48. William Colbert, Journal, 1:93.

CHAPTER 3
SANCTIFICATION

For early Methodists conversion was a threshold, not a finish line. Central to their spirituality was the conviction that the experience of justification/new birth was only the gateway into the journey of salvation. Their anticipation of what lay ahead contained both a progressive aspect—one was expected to grow continually as a Christian—and a climactic aspect—there was a distinct second crisis to be sought after conversion.

While these two aspects were combined in their formal understanding of sanctification as the second dimension to salvation, early Methodists clearly put greatest emphasis on the latter aspect. Indeed, they frequently used the word "sanctification" to refer specifically to the second crisis experience of God's saving grace. Accordingly, the present chapter will focus mainly on this climactic aspect of sanctification.

The first excerpt below, a sermon outline by Philip Gatch, is a good introduction to how sanctification fit within the order of salvation underlying American Methodist spirituality. In describing the "blessings" that Christ as Savior had opened, Gatch lays out a progression of convincing grace, convicting grace, converting grace, sanctifying grace, and persevering grace. These various forms of grace parallel the spiritual states that early Methodists expected all to pass through in the journey of salvation. Convincing grace awakens persons to their spiritual need, while convicting grace brings the deeper sense of anxiety and repentance that Methodists considered prerequisite to conversion (as we saw in chapter 2).[1] Converting

---

1. Although his manuscript outline is a little unclear, it appears that Gatch is using a bracket to stress the close connection of convincing grace and convicting grace in repentance.

grace then bestows the first climactic experience of salvation, as believers are assured of the pardon of their sins (justification) and enlivened by the new birth. The most interesting point, for present purposes, is how Gatch groups "sanctifying grace" and "persevering grace" under the larger heading of sanctification. Sanctifying grace is clearly being connected to a second specific experience of God's saving work, while persevering grace accounts for our continuation and growth in the new life made possible by grace.

What did early Methodists think happened in this second climactic salvation experience? They gave a variety of explanations. One set of these explanations focused on the overcoming or negation of some aspect of sinfulness that remains in new believers. The victory over this sin in human nature was described in images like overcoming self-will and self-love, mortification and crucifixion, burning vain desires, washing from heart uncleanness, an entire change of nature, and deliverance from indwelling sin.

Another set of explanations of this second climactic experience focused on what was being added to the initial work of salvation. The most central image was the bestowal of a new quality of love in the heart. In the experience of sanctification believers received a new capacity to love God entirely and to love other people as one's self.

"Holiness" was a synonym often used to describe what was experienced in sanctification. "Perfection" was another, particularly in the form of using "perfect" as an adjective to describe some spiritual quality obtained in sanctification, for example, perfect love or perfect resignation.[2] Other images used the language of offering: when sanctified, a person was making a total consecration of her or his whole self to God. Finally, picking up on another set of biblical images, many early Methodists spoke of this experience of sanctification as the "baptism with the Holy Spirit."[3]

---

2. "Christian perfection" was one of the key phrases of John Wesley for sanctification. The word "perfection" had a different meaning for Wesley and early Methodists than it tends to have today, although the term caused confusion even in the eighteenth century. Wesley had to clarify what perfection was not. Someone who was sanctified was not perfect in knowledge, free from ignorance and mistakes, or free from infirmities. A sanctified person still faced temptation and needed to continue to progress in grace, there being no static perfection. Cf. Collins, Scripture Way of Salvation, 172-73.

3. See Laurence W. Wood, The Meaning of Pentecost in Early Methodism: Rediscovering John Fletcher as John Wesley's Vindicator and Designated Successor (Lanham, Md.: Scarecrow Press, 2002), 293-311.

If this seems like a confusing array of overlapping images, it was. Rather than trying to subsume sanctification under a single term, it is best to think of it as an umbrella category that encompassed a complex of terms and images. This lack of precision reflects a people who were more concerned with the evangelical *propagation* of spiritual experiences than with detached explanations of them.

The actual degree of emphasis on the experience of sanctification in early American Methodist spirituality is a bit unclear. Some scholars have suggested that this emphasis was on the wane, especially during the latter period covered by this book (the 1810s).[4] In favor of this claim would be the occasional Methodist voice during this period lamenting that sanctification was not being spoken of enough. On the other hand, while the wide range of early Methodist sources that I have consulted suggest that the issue was not nearly as prominent as conversion and justification, it does occur quite frequently and in some powerful passages. Moreover, if the numbers that early Methodists reported are at all reliable (see below), the crisis experience of sanctification was quite a widespread phenomenon. One must also bear in mind that emphasis on this experience was central to early Methodist identity. It was one of the elements that clearly distinguished them within the range of heart-religion Christians in the late-eighteenth and early-nineteenth centuries.

The emphasis on sanctification served to distinguish Methodists on a variety of fronts. In one direction, it was their key rejoinder to a kind of popular Protestantism that nurtured a sort of spiritual passivity. If the sole sufficiency for salvation resides in Christ, this approach said, then humans could do nothing. This piety put emphasis almost exclusively on God's declaration of pardon and the imputing of righteousness. It held that God did not see people for who they really were; God saw them as if looking on Christ. This view was sometimes labeled "antinomian" (against the law) by early Methodists, because they saw its advocates stating that the law of God should be used only to convict people of their sinfulness, not as a positive guide for Christian living. Against this cluster of ideas, Methodists emphasized the experience of

---

4. For an example, see John L. Peters, *Christian Perfection & American Methodism*, rev. ed. (Grand Rapids: Francis Asbury Press, 1985), 97-98 and 188-89.

sanctification as God's way of actually and thoroughly transforming a human person.

In another direction, early Methodists emphasized the alternative of sanctification to the nominal Christian identity of many church members, particularly those in "formal" traditions. Methodists were convinced (often by reflection on their own spiritual journey) that members of these churches were prone to adopt the forms of religion, including a kind of outward obedience to moral standards, while lacking the inward power of godliness. In direct contrast, Methodists testified that the true power for obedience is love, not duty. It is a heart transformed by the love of God that makes possible the obedience that is truly acceptable to God.

On yet another front, early Methodists appealed to sanctification in exhorting each other out of spiritual complacency. They were convinced that one of the greatest dangers facing converted "professors of religion" was that they might get "settled on their lees," to use one of their turns of speech. The image is of becoming stagnant and still (lees were the dregs or settlings of liquor during fermentation and aging). Such stagnation risked spiritual disaster. Methodists found that exhorting one another onto sanctification was a way of unsettling any complacency that might have set in after conversion.

This raises the question of how early Methodists understood the connection between conversion and sanctification. At one level there was a strong logical connection, in that the new birth initiated sanctifying transformation. Regeneration was *initial* sanctification.[5] Indeed, the image of new birth cried out for the expectation of further growth and maturation.

But perhaps the more important connection was how their conversion experiences shaped their expectations for what it meant to *experience* sanctification. In comparing the typical conversion narrative to many of their sanctification testimonies, several parallels emerge. In both cases some initial trigger creates an awareness of a not-yet-experienced dimension of salvation. The awareness grows, as does the desire to experience this aspect of salvation. Awareness of sin in some degree is key to the growing desire and anxiety. Urgent prayer follows, as does continued participation in

---

5. This connection of new birth and sanctification is an aspect of John Wesley's theology. See Maddox, *Responsible Grace*, 176.

Methodist fellowship. Finally, usually after greater agony of spirit, the person breaks through to the sought-after dimension of salvation. A great sense of relief and joy comes with an inner sense of witness. Overall, the affective choreography of an early Methodist sanctification experience—both inward and outward—was very much like that of conversion.

The complexity of terms that early American Methodists used to describe sanctification, and the parallels between it and conversion, both suggest that multiple sources contributed to their understanding of this dimension of salvation. At least four sources should be noted: British Methodist roots, biblical proof texts, the experience of experimental religion, and the opportunities for testimonies in the rhythm of Methodist life.

At the most direct level, American Methodists inherited their focus on sanctification from their roots. Emphasis on sanctification had been a long-standing aspect of British Methodism, reaching its peak perhaps just before American Methodism began to proliferate in the 1770s. The language and understanding of British Methodists, conveyed through sermons, hymns, treatises, and testimonials, provided the basic material for the earliest American Methodists.

In comparison, it is evident that this British material provided the basic framework for American understandings of sanctification. Consider, for example, Kenneth Collins's summary of John Wesley's views.[6] Wesley thought of a second repentance that "professors" were to do over sin, especially the despair brought about by deeper awareness of one's basic sinful nature. Affirming a progressive nature to sanctification, Wesley also affirmed a second, distinct experience whose sole condition was faith. Inward witness (conviction) could follow. The emphasis was on the thoroughness of inward transformation brought about by the love of God and resulting in love for God and others. Wesley's writings were also reflected in what Americans emphasized they did *not* mean when

---

6. Collins, *Scripture Way of Salvation*, 155-90. It should be noted that Wesley's emphases on sanctification were not the only influence from British Methodism to reach the American church. For example, many Americans were drawn to John Fletcher's stronger equation of sanctification with the baptism of the Holy Spirit; cf. Wood, *Meaning of Pentecost*. Likewise, Randy Maddox has suggested that a greater emphasis on the crisis experience found in such British Methodists as Adam Clarke and Richard Watson proved amenable to the Americans; cf. Randy L. Maddox, "Holiness of Heart and Life: Lessons from North American Methodism," *Asbury Theological Journal* 51, 1 (1996): 151-72.

affirming sanctification. (While they affirmed that sanctification brought a renewal of love for God and neighbor, they insisted that it did not mean that one becomes like angels or like Adam before the Fall. It did not involve freedom from ignorance, mistakes, or infirmities. Nor did it exclude the possibility of sinning.)

American Methodist attraction to sanctification was not built simply on these British roots. As their surviving writings show, the Americans sought sanctification because they saw it as scriptural. Two sets of scriptures in particular created the tension out of which their desire for sanctification came. One set were those scriptures that spoke of God's promise of an aspect of salvation beyond forgiveness. As seen in the excerpts below, American Methodists highlighted those scriptures that speak of a new heart, a clean heart, purity in heart, death to sin, perfection, and sanctification itself. The second set of passages that drew their attention were those where God commanded something that these Methodists knew they could not fulfill within their own ability. Foremost among these passages was the call to love God with all one's heart, mind, soul, and strength and to love one's neighbor as one's self. Together, these two sets of passages convinced early Methodists that God intended to do more with sin than just forgive it.

If British roots and a scriptural perspective provided the basic fuel for American desire for sanctification, their commitment to "experimental religion" provided the form for how they experienced sanctification. What they learned of justification in their conversion—the internal spiritual rhythms culminating in a climactic new awareness, the range of affections, and the knowing of salvation by inward witness—they brought to their search for sanctification. This leaves little surprise that the expectation of a definitive, conscious, climactic experience of sanctification became increasingly standard. It was experimental religion that led Methodists to believe that the divine intention to provide true holiness could be inwardly experienced *now*.

The final factor that shaped the understanding of sanctification among early Methodists was the prominence in their organization of the practice of testimony. Between the required class meetings, special worship services, and general Methodist exhortation, an unsanctified Methodist had ample opportunity to hear other Methodists testify to sanctification. As in conversion, the potency of such testimonies was overwhelming. They were often the immediate triggers for new experiences of sanctification.

The excerpts that follow are intended to demonstrate sanctification's importance across early Methodism. They have been chosen specifically for their breadth with respect to period, region, race, gender, and status within the movement. In the first set of excerpts several preachers explain how sanctification fits into the order of salvation and give rationales for its importance. The next two sections explore the key terms used to name sanctification and the different ways of expressing its instantaneous nature as a discernable experience of salvation. We then are offered several accounts of Methodists actually experiencing sanctification. The chapter concludes with some excerpts illustrating how the "promise" of sanctification was offered in worship services, and how the dynamics of these services created the setting for experiencing sanctification.

SANCTIFICATION AS SALVATION

Early Methodists thought of salvation as progression through a series of experiences or states of grace. Philip Gatch, originally an itinerant preacher in Virginia and later a local preacher in Ohio, illustrates this understanding in this excerpt from a sermon outline. Gatch first details the progressive experiences of grace one can find in Christ: conviction, conversion, sanctification, perseverance, paradise, and finally, eternal glory. He then explains the differences between these experiences.

John 10:9, "I am the door: by me if any man enter in, he shall be saved, and shall go in and out, and find pasture." . . .
[I.] Because he [i.e., Christ] is a door, he opens to all the blessings of earth and heaven. He's said to be the Savior of the world, etc.
1. Then he opens to convincing grace }
                } or repentance
2. [To] Convicting grace   }
3. To converting grace   } or Justification
4. To sanctifying grace   }
                } or Sanctification
5. To persevering grace   }
6. To Paradise

7. To the fullness of eternal glory

    Again the necessity of entering in by Christ

[II.] Second How we are to enter in by Christ the door to these blessings set before us, etc.

    It is by faith. Ephesians 2:8 [and] Heb 11:6.

1. Into a state of penitence or repentance by which we are saved from the love and [attraction? word indecipherable in the manuscript] of sin
2. Into a justified state by which we are saved from the guilt of sin
3. Into a sanctified state by which we were saved from the remains of sin
4. Into the paradise of God by which we were saved from temptations and every other misery
5. Into the New Jerusalem by which we should be saved from our mortality.[7]

Thomas Coke and Francis Asbury, the first bishops of The Methodist Episcopal Church, added commentary to the book of discipline for the MEC published in 1798. One of their comments stresses the need for Methodist preachers to stir up desire for sanctification. Their explanation makes clear that initial experiences of salvation were considered merely thresholds to addressing the more fundamental issue: the heart's "self-will and self-love." Note in this passage the biblical proof texts used to support a doctrine of sanctification and the way that they root sanctification in the different offices of Christ: prophet, priest, and king.

Those who are more adult in grace, he [the preacher] must feed with strong meat. He must show them the necessity of being crucified to the world, and of dying daily, that "if they mortify not the deeds of the flesh, they shall die." He must not spare the remaining man of sin. He must anatomize the human heart and follow self-will and self-love through all their windings. And all this being addressed to the children of God, he must do it with great tenderness. "I protest by your rejoicing which I have in Christ Jesus our Lord, I die daily," says the apostle (1 Corinthians 15:31). "If ye live

---

7. Philip Gatch, sermon outline book, 20-21.

after the flesh ye shall die: but if ye, through the Spirit, do mortify the deeds of the body, ye shall live" (Romans 8:13). "Grow in grace, and in the knowledge of our Lord and Savior, Jesus Christ" (2 Peter 3:18).

And now he must again turn to the son of consolation. He must hold forth Christ as an all-sufficient Savior, as "able to save them to the uttermost that come unto God by him; seeing he everliveth to make intercession for them" (Hebrews 7:25). He must describe to them, in all its richest views, the blessings of perfect love. He must now declare how our great Zerubbabel is this moment able and willing to reduce the mountain into a plain.[8] And all the above he [the preacher] must endeavor more or less to introduce into every sermon which he delivers to a mixed congregation. "The very God of peace sanctify you wholly, and I pray God your whole spirit, soul, and body be preserved blameless unto the coming of our Lord Jesus Christ. Faithful is he that calleth you, who also will do it" (1 Thessalonians 5:23-24). "This is the will of God, even your sanctification" (1 Thessalonians 4:3).

He must preach the law as well as the gospel. He must hold forth our adorable Redeemer as a prophet to teach, a priest to atone, and a king to reign in us and over us. He must break the stony heart, as well as bind up the broken. But still holiness inward and outward must be his end. Holiness must be his aim. And antinomianism [see commentary above] and every doctrine which opposes holiness, he must contend with, until he gain the victory, or render his hearers utterly inexcusable. Who is fit for these things? O Lord God, help us all! Let us do our utmost, and leave the blessing to the Lord.[9]

In this sermon fragment, itinerant preacher Freeborn Garrettson addresses the need for sanctification as a saving experience beyond justification or conversion. He uses some of early Methodists' most fundamental terms for sanctification: pure in heart, conformity to the will of God, and perfect love.

---

8. See Zechariah 4:7. Zerubbabel was the governor of Judah upon the Jews' return from exile. In Old Testament accounts he is associated with the rebuilding of the temple in Jerusalem. The passage in Zechariah was an encouragement to Zerubbabel that it would not be by might or power but by God's Spirit that he would succeed in rebuilding the temple by leveling the mountain so that it would be a plain useful as a foundation for the new building. Coke and Asbury suggest that Christ is a new Zerubbabel who, by the Spirit of God, is able to accomplish the new work of sanctification, leveling all mountainous sins to do so.

9. *Doctrines and Discipline* (1798), 86-87.

What does our blessed Lord mean by the word "pure in heart"? How is this blessing attained? It is a common thing for people when first brought into gospel liberty [i.e., having experienced the new birth] to suppose the work is complete. But sooner or later, if faithful to the grace given, they are convinced that there must be a deeper work. This conviction is wrought in the heart by the Spirit of God. The law is pure and discovers impurity. There is now an earnest groaning for an entire conformity to the will of God. Faith apprehends the merits of Christ and obtains the evidence of perfect love. Those graces which were before immature, now are mature, filling the whole soul and governing the whole new man [sic]. The pure in heart are blest. They see God.[10]

Methodist advocacy of sanctification could be quite strong. It was not enough just to have one's sins forgiven. In this striking passage, Richard Allen, a Philadelphia preacher and eventual founding bishop of The African Methodist Episcopal Church, insists that holiness—the result of sanctification—is necessary for heaven. His main argument is that we are not fit for heaven until we have a "heavenly" character.

In the temper of every wicked mind there is a strong antipathy to the pleasures of heaven, which, being all chaste, pure, and spiritual, can never agree with the vitiated palate of a base and degenerate soul. For what concord can there be between a spiteful and devilish spirit and the fountain of all love and goodness? Between a sensual and carnalized[11] one, that understands no other pleasures but only those of the flesh, and those pure and virgin spirits, that neither eat nor drink, but live for ever upon wisdom, holiness, love and contemplation? Certainly till our mind is contempered to the heavenly state, and we are of the same disposition with God and angels and saints, there is no pleasure in heaven that can be agreeable to us. For as in the main we shall be of the same temper and disposition when we come into the other life as we are when we leave this, it being unimaginable how a total change should be wrought in us

---

10. Freeborn Garrettson, untitled, undated sermon on Luke 11:31, Garrettson Family papers (box 1, folder 20).

11. Allen means a human spirit that pursues the desires "of the flesh." The image is one from the Apostle Paul. See Romans 7 and 8, and 1 Corinthians 3.

merely by passing out of one world into another, and, therefore, as in this world, it is likeness that does congregate and associate beings together, so, doubtless, it is in the other world too; so that is we carry with us thither our wicked and devilish dispositions (as we shall certainly do, unless we subdue and mortify them here), there will be no company fit for us to associate with, but only the devilish and damned ghosts of wicked men, with whom our wretched spirits, being already joined by a likeness of nature, will mingle themselves as soon as ever they are excommunicated from the society of mortals.

For whither should they flock but to the birds of their own feather? With whom should they associate but with those malignant spirits, to whom they are already joined by a community of nature? So that, supposing that when they land in eternity, it were left to their own choice to go to heaven or hell, into the society of the blessed or the damned, it is plain that heaven would be no place for them [and] that the air of that bright region of eternal day would never agree with their black and hellish natures. For, alas, what should they do among those blessed beings that inhabit it? To those godlike natures, divine contemplation and heavenly employments, they have so great a repugnancy and aversion? So that, besides the having a right to heaven, it is necessary to our enjoying it, that we should be antecedently disposed and qualified for it. And it being thus, God has been graciously pleased to make those very virtues the condition of our right to heaven, which are the proper dispositions and qualifications of our spirits for it, that so, with one and the same labor, we might entitle ourselves and qualify ourselves to enjoy it.[12]

IMAGES FOR SANCTIFICATION

No single image or biblical metaphor sufficed to explain sanctification for early Methodists. In the following diary passage, Catherine Livingston, a Methodist in New York and eventual wife of Freeborn Garrettson, discusses her desire to be sanctified. Beyond the terms "perfect heart and willing mind," she articulates this desire by the image drawn from the Apostle Paul: crucifixion with Christ and a life hid in Christ.

---

12. Richard Allen, "A Short Address to the Friends of Him Who Hath No Helper," in *The Life Experience and Gospel Labors of the Rt. Rev. Richard Allen* (Philadelphia: Martin & Boden, 1833), 87-89.

I find myself more than ever engaged for sanctification. I desire to rest in nothing short of this great privilege. I want to serve my God with a perfect heart and willing mind. I have long seen a great beauty in this doctrine, and long to bear witness to the truth of it. I last night dreamed I was crucified.[13] Be it so, Lord Jesus! Let me die that I may live, and that my life may be hid with you.[14] Such a day of heaviness and travail of soul I have not experienced in a long time.[15]

In describing his experience of sanctification, Jeremiah Minter invokes the fulfillment of the prophecy in Ezekiel concerning God giving people new hearts and spirits.

I had now entered into my twenty-first year. I felt as great a desire to grow in grace myself, as to bring others to it. And believing from Scripture that there was a greater change of heart attainable than I had yet attained, a far greater degree of sanctifying grace unto full assurance of faith, I continued in prayer for it daily. And on the 11th of March 1787, the Lord fulfilled in me his ancient promise [from] Ezekiel 36:26, "A new heart also will I give you, and a new spirit will I put within you: and I will take away the stony heart out of your flesh, and I will give you a heart of flesh." And I felt the witness within that it was done. And my joy was full, yea was utterly unspeakable, and so full of glory, it seemed like overpowering life with heavenly happiness of soul. (1 John 1:4 [and] 1 Peter 18.) It was really like the visions of God. Love to God and souls, and courage to go on in preaching the Gospel, were as the overflowing of a river, bearing down all opposition from earth and Satan.[16]

Some references to sanctification in early Methodist writings are subtle. For example, it would be easy to miss the references in the following hymn entitled "Christ Our Salvation," unless one bears in mind the standard Methodist assumption of progression through various experiences of grace (conviction, justification, sanctification, eternal glory). Stanzas 3

---

13. Compare Galatians 2:20.
14. Colossians 3:3.
15. Catherine Garrettson, Diary, 1 December 1791, Garrettson Family papers.
16. Minter, *Brief Account*, 10.

and 4 deal with sanctification under biblical images of washing and burning. This hymn is also helpful for seeing how all salvation was rooted in the saving activity of God in Jesus Christ. As seen with this hymn in chapter 3, this rooting is the basis for adoring Christ.

1. When man was fallen far from God
Exposed to condemnation,
The Lord of glory interposed
And purchased our salvation.
He laid his richest glory by
And groveled in the garden.
'Twas love divine did him incline
To purchase for us pardon.

2. None could atone but Christ alone,
His Father's wrath diminish.
To make us kings and priests to God
Jesus has cried, "'Tis finished."
The work of man's salvation's wrought.
The sacrifice is accepted.
Now man may live for Christ hath died.
His pardon is contracted.

3. Come, Lord, and bring us to the pool
'Twas opened for uncleanness.
Bid us step in and be made whole
And cry no more our leanness.
For to bring fire on Earth he came,
O, burn my vile desires.
And then my mind shall be inclined
To join celestial choirs.

4. Like Moses' bush then may we burn
Without receiving harm.
And when thou dost to earth return
To sound the great alarm,
Then may our souls with thee arise,

Whatever may oppose us,
With Angels mount above the skies
And sing the song of Moses.

5. So be it, Lord, thy will be done.
Appear and be victorious.
The Spirit and the bride say, "Come,
And make us with thee glorious."
Then shall we walk with thee in white
And cast our crowns before thee,
With Abra'm sing, "our glorious King,"
And evermore adore thee.[17]

From Methodism's beginning one of the basic images for sanctification was perfect love for God and neighbor. The following poem, printed in the 1789 edition of the denominational magazine, honestly explores the human inability to accomplish this end on our own. As such the poem shows the sort of inward cry that many early Methodists prayed, asking God to sanctify so that the command to love with the entire heart might be fulfilled.

A Prayer
"Thou shalt love the Lord thy GOD with all thy heart."

Dost thou request a feeble worm,
To touch the sky, t' arrest the storm,
The mountains to remove:
Dost thou command what cannot be,
That thine apostate creature, thee
I should entirely love?

Have I ability t' obey,
Why should I then one moment stay?
Compelled, alas! I own,
Forced by ten thousand efforts vain,
There is no power in fallen man,
To love a GOD unknown.

---

17. Spiritual Songs (Edward Dromgoole papers), 11.

The power must then from thee proceed,
If thee I ever love indeed;
The thing thy laws enjoin,
Thy Spirit must in me fulfill,
Who seek, according to thy will,
The precious grace divine.

If all who *will* receive it, *may*,
I humbly for the blessing pray
To poorest beggars given:
With strength of infinite desire
I nothing but thy love require,
Of all in earth, or heaven.

What shall I say my suit to gain?
Father, regard that heavenly man,
Who groaned on Calvary!
Who paid my ransom on the cross,
Who ever lives to plead my cause,
And asks thy love for me.

In honor of th' incarnate GOD,
The gift he purchased with his blood,
Father, on me bestow!
That loving thee with all my heart,
And thus made ready to depart,
I to thy arms may go.[18]

SANCTIFICATION AS INSTANTANEOUS EXPERIENCE

One of the most important discussions among early Methodists was whether personal experience of sanctification comes instantly or gradually. According to Nathaniel Mills, it is both.

---

18. "A Prayer," *Arminian Magazine* (Philadelphia) 1 (1789): 548-49.

A Memorial which I wish read at my funeral and printed in the *Minutes*[19] (if thought proper) after my decease.

I was born in Newcastle County, in the state of Delaware, February 23, 1766. [I] pursued the follies of youth and the vice of the day in some degree (although not without frequent alarms of conscience) until the fifteenth year of my age, when by the mercy of God, I was awakened to a sense of my lost and perishing condition, partly through the instrumentality of the Methodists. I then became a habitually serious seeker of salvation until about the seventeenth year of my life [when] I obtained an evidence of pardoning mercy and a saving change through the infinite mercy of God and through the merits of our Lord and Savior Jesus Christ, to whom be all glory and honor, might, majesty, and dominion, both now and forever. Amen. Not long after I professed pardon (by a singular circumstance) I was convinced of inbred sin and sought the entire change of my nature, which I trust I found (in some good degree at least) about the twentieth year of my life. But as it respects sanctification, it is both gradual and instantaneous. There is often, if not always, a gradual change, a gradually increasing salvation in all holiness, both before, and after the instantaneous change, such it has been in my Christian experience.[20]

Other early Methodists emphasized the instantaneous nature of sanctification. Note, for example, Bishop Asbury's provocative advice in a letter of greeting to British Methodists.

If I were to judge myself worthy to write to the elder brethren in England, it would be [to say], "Seek pure hearts. Preach instantaneous salvation from all sin. Let every prayer, every hymn and sermon be seasoned with this wholesome, holy doctrine."[21]

As an instantaneous experience, the moment of sanctification could be identified as a milestone of one's spiritual journey. The following memorial of deceased preacher Hezekiah Wooster (d. 1799) is typical in identifying the date for his sanctification.

---

19. The published *Minutes* of the annual conferences, which included reports of every itinerant who had died that year.

20. Nathaniel Mills, papers.

21. Undated letter from Francis Asbury to Thomas Coke, *Methodist Magazine* (London) 25 (1802): 218.

The following lines were found among his papers after his death: Hezekiah Calvin Wooster was born, May 20, 1771; Convicted of sin, October 9, 1791; Born again, December 1, 1791; Sanctified, February 6, 1792.[22]

Understanding sanctification as an instantaneous, crisis experience also allowed early Methodists to count those who were sanctified on particular occasions. A good example is the following accounts tabulated for two camp meetings held on the Delmarva Peninsula in 1806. The number of sanctifications reported is particularly striking.

For a camp meeting held 13-17 June 1806:

Friday morning:	47 conversions;	39 sanctifications
Friday evening:	100 conversions;	75 sanctifications
Saturday morning:	82[23] conversions;	53 sanctifications
Saturday evening:	146 conversions;	76 sanctifications
Sunday morning:	156 conversions;	116 sanctifications
Sunday evening:	339 conversions;	122 sanctifications
Monday morning:	81 conversions;	68 sanctifications
Monday evening:	218 conversions;	56 sanctifications
Tuesday morning:	46 conversions[24]	

For a camp meeting held 8-12 August 1806:

Friday morning:	122 conversions;	84 sanctifications
Friday evening:	145 conversions;	82 sanctifications
Saturday morning:	95 conversions;	47 sanctifications
Saturday evening:	146 conversions;	59 sanctifications
Sunday evening:	92 conversions;	51 sanctifications

22. *Minutes of the Methodist Conferences* (1813), 222.
23. Perhaps 62; the manuscript is damaged and somewhat illegible.
24. Henry Boehm, Journal, 13-17 June 1806 and 8-12 August 1806.

Monday morning:	69 conversions;	32 sanctifications
Monday evening:	69 conversions;	25 sanctifications
Tuesday morning:	67 conversions;	17 sanctifications[25]

SANCTIFICATION TESTIMONIES

Early Methodists gave testimonies of religious experience as a kind of sacred history. These testimonies include the individual's account of experiencing conversion and, where appropriate, sanctification. The following testimony is from Jarena Lee, an articulate African American woman.

I continued in this happy state of mind for almost three months, when a certain colored man, by name William Scott, came to pay me a religious visit. He had been for many years a faithful follower of the Lamb; and he had also taken much time in visiting the sick and distressed of our color and understood well the great things belonging to a man of full stature in Christ Jesus.

In the course of our conversation, he inquired if the Lord had justified my soul. I answered, "Yes." He then asked me if he had sanctified me. I answered, "No; and that I did not know what that was." He then undertook to instruct me further in the knowledge of the Lord respecting this blessing.

He told me the progress of the soul from a state of darkness, or of nature, was threefold, or consisted in three degrees, as follows— first, conviction for sin; second, justification from sin; third, the entire sanctification of the soul to God. I thought this description was beautiful and immediately believed in it. He then inquired if I would promise to pray for this in my secret devotions. I told him, "Yes." Very soon I began to call upon the Lord to show me all that was in my heart which was not according to his will. Now there appeared to be a new struggle commencing in my soul, not accompanied with fear, guilt, and bitter distress, as while under my first

---

25. Ibid., 8-12 August 1806.

conviction for sin, but a laboring of the mind to know more of the right way of the Lord. I began now to feel that my heart was not clean in his sight [and] that there yet remained the roots of bitterness, which if not destroyed, would ere long sprout up from these roots and overwhelm me in a new growth of the brambles and brushwood of sin.

By the increasing light of the Spirit, I had found there yet remained the root of pride, anger, self-will, with many evils, the result of fallen nature. I now became alarmed at this discovery, and began to fear that I had been deceived in my experience. I was now greatly alarmed lest I should fall away from what I knew I had enjoyed. And to guard against this I prayed almost incessantly, without acting faith on the power and promises of God to keep me from falling. I had not yet learned how to war against temptation of this kind. Satan well knew that, if he could succeed in making me disbelieve my conversion, he would catch me either on the ground of complete despair or on the ground of infidelity. For if all I had passed through was to go for nothing and was but a fiction, the mere ravings of a disordered mind, I would naturally be led to believe that there is nothing in religion at all.

From this snare I was mercifully preserved and led to believe that there was yet a greater work than that of pardon to be wrought in me. I retired to a secret place (after having sought this blessing, as well as I could, for nearly three months, from the time brother Scott had instructed me respecting it,) for prayer, about four o'clock in the afternoon. I had struggled long and hard but found not the desire of my heart. When I rose from my knees, there seemed a voice speaking to me as I yet stood in a leaning posture: "Ask for sanctification." When to my surprise, I recollected that I had not even thought of it my whole prayer. It would seem Satan had hidden the very object from my mind for which I had purposely kneeled to pray. But when this voice whispered in my heart, saying, "pray for sanctification," I again bowed in the same place, at the same time, and said, "Lord, sanctify my soul for Christ's sake." That very instant, as if lightning had darted through me, I sprang to my feet, and cried, "The Lord has sanctified my soul." There was none to hear this but the angels who stood around to witness my joy, and Satan, whose malice raged the more. That Satan was there, I knew, for no sooner had I cried out "The Lord has sanctified my soul" than there seemed another voice behind me, saying, "No, it is too great a work to be done." But another spirit said, "Bow down for the witness—I received it—*thou art sanctified.*" The first I knew of myself after that I was standing in the yard with my hands spread out and looking with my face toward heaven.

I now ran into the house and told them what had happened to me, when, as it were, a new rush of the same ecstasy came upon me and caused me to feel as if I were in an ocean of light and bliss.

During this, I stood perfectly still, the tears rolling in a flood from my eyes. So great was the joy that it is past description. There is no language that can describe it, except that which was heard by St. Paul, when he was caught up to the third heaven,[26] and heard words which it was not lawful to utter.[27]

The following testimony is reported secondhand. The one sanctified is William Adams, a Virginian Methodist from the 1770s. The testimony was printed in the denominational magazine.

Sometime in the summer of 1777, as well as I can judge from my acquaintance with him (William Adams), as also from what I have heard at different times from his own lips, I have reason to think, that the Lord gave him a greater sense of the inward corruption of his heart, than ever he had seen or felt before: Though I believe he had known for some time, that there must be a deeper work wrought in his heart. But now he seemed all athirst for a heart perfectly devoted to God, crying, out of the fullness of his soul, to this effect:

> 'Tis worse than death my God to love,
> And not my God alone—[28]

---

26. See 2 Corinthians 12:2.

27. Jarena Lee, *Life and Religious Experience of Jarena Lee, A Coloured Lady* (Philadelphia: Printed and Published for the Author, 1836), 10-12.

28. Charles Wesley, "The Resignation," st. 4, *Hymns and Sacred Poems* (1740). This stanza became prominent in early Methodism because it was quoted by Jane Cooper in her testimony to sanctification, which John Wesley reproduced in *A Plain Account of Christian Perfection*, §24.

What particular means the Lord made use of to convince him so deeply of his inbred sin, I cannot assuredly say. However, on August the 17th, 1777, divine grace wrought such a mighty change in his soul, that he believed the Lord had saved him from all his inbred sin. He felt in his soul what (as he has often said since) he could never fully express with his lips....

At the last quarterly meeting he attended, many can testify of the humble confidence he expressed in the love feast. For my part, I acknowledged it exceeded anything that ever I heard drop from his lips until then. His words seemed like fire that flowed from a heart glowing with the love of Jesus and ran through many a happy soul then present. Here he declared before several hundreds of his brethren, that the Lord (since he came to that circuit) had taken away every doubt of his soul's being perfect in love and had given him that confidence which was stronger than death and all the power of darkness, which his last illness proved to be true to all then around him, as I shall hereafter relate. He well knew the blessedness of being with those Christians who have experienced a deliverance from the indwelling of sin and who are daily pressing after a growth in every grace of the Holy Spirit.[29]

Many of the sanctification accounts suggest parallels between the experience of conversion and that of sanctification. The following account, for instance, with its intense prayer under a deep sense of conviction, the transition in bodily posture, and the affective change from conviction to ecstatic joy, is similar to justification testimonies.

Sister Schuyler at Rhinebeck[30] experienced sanctification in a class meeting at my house. This was one of the most awfully solemn seasons I ever had. When I had done speaking to the class, I asked Sister Schuyler, to close our meeting by prayer. And she was led by the Spirit to pray for sanctification. Her gift in prayer at all times surpassed all I ever heard, [either] of man or woman. And at this time she excelled herself and everything I had ever heard. Her converse [i.e., conversation] with God, her thanksgiving for

---

29. "A Short Account of the Life and Death of William Adams, A Youth of Virginia," *Arminian Magazine* (Philadelphia) 1 (1789): 87, 90.

30. Rhinebeck is in New York state.

justification through the redemption that is in Jesus, and the faith that is by him, her confession of weakness of faith and depravity of our nature that rendered us so liable to err from the paths of holiness, [all] were expressed most feelingly. She portrayed the advantage of sanctification to assist us to serve the Lord perfectly and then in her appeal to the Lord for the sincerity of her motives and the fullness of his grace for all she asked for, she seemed to us to be conversing in the language of immortals. She implored the Most High to implant the blessing in her soul for the sake of Jesus Christ, who had redeemed us to himself that we should be a peculiar people, zealous of good works. She then cried out "O! Thou dost hear! Thou art nigh! O! Thy glory! O!!" and sunk forward in her chair with a sigh. For about four minutes we were all overwhelmed with divine glory and nothing was uttered by anyone but a sigh or a groan that indicated the joyful surprise of the Divine presence. After the lapse of about four minutes, she arose from her chair, before which she had continued kneeling and her expressions of thanksgiving to God, exceeded all she had ever expressed before.[31]

Richard Graves, another Virginian Methodist, testifies to an intense sanctification experience.

It has been about twenty years since I have been acquainted with the goodness of God, and nearly the same time since I had reason to believe that I stood in a state of acceptance with God. Still I have felt the war between nature and grace so strong, that I was afraid, many times, I should fall by the hands of my enemies, without some greater deliverance. I have many times had a pleasing view of a field of religion before me, of loving God with all my heart, but when I attempted to come to God for it, that I might rejoice ever more, pray without ceasing, and in every thing give thanks, it appeared to be something at a distance that I could not lay hold of.

So I have been for seven or eight years praying for a clean heart, and power over my enemies, sometimes hoping, sometimes despairing, until about the first of last June, when I was well convinced that I did not fully believe the doctrine of sanctification, for I thought, if I believed that there was such a blessing for me, and it

---

31. Billy Hibbard, *Memoirs of the Life and Travels of B. Hibbard* (New York, 1825), 237.

was absolutely necessary for me to prepare for heaven, I could not rest without it, that I should go into despair if I did not receive it. And now I began to pray in earnest that God would open my understanding, and give me to see and feel the need of pure love, and discover to me, as I could bear, the depth of inbred sin, that I might not rest satisfied with any thing short of that perfect love that casteth out fear.[32]

God did soon discover to me, as I had never seen before, the depth of my corruptions, and gave an inward hungering and thirsting after full salvation. I saw such a fullness in God's word, and such a willingness in him to give his love, that one evening after I had been pleading his promises, I felt a peace and strong confidence in him. A hope sprung up in my heart that God would cleanse me from my sins and give me power over my enemies. In this hope I went to bed and felt my heart still breathing after full salvation, where he poured down such love as I never felt before. In an ecstasy of joy, the language of my heart was, "Is God come to cleanse me from sin?" The impression was so great that it affected my body as I lay. The next day I felt such joy and peace, yet I was not assured that the work was wrought. Only one text ran greatly in my mind. I did not know where to find it until one told me that it was in the 17th chapter of John: "Sanctify them through thy truth; thy word is truth."[33] I read the chapter and found such a fullness in it of what my heart desired, that if ever I felt hunger for food, or thirst for water, I now truly hungered and thirsted after full salvation.

My faith was strong, but, though I saw believingly such a fullness in God's word and had such a taste and relish for spiritual things, yet I was not established in the faith. The language of my heart was, "Give me love or else I die." Indeed God did create in me such a hungering and thirsting after perfect love that nothing could satisfy but God himself. For near four weeks I felt such keen pain within, that I could almost say, I prayed without ceasing, but with little joy. Only sometimes I rejoiced in hope that God was near to cleanse me from my sins. It appeared to me to be worse than death, my God to love, and not my God alone. I thought my state was singular. I had such confidence in God. I believe I never had

---

32. 1 John 4:18.
33. John 17:17.

such power over sin nor lived so near to God for the time before. The things that I saw and had to do with in the world had no weight at all upon my mind, yet something kept me from stepping into the full liberty of God's children until I was brought into such distress as I never had felt.

It was on Monday, the second day of July 1799, [that] the Lord poured down his blessing into my heart. In the evening my happiness increased till I went to bed, with raptures of joy unknown, by an application of these words, "As far as the east is from the west, so far hath he separated thy sins from thee."[34] I slept but little that night [because] my joy was so great. I had no doubt then of God's hearing my prayer and filling my heart with pure love. I could truly say that Jesus was mine in all his offices, and I was his. In a few days my rapture of joy abated, and I had some temptation and struggle. Not that I had any reason to doubt of the work being wrought, but if it was consistent with such a work of grace for me to have such feelings, but I soon discovered the device of the enemy to rob me of my confidence, and the Lord multiplied my peace. I now, notwithstanding temptations, feel the abiding witness. My mind is stayed on God. Christ is my object. I am willing to take him for my portion. He is the fairest among ten thousand. He is altogether lovely.[35]

George White, an African American preacher in New York, describes the tremendous change he experienced in sanctification. He begins by describing a worship service prior to his experience.

Many who knew not Christ were awakened and converted in a most extraordinary manner, being smitten to the earth by the power of God, which, with a number of other circumstances, led me more fully than ever, to reflect upon the importance of the work I had undertaken for Christ's sake, which exercised my mind to that degree under a sense of the necessity of a clean heart, that I could not rest until God should sanctify my soul, and thereby, the better prepare me for his service.

---

34. See Psalm 103:12.

35. "The Experience of Richard Graves, of Dinwiddie County, state of Virginia, who departed this life in the month of May, 1800. Transcribed from his own writing," in *Extracts of Letters, Containing Some Account of the Work of God Since the Year 1800, Written by Preachers and Members of the Methodist Episcopal Church, to Their Bishops* (New York: J. C. Totten, 1805), 21-23.

Under these exercises, I returned to the city of New York, and in the month of May, 1806, at a meeting held in my own house, I fell prostrate upon the floor, like one dead. But while I lay in this condition, my mind was vigorous and active. And an increasing scene of glory opened upon my ravished soul with a spiritual view of the heavenly hosts surrounding the eternal throne, giving glory to God and the Lamb with whom all my ransomed powers seemed to unite in symphonious strains of divine adoration, feeling nothing but perfect love, peace, joy, and goodwill to man, pervading all my soul, in a most happy union with God, my all in all. Every doubt, fear, and terror of mind were banished, and heaven opened in my bosom.

In this memorable hour, I have no doubts but God sanctified me to himself, by the power of the Holy Ghost. For, from this time, what had before appeared like insurmountable difficulties, were now made easy, by casting my whole care upon the Lord. And the path of duty was only the path of pleasure. I could pray without ceasing, and rejoice evermore; and my stammering tongue was more than ever loosed to declare the truth of God with greater zeal and affection. At the same time that I received this inestimable blessing, there were many others who were awakened, converted, and made happy in the pardoning love of Christ. The memory of that glorious day will never be erased from my mind.[36]

Nancy Caldwell describes her journey toward sanctification, noting all the influences and reading which led to the experience.

One morning a stranger, a Methodist preacher, called and took breakfast with us. After breakfast, while he was praying, I was deeply affected. He wished to know the state of my mind, and I readily told him. Said he, "Sister, you have need to be sanctified. Pray for conviction for you must be convicted for holiness as much as you were for justification." This was truly a "word fitly spoken,"[37] and it did not fall without effect for the blessed Spirit applied it to my heart. I felt that nothing short of sanctification would prepare me to do and suffer the will of God. The language

---

36. George White, *Brief Account*, 14-15.
37. See Proverbs 25:11.

of my soul was, "Create in me a clean heart, O God, and renew a right spirit within me."[38] In this frame of body and mind I continued to labor and suffer. Having none to encourage or instruct me, I found my way alone in the twilight. I have often wondered that my Bible was so sealed to me while this doctrine is so clearly revealed in it. About this time the life of Mrs. Hester Ann Rogers[39] was put into my hands and proved of great benefit to me, throwing much light upon the scriptures. This was the only book having a direct reference to the subject of holiness that I had then seen; and it was, indeed, a treasure to me. This, with the book of God [i.e., the Bible], was my only resort. . . .

I then became convinced that nothing short of a clean heart, and perfect resignation to the will of heaven could render my situation tolerable. At this crisis I took my Bible and opened at Psalm 73. The precious words were so applied to my heart that they seemed new and I could hardly realize that I had ever read them before. It spoke volumes to me at that time. What could have been more to the point than this? "Truly God is good to Israel, even to such as are of a clean heart, etc."[40] A *clean heart*! This was the burden of my prayer. For this "I cried unto the Lord and made supplication to my God, day and night without ceasing."[41] Again: "For I was envious at the foolish, when I saw the prosperity of the wicked."[42] I had just heard of the health and prosperity of my neighbors. I cannot say that I was envious, but I contrasted my own situation with theirs while the shades of earthly misfortune gathered around me, without a beam of light to gloom. . . .

It was impressed upon my mind that if I would bear every cross and perform every known duty, the blessing should be mine and that I should be spared to my family. In the strength of the Lord I resolved to do so. My Heavenly Father has ever held me to this promise. The next day, being alone, there were three questions suggested to me as forcibly as though I had heard an audible voice.

---

38. Psalm 51:10.
39. An eighteenth-century British Methodist whose dramatic spiritual biography was widely read.
40. Psalm 73:1.
41. Compare 2 Timothy 1:3.
42. Psalm 73:3.

The first was, "Are you willing to come out and separate your-self from all the professors around you?"[43] It was a very low time in the church. Very little, I think, was said or thought of full salvation. No one whom I knew professed it, and even the preacher in charge was an entire stranger to it.

I was aware that, in order to retain it, I must bear a public testimony, and, consequently, be marked for my singularity, if not judged assuming. For a moment nature shrank from this. I was at once reminded of my promise. I readily raised my heart and eyes to heaven for help. I think I can say to the praise of God that I was answered in a minute and was so strengthened that I surmounted every obstacle, and, having respect unto the recompense of rewards, resolved to perform my repeated vows, regardless of what any might say or think.

The second question was, "Will you pray in your family?" My husband, though a professor of religion, had neglected this duty. Our family was principally composed of those who were without religion, and I so deeply felt my weakness and insufficiency that the cross appeared like a mountain. I do not say it was like plucking out an eye or amputating the limbs from the body, but it seemed a natural impossibility. I took the *Christian Pattern* by Kempis, and opened at the twelfth chapter of the second book, commencing thus: "This speech seemeth hard to many, 'Renounce thyself, take up thy cross and follow Jesus;' but it will be much harder to bear that last sentence, 'depart ye cursed into everlasting fire'."[44] With what power were those words applied to my heart! Here lay the cross before me, and darkness on either side. I was again reminded of my promise to perform every known duty. At the same time, I felt that I was perfect weakness. O how were these words verified: "Without Me ye can do nothing."[45] I again cried unto God with all the fervency of my spirit for strength to resolve and grace to perform, and as suddenly did prayer prevail. I was enabled to resolve, having the assurance, "My grace is sufficient for thee."[46] Here I solved the question.

---

43. By "professors" she means those who claimed a particular spiritual state, not an academic role.

44. Thomas à Kempis was a medieval writer who influenced John Wesley, Methodism's founder. Wesley republished an edition of *A Treatise on the Imitation of Christ* by à Kempis under the title *The Christian's Pattern,* and this work was widely read by Methodists.

45. John 15:5.

46. 2 Corinthians 12:9.

The third question was, "Will you fall upon your face and make the sacrifice?" I had never imitated my Savior in this. I immediately threw myself at the feet of my God and lay as a helpless infant. I then consecrated soul and body, time and talents, for time and eternity. Here the struggle ceased and a calm peace ensued. Being greatly exhausted, I retired, and slept more quietly than for many nights.

I awoke in the morning much distressed in body, and could hardly ascertain what latitude I was in but soon the day-star arose in my heart.[47] My soul was illuminated.

March 1, 1806. This was truly a memorable day. As yet my joy was not full. In the course of the forenoon I asked for Baxter's *Saints' Rest*,[48] and opening it at page 383, I read through, as I was able, to the end. Here was language exactly suited to my case. Nothing could be more to the point. I shall notice some of the sentiments interspersed, beginning as follows: "Away then, O my drowsy soul, from this world's uncomfortable darkness. The night of thy misery and ignorance is past; the day of glorious light is at hand. This is the day-break betwixt them both, and though thou see not yet the sun itself appear, methinks the twilights of promise should revive thee. Come forth then, and leave these earthly cells, and hear the Lord that bids thee rejoice and 'again rejoice.'"

By this time my cup was full. My soul was in a rapture. I broke out in praise to God, but had no one to join me, as the religious members of the family were strangers to the joys of full salvation.

Here I learned that though perfect love differs not in its *nature* from pardoning love, it yet differs much in *degree*.[49]

Lucy Watson testifies to sanctification. She ends her description by noting how she failed to continue in that state. The "problem" was inherent in early Methodists' understanding of grace and salvation. One could never stand still in an experience but had to press on to deeper levels of maturity in grace.

---

47. See 2 Peter 1:19.

48. Richard Baxter was a seventeenth-century Puritan author, whose most famous work was *The Saints' Everlasting Rest*. Wesley found this work so helpful that he again republished it and circulated it among early Methodists.

49. James O. Thompson, ed., *Walking with God: Leaves from the Journal of Mrs. Nancy Caldwell* (Keyser, W. Va.: For Private Distribution, 1886), 26-32.

After hearing and reading much of sanctification, I began to feel the want and the necessity of it. One night, as I was going to prayer meeting, I thought, "Now, I will give up the world and all its perplexing cares and give myself wholly to the Lord." (Previously I had felt some anger rise against my hired woman.) And while one was praying and mentioned that Christ might appear "in the greatness of his strength, with his garments rolled in blood,"[50] just then, I saw him, by the eye of faith, pass by in that appearance, and gave me a touch with his hand, when I felt as if my heart was taken out, and I was so filled and melted with divine love that I sunk down exhausted to the floor. When I rose to go home, my body was still weak and for sometime I was overwhelmed with love. I dare not say I was sanctified, but when I would feel my peace to flow as a river, I would think, "What can this be but perfect love?"

I was as happy in body and mind as an infant. At my laying down at night, I would purposely keep myself awake by the hour for the purpose of sweet meditation. At sometime, I would see, as if I stood between time and eternity and looking into the world, how trifling seemed all the things it possessed and how vast were all those of eternity.

How it was that I did not continue in that state I cannot say, but I believe it might be by thinking more highly of myself then I ought to have done. However, so it was, that I wandered from this central point and the consequence was that the rod was upon me. "Whom the Lord loveth, he chasteneth and scourgeth every son whom he receiveth"[51] into his family of whole hearted Christians.[52]

Rachel Buff testifies to her sanctification experience. Questions raised by her initial hearing of Methodist preaching on sanctification are answered by her study of the Bible.

Sometime after this, they began to preach sanctification. At first, I did not so clearly understand it, but, adored be the name of the Lord, he soon gave me to see that this was what my soul wanted. I perused the holy scriptures and found that the doctrine of perfection or holiness was required if ever I got admittance into the New

---

50. Compare Isaiah 9:5.
51. See Hebrews 12:6.
52. Lucy Fanning Watson, "Experiences," 94.

Jerusalem. At that time, many all around were crying out against Perfection (they did not plead for Adamic but Christian Perfection which is the love of God filling the soul and governing all our actions, thoughts, and words).[53] I read in the fifth chapter of Matthew where our Lord says, "Be ye perfect, etc."[54] The Lord by the prophets says, "I will sprinkle clean water upon you, etc."[55] Paul says, "As many of you as are perfect, etc."[56] The apostle [also] prays for sanctification of soul, body, and spirit.[57]

From the very time I was convinced it was my privilege I began to hunger after it, and, blessed be God, I saw a great beauty in it and was determined not to rest short of it. And I believe from the time that I saw it to be my privilege there was a struggle in my soul for it, and the work of grace was progressively deepened and carried on. I was conscious I daily died to the world and was given up to God. . . . I saw the purity of the law, the purity of God and heaven, and was sensible that my heart was impure. Holiness was my aim. I was determined not to rest without the blessing. The foul spirit came in like a flood and [I] thought he would sweep me away but my dear master stood my friend and bruised the devil beneath my feet. . . . At a particular time I seemed to have faith to believe I should receive the blessing. I humbled my soul at the feet of Jesus and cried to him for the blessing. I went to the throne with humble boldness. I knew my dear Jesus was pleading my cause and I was sensible I could have access to the Father in no other name. In the evening while agonizing in prayer, I threw myself wholly on the Lord saying, "Lord, here I am. Make me just as thou wouldst have one to be." Glory to God! In a moment all my distress was gone. My blessed Jesus came and brought his heavenly Father with him. I was enabled to praise the Lord aloud for the great things he had done for my poor unworthy soul. My soul was so filled with love [that] I have faith to believe that all inbred sin was destroyed.

O! What a blessing it is not only to know to feel my sins forgiven but to be blest with an antepast of heaven.[58]

---

53. Eighteenth-century Methodist preachers repeatedly clarified that they did not believe we can achieve the absolute perfection that Adam had in Eden (pure in expression and free from any mistake). What they proclaimed was a perfection of love and intent, which allows for infirmity and mistakes.

54. Matthew 5:48.

55. Ezekiel 36:25.

56. Philippians 3:15.

57. Compare 1 Thessalonians 5:23.

58. Rachel Buff, "The Experience of Rachel Buff of Talbot County, Maryland."

OFFERING SANCTIFICATION IN WORSHIP

From their beginnings, early Methodists invited worshipers to move toward experiencing sanctification. In this 1777 letter, for instance, a Virginian Methodist describes how she or he was invited to sanctification and, bit by bit, progressed toward it. The writer eventually experienced sanctification. Talking about sanctification and watching others experience it helped create an expectation for the experience and an anticipation of what the experience would be like.

In the year [17]76, the first of May, at quarterly meeting, my God convinced me more clearly of the need of purity of heart by raising up some living witnesses who testified that great change was wrought in them, and [they] could rejoice in his perfect love. Mr. Shadford[59] and yourself exhorted before the love feast and greatly enforced the necessity of sanctification. It reached my heart with power. I saw the blessing was attained by simple faith, the same as justification. I concluded I should never rest without it. In time of love feast my heart was harder than I had felt it, from the time I first had faith in Christ. But, glory to God forever, after meeting was over, in conversing with one of the brethren[60] my soul seemed swallowed up in love, and I enjoyed more of God in my heart than ever I had done before. I had some hopes I loved God with all my heart, but the next day found my heart hard and unbelieving. May 3 [1776]. I went to a watch night, with expectation I should receive what my soul longed for.[61] The Lord was with us of a truth. Glory to his Name. Twelve found peace before morning. The concluding prayer was much for sanctification.[62]

Some Methodist preachers became quite adept at inviting people to experience sanctification and creating an environment in which many found the experience. Benjamin Abbott was one of those. The following is Abbott's description of his sanctification ministry in New Rochelle, New York.

---

59. George Shadford, one of the first itinerant preachers.
60. Early Methodists called each other "brother" and "sister."
61. A watch night was a preaching service lasting several hours; cf. chapter 6.
62. Letter dated November 1777 from unknown writer to Edward Dromgoole, Edward Dromgoole papers.

That evening, there came as many as twelve to me, and said that they wanted clean hearts. "Well," said I, "if this is your desire, I have no doubt but you will receive the blessing before you leave the house." I began to tell them what the Lord was doing and what I had seen of his work through the land, and exhorted them to let every breath be prayer, as if it were the last. And then [I] gave out a hymn and went to prayer, and four of the men fell to the floor and struggled about as long as they would have done if their heads had been cut off. This frightened the women who thought they never would come to. . . .

They lay near one hour and then one of them turned himself and began to praise God who had sanctified his soul and body. And then another and so on until they all four professed sanctification. Then [they] shouted and praised God for what he had done for them. I exhorted the remaining eight to be much engaged, and the Lord would sanctify them also. They wept much but did not receive the blessing. There was a girl, about twelve or thirteen years old, that was struck down when the men were but no notice had been taken of her. Afterward I called for a light to see where she was, and, when we found her, she was laying in the corner of the house like a dead person. I told them to let her alone and the Lord would justify her soul. She lay about three hours, and, when she came to, she said the Lord had pardoned her sins and she had such a peace in her soul that she never felt before. When then all joined in singing and prayer and then parted, it being about twelve o'clock at night.[63]

Benjamin Abbott describes a similar scene at an annual conference. The fact that Abbott smokes a pipe is interesting—while later sanctification advocates spoke strongly against tobacco use, such use was widespread in early Methodism. People began to experience sanctification after Abbott shared a love feast testimony and then "claims the promises," i.e., suggests that God promised sanctification in the Bible.

Our conference went on from day to day in brotherly love and unity. There was preaching by one or another every night. I was

---

63. Ffirth, *Experience . . . of the Rev. Benjamin Abbott*, 150.

sitting one day in the kitchen, where I put up, smoking my pipe, being tired of confinement in conference so long, and the Spirit of the Lord came upon me in a miraculous powerful manner so that I was fully convinced that something great would be done at the conference. Next day, Bishop Asbury opened the love feast. Then brother Whatcoat[64] spoke. And, when he had done, I arose and told them my experience. The people gave great attention, and, when I came to the account of my sanctification, down dropped one of the preachers and did not rise until the Lord sanctified his soul. I then claimed the promises, and in a moment the house was filled with cries, and screeches, and wonderful shouts! Several went among the people, to those whom they found in distress, to admonish, exhort, and pray with them. Afterward, six told me that God had sanctified them, and, I think, seven that God had justified them. Three had to be carried home that evening who were not able to go of themselves.[65]

Itinerant preacher Thomas Mann conducts the same sort of ministry at the end of the Lord's Supper. As in Abbott's descriptions above, testimony of personal experience seems the trigger.

[At] nine o'clock we had [the] sacrament. I told in part what God had done for my soul and told them at the concluding all that believed in the doctrine of sanctification to come up and let us pray for the blessing. And many came, and we had a powerful time. Sister Isabell Owen got uncommonly happy.[66] I expect she knew nothing of this world for one hour or more. Some people perhaps would have called it "the dance."[67] I suppose it was the same exercise. Perhaps God sanctified her soul, and others appeared very happy. And my poor soul was happy.[68]

---

64. Richard Whatcoat, one of the elders sent over by John Wesley in 1784 and eventual bishop of The Methodist Episcopal Church.

65. Ffirth, *Experience . . . of the Rev. Benjamin Abbott*, 163-64.

66. "Happy" is the term Methodists used for a strong, joyful feeling of God's grace.

67. In the last of the eighteenth and early nineteenth centuries, experiences of God's grace often produced physical movement like dancing or jerking.

68. Thomas Mann, Journal, 18 November 1805.

CHAPTER 4
HEAVEN AND HELL

Early Methodists' assumptions about the nature of heaven and hell were in line with over a millennium of Western Christian teaching on these two realms. Even the disagreements between Protestants and Catholics had concerned less the nature of heaven and hell than the question of who would reside in either realm and why. If there was anything distinctive in early Methodist piety on this front, it was the same qualities that characterized their spirituality in general: a connection to evangelism, a strong link to affections, roots in the popular thought of average people, and a tendency toward ecstatic spirituality.

In keeping with this long tradition, early Methodist hope for heaven was primarily God-centered or, more specifically, Christ-centered.[1] Thus, for example, the true happiness of the heavenly state was not its beauty or peacefulness, but the fact that people would continually be in God's presence. Likewise, the fundamental activity of heaven was anticipated to be worship, understood as the unending adoration of God (sometimes focused on God the Father, or on Jesus Christ, or on both).

In another resonance with tradition, Methodists emphasized the social nature of heaven. Their accounts describe heaven as a crowded place involving fellowship with God and with all who

---

1. See the characteristics of the typical theocentric model of heaven generally held from the sixteenth century forward in David W. Lotz, "Heaven and Hell in the Christian Tradition," *Religion in Life* 48, 1 (Spring 1979): 178.

enjoyed God's grace and rule. When they departed this life, early Methodists expected to enjoy the company of saints, biblical figures, previous generations of Christians, and even angels. Added to this general joy was the specific joy of reunion with other Methodists they had known on earth, as well as with family members.

Adding an emphasis less common in tradition, early Methodists claimed that enjoyment of these central characteristics of heavenly blessedness—fellowship and worship—need not be postponed to the afterlife. One of their favorite ways to describe the sense of loving fellowship that they felt among themselves, and to describe the enjoyment of God's presence that they felt in worship, was to say that they were *already* experiencing something of heaven. For example, Ezekiel Cooper once described a 1790 Baltimore worship service as the "suburbs of heaven."[2] Similarly, William Watters rejoiced after another service, "I was as in a little Heaven below, and believe Heaven above will differ more in quantity than in quality."[3]

Methodist views of hell were also derived from long-standing strands in Western Christian piety. It was common in the Western tradition, for instance, to distinguish two main facets of the punishment suffered in hell: the punishment of loss *(poena damni)*, and the punishment of sense *(poena sensus)*.[4] Early Methodists clearly affirmed that both would be present, without end, relief, or interruption. They stressed that the foremost punishment of loss was the deprivation of intimate fellowship with God, and all the benefits that derive from this fellowship. They warned of inward sensible punishment in the form of the deepest sort of turmoil and pain without relief. Then there was the threatened outward sensible punishment of sheer physical pain, usually associated with fire.

The continuity between early American Methodist spirituality and general Western Christian spirituality with respect to heaven and hell makes it difficult to ascertain how much Americans depended upon John and Charles Wesley on these topics. After all, the Wesleys' views were also solidly within the general Western

---

2. Ezekiel Cooper, "An Account of the Work of God at Baltimore, in a Letter to ————," *Arminian Magazine* (London) 13 (1790): 409.

3. William Watters, *A Short Account of the Christian Experience, and Ministereal Labours, of William Watters* (Alexandria: S. Snowden, 1806), 75-76. For more on this aspect of Methodist spirituality, see Ruth, *A Little Heaven Below*, 145-54.

4. Lotz, "Heaven and Hell," 85.

stance.[5] Nonetheless their influence can be seen in a few relatively distinctive aspects of Methodist teaching. Perhaps the most important is the emphasis on holiness as the necessary condition for attaining heaven. John Wesley insisted that the new birth was strictly necessary for eternal salvation.[6] Inward holiness began in the new birth and, "without holiness" (to quote a favorite early Methodist proof text on both sides of the Atlantic) "no one will see the Lord" (Hebrews 12:14). Wesley took "see the Lord" to mean seeing the face of God in heaven. This connection of heaven and holiness recurred in early American Methodists, sometimes in even stronger form. One could not be one kind of person this side of death and expect a radical transformation, disconnected from one's basic character, on the other side. The inward trajectory begun here was continued in heaven or hell.

What will probably strike present-day readers as most surprising is that contemporary non-Methodists did not judge this aspect of early Methodist spirituality as excessively harsh. In reality, Methodist expectations about heaven and hell were in sync with most of their culture. This resonance facilitated the appropriation of Methodist spirituality. When they called for people to "flee from the wrath to come," Methodists generally did not have to convince people that God's wrath was coming.

This popular discomfort about God's coming judgment and the prospects of heaven and hell that followed was linked to a heightened awareness of life's fragility. The combination of a view of God as a righteous Judge and the ever-present threat of death was potent. What one historian has noted about contemporaneous British Methodism could be said about American Methodists from the same period: "Methodism appealed to the common people... because it took seriously their fears and uncertainties of living in a world liable to unpredictable disasters and unfortunate death."[7]

---

5. For the views of John Wesley, see Thomas C. Oden, *John Wesley's Scriptural Christianity* (Grand Rapids: Zondervan, 1994), 345-59; and, especially, Bruce Rodger Marino, "Through a Glass Darkly, the Eschatological Vision of John Wesley" (Drew University Ph.D. dissertation, 1994).

6. John Wesley, "The New Birth," §III.3, *Works of John Wesley* (Nashville: Abingdon, 1985), 2:195-96.

7. Charles H. Goodwin, "The Terrors of the Thunderstorm: Medieval Popular Cosmology and Methodist Revivalism," *Methodist History* 39, 2 (2001): 107. Goodwin's article is an interesting study of how early Methodists used the fear created by thunderstorms to tap into the deeper fear of God's judgment.

Not surprisingly, contemplating death along with the fear of how God would execute judgment and punishment was often a contributing factor in conversion.[8]

Early Methodists did not mention hell to create fear for fear's sake, but to awaken people out of their negligence and spiritual apathy. They considered raising this issue to be a gracious act because it provided a contrasting backdrop to the real center of their heart's desire: the offer of how God had provided a way to heaven in Jesus Christ. If God was about to bring righteous wrathful judgment, God had also graciously provided a way of salvation through Jesus Christ. The joys of God's heaven and grace were accentuated by contrasting them to the torments of hell. In other words, Methodists did not focus on God's judgment to preach people into hell. They shared the common assumption that people were already well on their way to hell, and longed to offer them God's grace.

The prominence of heaven and hell in Methodist spirituality had several effects beyond bolstering evangelistic drive. One significant effect was the fostering of a sense of detachment from the world.[9] In light of what they expected to experience when in God's intimate presence, the present world in all its unstable quality did not appear worthy of deep human longings. Their hope encouraged them to persevere in faithfulness to Christ.

Methodists often sought to capture this sense of singular faithfulness, detached from the world's allures, by speaking of the present Christian life as a journey or pilgrimage. (Again, they were pulling on antecedents elsewhere in Christianity, including Puritanism.) Using a biblical typology of heaven as the city Zion, Methodists characterized earthly life as a pilgrimage to God's holy city. Their journey as "Zion travelers" called for faithfulness, but in their estimation such return to God's presence was worth far more than everything else.

The excerpts selected and organized below reflect the sharp dichotomy between heaven and hell that existed in early Methodist spirituality. Two types of material predominate in the collection: poetic/hymnic materials and accounts of visions and dreams. Like

---

8. Compare the figures from Michael R. Watts in *The Dissenters* (Oxford: Clarendon Press, 1995), 2:72.

9. For Puritan and Wesleyan roots of this piety, see Colleen McDannell and Bernhard Lang, *Heaven: A History* (New Haven, Conn.: Yale University Press, 1988), 171-77.

many aspects of Methodist spirituality about which they felt deeply, there was something about contemplating heaven and hell that lent itself to rhyme and meter. While ecstatic material has appeared in the prior chapters, these selections on heaven and hell can hint at how widespread such experiences were among early Methodists—across the range of ministerial status, gender, and race.

LONGING FOR HEAVEN

Lucy Watson's little hymn book contains the following song entitled "The Believer's Triumph." For Watson heaven means a greater enjoyment of Jesus Christ, an enjoyment that passes anything earth can offer. The concluding stanza places this hope for heaven within a larger framework of the return of Christ and resurrection of the body.

What hath the world to equal this,
The solid joy, the heavenly bliss,
The joys immortal, love divine,
The love of Jesus ever mine?
Greater joys we're born to know
From terrestrial to celestial
When I up to Jesus go.

When I shall leave this house of clay,
Glorious angels shall convey,
Upon their golden wings shall I
Be wafted fair above the sky,
Then behold him free from harm
Beauty vernal, Spring eternal,
In my lovely Jesus' arms.

Then in sweet silent raptures wait,
'Til the Saints' number are complete,
'Til the last trumpet God shall sound,
Break up the graves and tear the ground.
Then descending with the Lamb

Every spirit shall inherit
Bodies of immortal frame.[10]

"Fair Zion," a hymn in Edward Dromgoole's manuscript hymnal, also weaves together hope for heaven with a resurrection of the body at Christ's second coming. Further, it illustrates a common use of an Old Testament image as a type: heaven is identified as Canaan. Thus a Christian who dies and goes to heaven is entering it as the promised land.

Arise and shine, O Zion[11] fair.
Behold, thy light is come.
The glorious conquering king is nigh
To take his exiles home.
The trumpet thundering through the sky
To set poor captives free.
The day of wonder now is come
The year of jubilee.

Ye heralds blow your trumpets loud
Throughout the earth and sky.
Go spread the news from pole to pole
Behold the judge is nigh.
Blow out the sun, burn up the earth,
Consume the rolling flood.
While every star shall disappear,
Go turn the moon to blood.

Arise ye nations under ground.
Before the judge appear.
All tongues and languages shall come
Their final doom to hear.
King Jesus on his dazzling throne,
Ten thousand angels round,
While Gabriel with his silver trump
Echoes a doleful sound.

---

10. Lucy Watson, Hymns and Poems (1786).
11. Zion is used as an image for the church.

The glorious news of gospel grace
With sinners now is o'er.
The trump in Zion now is still
And to be heard no more.
The watchmen all have left their walls
And with their flocks above
On Canaan's happy shore they sing
And shout redeeming love.

Go on ye pilgrims in the Lord
Whose hearts are joined in one.
Lift up your hands with courage bold,
Your race is almost run.
Above the clouds behold him stand
And smiling bids you come
While angels beckon you away
To your eternal home.

To see a pilgrim as he dies
With glory in his view,
To heaven he lifts his longing eyes
And bids the world adieu.
While friends are weeping all around
And loath to let him go
He shouts with his expiring breath
And leaves them all below.

O! Christians are you ready now
To cross the narrow flood
On Canaan's happy shore behold
And see your smiling God?
The dazzling charms of that bright world
Attract my soul above.
My tongue shall shout redeeming grace
When perfected in love.

Go on my brethren in the Lord
I'm bound to meet you there.

Although we head uncharted ground
Be bold and never fear.
Fight on, fight on, you conquering souls
The land it is in view.
And when I reach fair Canaan's land
I hope to meet with you.[12]

*In a poem entitled "Longing to Be Dissolved and Be with Christ,"
Virginia Methodist Sarah Jones speaks of her desire to go to heaven. Her
reason is plain: closer communion with Christ.*

How long shall I weep in this prison of clay?
Shall tears flow like rivers to see endless day?
My groans can't be uttered, I faint to be gone.
My days pass in sighing, I languish and mourn.

All earth and its glories are darkness to me
While Jesus and angels I'm waiting to see.
My soul pants in sorrow, my heart melts in pain
Because in this valley of tears I remain.

I fly through this desert and anxiously cry,
"Have you seen Christ my Savior? To find him I'd die."
My life rolls as evening, no comfort beside
But my heaven's in Jesus and him crucified.

What passion can equal this hoping to find
All the image of Jesus and his quiet mind?
"My earth sinks before it; how shall I attain?"
Is my language at midnight. How shall I obtain?

In prayer and in praises, I still upward rise
And passing all treasures encompassed by skies.

---

12. Spiritual Songs (Edward Dromgoole papers), 19-20.

I grasp at the nature and fullness of God
And take for my portion the truth of his word.

Though still I'm imprisoned, through Jesus I'll speed.
Though crushed by distresses, I'll lift up my head.
In fighting and running, my pleasures increase,
And I soon shall be perfect when sorrow shall cease.

Then on wings of angels my Jesus I'll meet
And gaze on my treasure and fall at his feet.
With raptures of joy in glory I'll tell
That Jesus' image my spirit doth fill.[13]

In early Methodist piety heaven is not just about an individual encounter with Jesus Christ. As is evident in this excerpt from Richard Allen (eventual founding bishop of the African Methodist Episcopal Church), they anticipated a reunion and expansion of the deep Christian fellowship that they were currently experiencing on earth.

When, therefore, we shall leave this impertinent and unsociable world, and all our good old friends that are gone to Heaven before us shall meet us as soon as we are landed upon the shore of eternity, and with infinite congratulations for our safe arrival, shall conduct us into the company of patriarchs, prophets, apostles and martyrs and introduce us into an intimate acquaintance with them, and with all those brave and generous souls, who, by their glorious examples, have recommended themselves to the world; when we shall be familiar friends with angels and archangels; and all the courtiers of heaven shall call us brethren and bid us welcome to their Master's joy, and we shall be received into their glorious society with all the tender endearments and caresses of those heavenly lovers; what a mighty addition to our happiness will this be! There are, indeed, some other additions to the happiness of Heaven, such Heaven, or the upper and purer tracts of the ether, which our Savior calls Paradise.[14]

---

13. Ibid.
14. Allen, *Life, Experience, and Gospel Labors*, 87.

EXPERIENCING HEAVEN IN WORSHIP

Seeking terms strong enough to describe their wonderful experiences in worship, Methodists often spoke of these times as an experience of heaven now. As a first example, consider this hymn that speaks of the required weekly meetings for fellowship and accountability (class meetings) as an experience of heaven.

This is the place where Jesus meets
The purchase of his blood.
Here, Lord, we sit in heavenly seats[15]
Beside the crimson flood.

Rise, gather manna[16] round the camp.
Come, taste of angels' bread.
Come, now supply your every want.
Lift up your drooping head.

Here, Lord, we drink the living stream.[17]
We long, we thirst for more.
Come to the fountain, wash, be clean
From sin or Satan's power.

In holy love let us begin
This day our heaven below.
Renounce the world, the flesh, and sin.
Lord, [give] life and light below.
'Tis heaven to meet our Jesus here,
To praise redeeming love.
Glory to God, we shall appear
To praise in worlds above.

With shining millions clothed in white,
All prostrate at thy feet,

---

15. See Ephesians 2:6.
16. Manna is the bread God provided to feed the Israelites in the wilderness. See Exodus 16.
17. See John 4:10-11.

In that blest world of love and light
No more to part we meet.[18]

In the following worship experience, James Horton's vision connects earthly and heavenly worship. The occasion is a love feast, a service involving the sharing of simple food and a time of testimonies.

While the brethren were passing the bread and water around, the enemy [Satan] tempted me and tried to rob me of my faith. I bowed down my head and lifted up my heart to the Lord, and he gave me victory. I was greatly blessed—my soul was so filled with the love of God, that for some time I was lost to all that was passing around me. It appeared to me that I was taken up into heaven, and there I saw the Lord upon his great white throne, and he spoke to me in melting language, thus: "Behold, dear child, none but the pure in heart can come here." And there I saw the shining happy millions flaming around his throne in such immortal beauty that my tongue cannot describe it. If I had really been translated to glory, it appeared to me I could not have been happier. When I came to my recollection, I was standing up on my seat with my hands uplifted, and when I looked down upon the people around me, they looked like the shining ones in whose company I seemed to be the moment before in the heavenly world. I spoke to them, and the power of God fell upon them, and the people fell under it in every direction.... Being unable to hold my peace, I went to the window and began to exhort the people that were out of doors, and the Lord took hold of them. Father Garrettson[19] then said, "Brother Horton, go out of doors and do your duty"; so I left the love feast, went out at the window,[20] and continued exhorting; many fell to the ground. When I became exhausted I leaned against the church, and then began again. I continued till the love feast closed.[21]

---

18. Ebenezer Hills, Hymnal, hymn 45.

19. Freeborn Garrettson, who had responsibility for leading this service as a presiding elder. "Father" was a term of respect for mature, influential Christian men. "Mother" was the comparable term for women.

20. Love feasts were closed to nonmembers. Horton is addressing those waiting outside the building for the public preaching service to begin.

21. James P. Horton, *A Narrative of the Early Life, Remarkable Conversion, and Spiritual Labours of James P. Horton, Who has been a Member of the Methodist Episcopal Church Upward of Forty Years* (Printed for the author, 1839), 85-86.

VISIONS OF HEAVEN

Visions of heaven were common. William Ormond mentions two visionaries with whom he had contact in passing references in his journal.

I came to bro. Arnold's and preached.... A young woman is here who tells that she had great views of heaven and hell when she lay for 13 days without eating or drinking. These things are too little regarded by the careless world....

[I] had a powerful time (while preaching). One young man struggled under conviction a long time, and a young sister lay with her eyes open till some time in the night, and when she arose talked of the views of heaven she had.[22]

Fanny Newell recounts her vision of heaven experienced at an 1809 camp meeting.

I took my seat to hear preaching, but I heard none at this time; for before preaching, Brother T. Merritt, the secretary of the meeting, was taking down the names of those who had experienced justification, and those who had obtained that second blessing—sanctification.[23] He sent for me. Accordingly I went, and stepped upon the seat before the preachers' stand, and he said to me, "Have you experienced sanctification?" I answered, "No," for I did not then understand what sanctification was, but I felt as I never did before. These words were scarcely uttered, when I felt a spark of divine power which took away all my bodily strength, and the last words which I heard were—"she is going"—but that moment I was caught up to the third heaven and heard things unspeakable, some of which I shall attempt imperfectly to relate.

I was entirely insensible to all that passed around me in this world, and according to the best account that I have since obtained, I remained so between three and four hours. Brother T. Robinson stated that he was about to go home, but was detained on my account, being unwilling to go and leave me in this apparently lifeless situation. Knowing that my friends would be over anxious about me, he waited the event.

---

22. William Ormond, Journal, 18 August 1802.

23. The practice of counting the number who experienced justification and sanctification at camp meetings is noted in chapter 3.

I was dead to all below, yet my mind was active and sensible, led on with ravishing delight to those joys that beggar all language, and far surpass description. In the first place I seemed to be transported by bright angels, as it appeared, and was impressed on my mind, for I saw no other appearance or form than bodies of light, and in color more like the sun than that of fire; and it appeared to me that by their power they bore me upward to the paradise of God. I thought that I came into the celestial city, and saw God and his throne, and as I came to the place I saw countless armies of shining spirits, who were praising God, and giving glory to the Lamb. I saw no distinct form or appearance of God, or angels, or glorified saints, but bodies of light, and those which were nearest the throne of God were the largest, and as they were seated farther distant from the throne, they were different in bigness and brilliancy. They sang praises in loud strains but I could not sing with them or learn their song. But now and then I could distinctly hear and understand these well known expressions: Hallelujah!! Glory to God in the highest!! I longed to join them in singing one of those heavenly anthems; and one of them said to me you shall, and immediately I struck in and sang so as I never did before or since.

Having enjoyed this delightful place a short time, I was again borne on the wings or rather powers of the bright shining ones back to earth again and came to a place where I had a view of Christ, as though he was nailed to the cross, his arms extended, and he interceding for dying men and women. And his cry was most affecting, enough to break the hardest heart of stone, whilst he said, "Father, spare them, spare the barren, those that bear no fruit spare a little longer; for I have died, O! Father, spare them." O yes I saw and—O amazing sight!—in speechless wonder I lay low at his adorable feet. And O how was my soul filled when he owned me for his child! I could then with the utmost confidence say, "Abba, Father." In short I was so filled with God and glory, that I cried out, "O Lord, enlarge my scanty vessel, or let it break." After this view I was moved on to life and activity (I mean temporal life and the activity of my bodily powers).[24]

---

24. Fanny Newell, *Memoirs of Fanny Newell; Written by Herself, and Published at Her Particular Request*, 2nd ed. (New York: Francis S. Wiggins, 1833), 54-56.

Itinerant preacher David Dailey questions a girl in his Delmarva peninsula circuit about her vision of heaven.

A month or two ago as I was preaching in the meeting house in Snowhill a young girl by the name of Hetty Clogg, who never had professed religion, fell.[25] This was Tuesday night. She was carried to the house of her mother, apparently in a senseless state, in which state she remained until about the middle of the next day at which time she began to take some notice, and after a while faintly answer questions but still lay helpless upon the bed. The morning following, which was Thursday, I was in town and went to see her with other Methodist friends. We sang hymns and I prayed. She said nothing [but] only in answer to question.... Some of the questions to her and her answers were as follows.

Q. Are you happy?[26]

A. Yes, sir.

Q. Have you been happy all the time you have lain here?

A. Yes, sir.

Q. Where have you been?

A. I've been to heaven.

Q. What did you see there?

A. I saw angels.

Q. Did they say anything?

A. Yes, they held up their hands, and prayed for me.

Q. Did you see no men there?

A. Yes, sir.

Q. What did they do?

A. They sang, and held up their hands.

Q. How long have you been gone?

A. A half a day, and a half a night.

Q. Did you see anybody that you knew there?

A. Yes, I saw my aunt and little sister.[27]

Methodists experienced heaven not only in visions but also in dreams. Here Catherine Garrettson describes her 1791 heavenly dream. Garrettson

---

25. To profess religion is a Methodist way of saying one has been converted and can profess saving faith in Jesus Christ. Falling was a common phenomenon; see chapter 5.

26. "Happy" is a Methodist term for being joyful after having experienced God.

27. David Dailey, Diary, 27 April 1817.

is able to interpret the dream by using information gained from the
dreams of Freeborn Garrettson, her future husband.

I awoke from a dream which I think too remarkable to pass
unnoticed. I thought I saw my Grandfather Beekman, and going
up to him, I took both his hands and asked him several questions.
I said, "Shall we meet?" He smiled and answered, "Yes." He told
me I was very near him. I said, "Are you happy?" And before he
could reply I awoke but was persuaded he was.

I again fell asleep and resumed my dream. I was in the same
street and alone; I walked on, and saw a gentleman who died
sometime since. A moral man, and I fear nothing more. I saw distress pictured in his face and manner. I spoke to him and heard him
pathetically exclaim, "Nature, nature, nature. Following thee leads
not to peace." Coming up to me he said, "You do not follow
nature." I said, "Sir, are you happy?" "No" was his answer. I then
walked from him as fast as I could. I found I had lost my way, and
kneeling down in the street begged of the Lord to direct me, and
rising I pursued my way. It was dark as death and I was going up
a steep hill up to my knees in mud. I heard a voice of a person
singing who appeared by the sound to be just ahead of me. I cried,
"Sister,[28] if it is possible for me to get to you, help me for I am stick-
ing in the mud and know not what lies before me." In an instant I
found myself at the door of a cottage, [through] which, the woman
opening, I entered with her. Here were two others who received me
with joy. And, all four of us joining hands, I kissed them all and
found myself happy. The ceiling of this blessed place was white
linen, studied with crystal stars. One of them asked me if I knew
where I was. I said, "Yes, I was in the place of sanctified souls."
That I know this [was] from a dream of Mr. Garrettson, who after
knocking at the door of such a cottage was told, "Come in thou
blessed of the Lord." While I was thus conversing with one of the
Sisters, two men came in. They sat on a high seat covered with
white linen and their feet rested on a lower seat with the same cov-
ering. I was brought to the one but did not know him. When I
looked up at the other I found him to be Robert G. Livingston.[29] He

---

28. A term Methodists used to designate a Methodist woman.
29. Another of Garrettson's relatives.

was arrayed in robes of the purest white, tied with blue ribbons. His face was pale or, rather, white as a lily, and there was in his whole appearance that which fully convinced me he was a glorified being. I sunk to the floor in speechless ecstasy. When I came to my speech I clapped my hands, giving glory to God for the wonders of redeeming love.

I now advanced to him, and taking his hand, which was white as the new fallen snow, and soft as down, I told him I had seen his wife and children. He threw himself down as I spoke and covered his head with a mantle of white linen, spotted with silver. I said they were negligent of their future state.[30] He uttered a deep groan.

I awoke praising the Lord and fully believing this dear relative is in glory and that the Lord will soon sanctify my soul. Difficulties I suppose lie before but I cannot pay too dear for such a blessing. Glory to God for this revelation of his blessed will.[31]

Freeborn Garrettson (Catherine's eventual husband) records a dream early in his itinerant ministry. In this 1780 dream, he encounters both heavenly and hellish realms.

I went to bed very happy, but my night visions were uncommonly strange. I thought I was taken dangerously ill, and expected shortly to be in eternity. I doubt not, but I felt just as dying persons do. I appeared to be surrounded with thousands of devils, who were all striving to take from my confidence and for a time it seemed almost gone. I began an examination from my first awakenings,[32] then my conversion, my call to preach, the motives which induced me to enter this great work, my intention, and life from the beginning. In the time of this examination, every fear was dismissed, and every fiend vanished; and a band of holy angels succeeded with the most melodious music that I ever heard. I then began to ascend, accompanied by this heavenly host; and thought every moment the body would drop off, and my spirit take its flight. After ascending a vast height, I was overshadowed with a cloud as white as a sheet. And in that cloud I saw a person the most

---

30. She means that these people had not been converted and were unconcerned about living as Christians.

31. Catherine Garrettson, Diary, 31 August 1791.

32. His initial realization of his need to repent, in response to hearing the gospel.

beautiful that my eyes had beheld. I wanted to be dislodged from this tabernacle, and take my everlasting flight. That glorious person, more bright than the sun in its meridian brilliancy, spoke to me as follows, "If you continue faithful to the end, this shall be your place, but you cannot come now. Return, and be faithful. There is more work for you to do." Immediately I awoke, and my spirit was so elevated with a sense of eternal things, that I thought I should sleep no more that night.[33]

Virginia Methodist Sarah Jones describes two ecstatic experiences of heaven while praying in 1792. The experiences are so intense that Jones must use very poetic images to describe them. The first occurs while in private prayer staying in the home of other Methodists during a quarterly meeting, an important worship setting for a circuit. The other occurs while Jones seeks to focus in prayer on an early summer day.

I passed the evening at Brother Speed's in paradisiacal delights. Heavenly raptures poured bright moment[s] through all my moving powers while awful, lasting, solemn thoughts of heaven and meeting God and friends surrounded me. Loud thoughts of glory thundered through my heart while Jesus lifted the veil and gave me a glimpse of his shining seat [of] mercy. And goodness was the habitation of his throne while gentle love imprisoned me in sweet embrace [with] golden bows. The kindness of Brother and Sister Speed to the preachers and members should be had in lasting memory. May Jesus reward them. Until eleven o'clock in a silent, sweet palace, a private chamber, I sat with Jesus and angels happy beyond expression, [shedding] tears of happiness.[34]

I had hard work to get engaged although nature's beautiful landscape strove to help me. It appeared to me as if the blessing would come in reach almost and my eager soul would reach hard after but could not fully touch it. I talked too free and simple to my best friend. [I wish?] to communicate in writing but it stands on record in the courts of heaven. My peace is always running as the sea, in dashing flood [and] tides divinely great. But, oh, I wanted a higher swell and

---

33. Robert Drew Simpson, ed., *American Methodist Pioneer: The Life and Journals of The Rev. Freeborn Garrettson* (Rutland, Vt.: Academy Books, 1984), 107-8.
34. Sarah Anderson Jones, Diary, 10 March 1792.

fixed not to give over the plea until prevailing. I triumphed. The way I know was to look earnestly to God. Let me just say (there is much implied in looking) to look aright has never failed yet neither ever will it. In deep agony the cloud burst and such streams of glory lighted from the flaming eyes of Jehovah Jesus it stunned my senses. Tangling blazes lifted me with fiery springs to the eternal worlds and I was in truth so elevated and transported I felt my body awkward in holding my soul. It [the soul] felt her prison strange while the whole earth as far I could see looked changed. The walls of my tabernacle trembled as I looked on the trees, crying "Art thou all kindled pouring ethereal flame?" While yet more lively wonders set in love would fasten on my rapid mind, sinking to the center of my bliss. Surprised I really was and could hardly walk or live! Ah, much was answered me. Glory bloomed as bright as worlds of fire and chains.... Up tracing [ascending] I joined ten thousand unanimous in soul to strain their chord of music severe of infinite delights. Boundless love and perfect wisdom formed the finished subject for nations and kingdoms to dwell upon in one eternal song.... I was lost in the field of happiness, shouting "Glory to God!" [I was] with heaven in my soul until near eleven o'clock although [I] had to keep it somewhat concealed until [my] company was all to bed. I cannot tell how I was blest.[35]

THE DREAD OF HELL

In a handwritten book filled with theological reflections, itinerant preacher Ezekiel Cooper compares hell to heaven.

What is hell?
1. A place of darkness, [a] deep pit
2. A place where vengeance and wrath falls
3. [A place] of torment to soul and body
4. [A place] of miserable reflection, fright, and fear
    1) On [one's] past conduct in sin
    2) [On one's] slighting gospel offers [i.e., rejecting offers of the Gospel], etc.

What is heaven?

---

35. Ibid., 14 June 1792.

1. God's residence
2. [A] place of light and glory
3. [A place] of delight or happiness
4. [A place] of praises
What makes hell?
1. The absence of God
2. The fury of his anger
3. The rage of [one's] conscience[36]

Methodists sang of hell's terror too. In the following hymn entitled "The Sinner's Doom," the stanzas fuse several biblical images together to speak of the eternal damnation of unrepentant sinners. God declares the punishment while righteous angels and saints agree with the sentence. The scriptural allusion is to Matthew 25:31-46, the separation of the goats from the sheep.

> Behold the sinner[s], they must stand,
> Trembling and pale appear,
> A ghastly throng on the left hand,
> Their awful doom to hear.

> "Depart ye cursed into hell
> With devils to remain.
> There with the damned ghosts to dwell
> In horror and in pain."

> "Eternal fire a just reward
> For sin," the Judge proclaims.
> Angels and saints the sentence hear
> And all must say, "Amen."[37]

Ebenezer Hills includes another contemplation of hell's agonies, this time as a warning to sinners, entitled "Awakening." The hymn employs a variety of images to shock a sinner into a spiritual awakening. The prospect of hell includes the captivity by devils, excruciating pain and discomfort, and, worst of all, eternal estrangement from God.

---

36. Ezekiel Cooper, "His Book," 24-25.
37. Ebenezer Hills, Hymnal, hymn 8.

Sinners, attend and hear the worst:
An awful doom awaits.
From God forever be accursed
Attend your awful states.

While devils drag your souls away
To hell's eternal pain,
Horror, despair, and sad dismay
Eternal to remain.

Under the wrath of God to dwell,
A God incensed at sin,
Engulfed in one eternal hell,
Your torment will begin.

But never, never have an end,
How can you bear the sound?
No God, no Jesus for a friend,
Inputting devils round

Deride your torment, mock your pain,
With hellish malice full.
Malicious spite forever reigns
In your tormented soul.

Against that God whose awful sight
As torment every breath,
In darkness through eternal night,
Sunk in eternal death.

Hell from beneath gasps to receive
Her long devoted prey.
There, sinner, can be no reprieve
So one eternal day.

Companions devils, liquid flames,
In one eternal flood.

No water drops to ease your pains
Nor no atoning blood.[38]

In this 1788 sermon, itinerant preacher James Meacham discusses a sharp dichotomy between the righteous and the ungodly, both in terms of character and in terms of ultimate destiny. Meacham records his sermon in outline form, a very common practice. One can sense the rising intensity as Meacham preached the sermon, combining his 1 Peter text with images from 2 Peter 3 and Matthew 25.

[I preached at] Brother Dews [on] 1 Peter 4:18: "And if the righteous scarcely be saved, where shall the ungodly and sinners appear?"

First: Who the righteous are

Second: How they are scarcely saved and what from: from pride, love of the world, and from the many stratagems of Satan

Third: The difference between the ungodly and the sinner: the ungodly are the wretched self-deceivers who labor to establish their own righteousness as the ground and bottom of their acceptance with God; the wicked are profaners [of] heaven, daring hell, [and] deserving wretches.

Where shall they appear?

First: When God comes to wake up his jewels [i.e., Christians] and take his exiles home, they shall appear behind while the glaring sun is turned into darkness [and] the moon into blood. [There shall be] the stars dropping ... [while] the forked lightning is darting through the skies, the elements melting, the earth tattering for the great day of the Lord is come. And who can abide it?[39]

Second: [They shall appear] at the left hand of God.[40]

Third: [They shall appear] in hell.[41]

VISIONS OF HELL

Dreams and visions of hell were common for early Methodists. They often occurred as part of their journey toward conversion. Nancy Caldwell

---

38. Ibid., hymn 54.
39. See 2 Peter 3:10 and Joel 2:11.
40. Matthew 25:14.
41. James Meacham, Memorandum Book, 1 February 1788.

describes such a role for her vision of hell. It comes while she is young, under the initial stages of conviction for sin.

One evening in particular, while my father was at prayer, I strongly feared that I had lost my conviction, and felt that if this were so, my situation was worse than ever before. The pleasures of the world were presented to my view, and I harbored the vain thoughts, though conscious that I was doing wrong. Immediately, though my eyes were shut, I seemed to see before me a precipice, and a person on a headstrong beast rushing violently down the awful steep. Being extremely anxious to know what it meant, it was shown to me to represent the dreadful situation of every impenitent sinner, who is led captive by Satan at his will. And I was convinced that if I yielded to temptation, and stopped short of con- version, Satan would, in like manner, carry me down into the pit of eternal ruin. I think this was a stimulus to duty, and, truly, vanity had then no more place in my heart. Some time after this, being alone in deep meditation, I might have said, with the poet,
"My thoughts on awful subjects roll,
Damnation and the dead."[42]
I never, at any other time, had such a sense of the torments of the lost. I seemed to hear their shrieks, and I soon left the room, much agitated. To some, this would appear a phantom, but to me it is a reality, and, I believe, from the Lord.[43]

In a dream George White, an African American Methodist in New York City, glimpses the terrible agony of those in hell. His description is vivid, intending to awaken fear. Like much of early Methodist spirituality, a commitment to evangelism is an essential part of White's dream as he is commissioned at the end to go save people from this end. The sense of urgency is heightened by the arrival of some unsuspecting gentry, sur- prised by the terrors of hell.

Sometime after this, I had the following most affecting, interest- ing, and frightful dream, or night vision. After the usual religious exercises in my family, I retired to rest at the late hour of about two

---

42. Opening stanza of a hymn by Isaac Watts, an eighteenth-century British hymn writer.
43. Thompson, ed., *Walking with God*, 22-23.

in the morning and falling to sleep, the place of the future torment of the wicked was presented to my view, with all its dreadful horrors. It was a pit, the depth and extent of which were too vast for my discovery but perfectly answering the description given of it in holy writ—a lake burning with fire and brimstone—which has enlarged her mouth without measure, and is moved from beneath, to meet the wicked at their coming.

The descent in this place of misery was by a series of steps, the top of which was near the surface of the earth. In it, I saw vast multitudes of souls, suffering the torments of the damned; out of whose mouths and nostrils issued flames of fire; and from these flames an impenetrable cloud of smoke continually ascended; and being attended by a guide, he made me take particular notice of what was passing, in, and about this hideous gulf, upon which I beheld an host of evil spirits continually employed in leading human souls to the place of descent into this bottomless pit, at which they were received by other devils, who awaited their coming, and dragged them headlong down the steps, to meet their final doom.

But one, which I particularly observed, and doubted from its smallness and singular appearance, whether it was a human being, had no sooner arrived at this place of misery, than it assumed the features and size of a man, and began, with all the other newcomers, to emit flames of fire, from the mouth and nostrils, like those I had seen there at first.

I next beheld a coach, with horses richly furnitured, and full of gay, modish passengers, posting to this place of torment; but, when they approached the margin of the burning lake, struck with terror and dismay, their countenances changed, and awfully bespoke their surprise and fear.

But having myself, while engaged with my conductor, stepped upon the top of the descent, and apparently burnt my feet, which he observing, said to me, "Go and declare what you have seen."[44]

In the 1760s and 1770s future Methodist preacher Benjamin Abbott had a series of dreams that led to his conversion. Abbott's dreams are noteworthy for the level of detail the give about hell and for how they culminate

---

44. White, *Brief Account of the Life*, 9-10.

with his conversion at the edge of a dream. Abbott's appeal for the Lord's Supper as the climax of his conversion is not surprising since desire for the sacrament was a standard part of eighteenth-century evangelical piety.

About the thirty-third year of my age [ca. 1766], I dreamed that I died and was carried to hell, which appeared to me to be a large place, arched over, containing three apartments with arched doors to go from one apartment to another. I was brought into the first, where I saw nothing but devils and evil spirits, which tormented me in such a manner, that my tongue or pen could not express. I cried for mercy but in vain. There appeared to me a light like a star, at a great distance from me. I strove to get to it but all in vain. Being hurried into the second apartment, the devils put me into a vice and tormented me until my body was all in a gore of blood. I cried again for mercy but still in vain. I observed that a light followed me, and I heard one say to me, "How good does this light appear to you?" I was soon hurried into the third apartment, where there were scorpions with stings in their tails, fastened in sockets at the end thereof: their tails appeared to be about a fathom long, and every time they struck me, their stings, which appeared an inch and a half in length, stuck fast in me, and they roared like thunder. Here I was constrained to cry again for mercy. As fast as I pulled out the sting of one, another struck me. I was hurried through this apartment to a lake that burned with fire. It appeared like a flaming furnace and the flames dazzled like the sun. The devils were here throwing in the souls of men and women. There appeared two regiments of devils moving through the arches, blowing up the flames. And when they came to the end, one regiment turned to the right and the other to the left, and came round the pit, and the screeches of the damned were beyond the expression of man. When it came to my turn to be thrown in, one devil took me by the head and another by the feet, and with the surprise I awoke and found it a dream. But O! what horror seized my guilty breast! . . .

About five or six weeks after this, I dreamed that I died and was carried into one of the most beautiful places I ever saw. And my guide brought me to one of the most elegant buildings I ever beheld, and when we came to it the gates opened to us of their own accord, and we went straight forward into the building, where we were met by a company of the heavenly host, arrayed in white raiment down to their feet. We passed on through the entry until we came to a door on the right, which stood about half open. Passing a little forward, we made a stand before the door. I looked in, and saw the Ancient of Days sitting upon his throne, and all around him appeared a dazzling splendor. I stood amazed at the sight. One stepped forward to me arrayed in white, which I knew to be my wife's mother, and said to me, "Benjamin, this place is not for you yet" so I returned, and my guide brought me back. I awoke with amazement at what I had seen, and concluded that I should shortly die, which brought all my sins before me and caused me to make many promises to God to repent, which lasted for some time; but this wore off again, and I went to my old practices....

That night [1772] I lay alone, expecting to sleep little, but to pray and weep all night. Whenever I fell into a slumber, it appeared to me that I saw hell opened ready to receive me, and I just on the point of dropping in, and devils waiting to seize me. Being thus alarmed, it would arouse me up, [with me] crying to the Lord to save me. And thus I passed the whole night in this terrified unhappy condition. Just at the dawning of the day, I fell into a dose more like sleep than any I had during the whole night, in which I dreamed that I saw a river as clear as crystal, in the midst of which appeared a rock, with a child sitting upon it, and a multitude of people on the shore, who said the child would be lost. I then saw a small man on the bank of the river, whose hair was very black, and he and I wrestled together. I heard the people cry out, "The child is lost." And looking round, I saw it floating down the river, and when it came opposite where we were, it threw up its wings, and I saw it was an angel. The man with whom I wrestled told me there was a sorrel or red horse chained head and hind foot in the river and bade me go down and loose him. The people parted to the right and left, forming a lane for me to pass through. I immediately hastened to the river, and went in, the water running over my head. And without receiving any kind of injury, I loosed the horse, and immediately I sprang out of the water like a cork or the bouncing of a ball. And at that instant I awoke, and saw, by faith, the Lord Jesus Christ standing by me, with his arms extended wide, saying to me, "I died for you." I then looked up, and by faith I saw the Ancient of Days, and he said to me, "I freely forgive thee for what Christ has done." At this I burst into a flood of tears, and with joy in my heart, cried and praised God, and said, "O! that there were a minister to give me the Lord's Supper!" Then by faith I saw the Lord Jesus come to me as with a cup in his hand, and he gave it to me, and I took it and drank thereof. It was like unto honey for sweetness. At that moment the Scriptures were wonderfully opened to my understanding. I was now enabled to interpret the dream or vision to my own satisfaction, that is, the river which I saw represented to me the river of life proceeding from the throne of God, spoken of by the psalmist (Psalm 46:4) and also in Revelation 22:1. The numerous company on the shore represented the angels of God, standing to rejoice at my conversion, according to Luke 15:1-7. The sorrel or red horse, I thought was my own spirit or mind, fettered with the cords of unbelief, or the chains of the devil. The color represented the carnal mind, or nature of Satan, which was stamped upon me, and thus I was plunged into the river, where the cords of unbelief were immediately loosed by faith, and my captive soul set at liberty. And my bouncing out was a representation of the lightness of my heart, which sprang up to God, upon my instantaneous change from nature to grace. The man at whose command I was loosed, was Christ. Thus I was set at liberty from the chains of bondage, and enmity of the carnal mind....

All the time of my conviction I used to consider what Church or society I should join, whether the Baptist, Presbyterian, or Methodist; but at this time the Lord said unto me, "You must join the Methodists, for they are my people, and they are right."[45]

---

45. Ffirth, *Experience ... of the Rev. Benjamin Abbott*, 7-9, 17-19.

CHAPTER 5
SHOUTING AND OTHER ECSTATIC EXPERIENCES

Writing on the ecstatic quality of early Methodist spirituality, John Wigger says: "While early American Methodism cannot be reduced to enthusiasm, neither can it be understood without. Early Methodism without enthusiasm would be like *Hamlet* without the ghost or *Macbeth* without the witches."[1] Wigger's assessment is perceptive. Early American Methodists lived in a supernatural world. The supernatural realm and the possibility of having an ecstatic experience within it were not on the periphery of their piety. These things occupied the center of their spirituality until well into the nineteenth century. Methodists expected and desired encounters with God and other spiritual beings through visions, dreams, miracles, signs, and wonders. This supernatural quality saturated even their regular religious life in times of prayer and worship as Methodists shouted, fell, and danced in overwhelming experiences of God's wrath, grace, and presence.

These ecstatic experiences tended to fall into several overlapping types. The basic level of experience was an overwhelming sense of joy in knowing the graciousness of God, often after an agonizing time of acute awareness of God's wrath. Methodists called

---

1. Wigger, *Taking Heaven by Storm*, 123. Wigger is using "enthusiasm" in a nontechnical manner here to refer to supernatural or ecstatic dimensions of their spirituality.

experiencing this joy "getting happy." It occurred as part of their conversion experiences as well as being a regular goal in worship. Shouting was also very common; it was pervasive enough that Methodists sometimes referred to themselves as "shouting Methodists." In addition, early Methodists commonly experienced a palpable, almost tactile, sense of God's presence. Physical demonstrations were frequent—whether clapping, jumping, convulsing, or even dancing, singularly or as a group. Spiritual ecstasy could also have the opposite effect—causing falling, loss of bodily power, and even loss of speech for varying periods of time. At deeper levels, Methodists regularly experienced dreams, visions, signs, and miracles, all taken as evidences of God's touch on their lives.

There was no single cause or trigger for Methodist ecstasy. For instance, outbreaks of ecstatic experiences occurred in early Methodist worship at a variety of different spots in the services. The range with which spiritual ecstasy permeated their worship defies simple cause-and-effect explanations. Indeed, on one occasion, a preacher reported that happiness erupted just from the sheer act of assembling, before a single preacher had arrived or worship had begun.[2]

While the causes were complex, early Methodists did recognize that certain practices and conditions fostered ecstasy. Indeed, as Ann Taves has noted, they intentionally moved ecstasy from the spontaneous "incidental flux of events" into the expected "realm of sacred ritual."[3] One way in which they did this was to develop a system of biblical typology to identify and locate ecstasy within sacred history.[4] Many images emphasized God's powerful presence dwelling within or among the people of God. Some of the most used images included: a new Pentecost (an outpouring of God's Spirit), a "shout of a King in the camp" (referring to the entrance of the ark of the covenant into the Israelite camp; see 1 Samuel 4:5-7), and the experience of heaven here and now (a theme developed in the previous chapter).

Expressions of ecstasy were not confined to corporate worship settings. To return to an extreme example, Sarah Jones could fall into rapture in almost any setting, triggered by almost any activity

---

2. R. Garrettson, "An Account of the Revival of the Work of God at Petersburg, in Virginia," *Arminian Magazine* (London) 13 (1790): 303.

3. Taves, *Fits, Trances, & Visions*, 209.

4. See Ruth, *A Little Heaven Below*, 76-77, and Taves, *Fits, Trances, & Visions*, 104-13.

including, as she reported on one instance, reading the journal of John Wesley.[5] Of course, her regular rigorous practices of sleep deprivation, vegetarian diet, and fasting probably contributed to her propensity. While most other Methodists likely did not push themselves as hard as Jones, many of them still report having experienced rapture, dreams, and visions frequently.

How did ecstasy come to be such a part of early Methodist spirituality? At least three interrelated factors played a role. One was that the Methodists' surrounding culture was firmly convinced of the reality of the supernatural realm. Methodists tapped into beliefs latent in popular religiosity and, to some degree, institutionalized them.[6] The church-state forces that helped restrain popular interest in such supernatural experience in England were not nearly as present in America.[7]

A second factor was the significant number of African Americans that became involved in early Methodism. As Dee Andrews notes, early black Methodists were able to translate prior forms of supernatural belief and ritualized ecstasy from West African religions into congenial "revivalistic counterparts."[8] Given the interaction of black and white Methodists (worship routinely was more integrated then than now), the spiritual aspects latent in black spirituality supported and shaped early Methodist ecstasy. Indeed, the self-validating quality of ecstatic spirituality (if one was predisposed to value such

---

5. Sarah Anderson Jones, Diary, 4 April 1792. For information on other comparable Methodist women, see Diane H. Lobody, "'That Language Might Be Given Me': Women's Experience in Early Methodism," in Richey, et al., eds., *Perspectives on American Methodism*, 127-44.

6. Andrews, *Methodists and Revolutionary America*, 81.

7. See Wigger, *Taking Heaven by Storm*, 105, 111; and Andrews, *Methodists and Revolutionary America*, 6, 80. It is also significant that American Methodists did not live under the shadow of the Thomas Maxfield and George Bell controversy in British Methodism in the early 1760s. For more on the excesses of these two preachers, and the reactionary caution they sparked about both perfection teachings and exuberant forms of worship, see Henry D. Rack, *Reasonable Enthusiast: John Wesley and the Rise of Methodism*, 2nd ed. (Nashville: Abingdon, 1992), 338-41 and Gareth Lloyd, "'A Cloud of Perfect Witnesses': John Wesley and the London Disturbances 1760–1763," *Asbury Theological Journal* 56, 2 (2001): 117-36.

8. Andrews, *Methodists and Revolutionary America*, 81. See also Taves, *Fits, Trances, & Visions*, 78-79; Theophus Smith, "The Spirituality of Afro-American Traditions," in *Christian Spirituality*, ed. Louis Dupré and Don E. Saliers (New York: Crossroad, 1998), 387. Cf. Sylvia R. Frey and Betty Wood, *Come Shouting to Zion: African American Protestantism in the American South and British Caribbean to 1830* (Chapel Hill: University of North Carolina Press, 1998) for general background.

experiences, who could argue against a direct contact with God's spiritual realm?) gave African Americans more influence in Methodism than they exerted in more established churches. The same seemed true for women.[9]

The third factor encouraging the ecstatic, supernatural elements in early Methodist spirituality was a basic emphasis on "experimental religion" (see chapter 2). The affirmation of an experiential knowing of grace was the bedrock for the early Methodist propensity for the ecstatic. They knew God was present when they *felt* God present, and many of them seemed to assume that deeper experience of God's presence was directly correlated to stronger feeling.

Emphasizing experimental religion as the theological backdrop to American ecstatic, supernatural spirituality connects it to similar strains in eighteenth-century British Methodism. Indeed, what occurred in Methodism was part of a larger phenomenon of experimental religion at the time, which extended from Jonathan Edward's New England, to the ministry of George Whitefield (an Anglican evangelist), to Presbyterian sacramental occasions, and even to more heterodox forms of Christianity like the French Camisard prophets and the Shakers.[10] Ecstatic American Methodists had much company in the eighteenth and early nineteenth centuries. The difference in American Methodism, at least in relationship to British Methodism, was the pervasiveness and intensity of the ecstasy.

Eventually, internal dissent arose within American Methodism. Initially the dissenters' particular concern was the ritualized pursuing of worship ecstasy. By the early nineteenth century some were complaining about how "mechanical" worship ecstasy seemed to have become. They began to work to eliminate the practices associated with liturgical happiness. The result was an earlier form of "worship wars." By 1809, for instance, there were two distinct parties in the Annapolis, Maryland, society—the shouters and

9. Cf. Wigger, *Taking Heaven by Storm*, 110.

10. See Taves, *Fits, Trances, and Visions*; and Clarke Garrett, *Spirit Possession and Popular Religion From the Camisards to the Shakers* (Baltimore: Johns Hopkins University Press, 1987). For Presbyterian sacramental occasions, see Leigh E. Schmidt, *Holy Fairs: Scottish Communions and American Revivals in the Early Modern Period* (Princeton: Princeton University Press, 1989).

the anti-shouters.[11] By that time caricatures were firmly in place. In 1813, for example, itinerant preacher Joseph Frye, moving from Baltimore to ride a circuit in Virginia, wrote home with amusement that the people in his circuit thought he would not like shouting, having come from a city station. Frye contradicted their stereotype, telling them "when I get happy shout as much as you please. I don't care if you jump as high as the house or up clear into heaven."[12]

Notwithstanding Frye's enjoyment of shouting, the initial salvos against ecstasy grew into a full-scale assault by some. In particular, John Fanning Watson, a Philadelphia Methodist concerned with middle-class respectability, started writing vigorously and systematically against ecstasy in the 1810s (see excerpt below). Over time Watson's viewpoint gained ground. Higher economic levels, increased education for preachers, and a growing desire for social respectability all contributed to diminishing the extent of exuberant ecstasy among American Methodists. Such spirituality filtered to the margins of the Methodist Episcopal Church while remaining stronger, at least initially, in movements and churches branching off from this main trunk.

The twenty-six entries below reflect the experiences or opinions of nineteen different Methodists on ecstatic experiences. The first set provides descriptions of the most common ecstatic phenomena: getting "happy," shouting, and falling. Next come three detailed accounts of experiences of rapturous ecstasy. Attention then turns to accounts of visions and dreams. Note in this set how the visions and dreams were regularly connected to Methodist concerns for salvation and evangelism. The final set gathers accounts of other, less frequent, ecstatic phenomena in early Methodism (heavenly signs, visitations, healings, and demon-possession).

The material has been selected to show the breadth of Methodists who had ecstatic experiences. It is inclusive of ministerial status, race, and gender, and demonstrates geographic breadth as well. Exuberant religious expression has often been too closely linked with the so-called frontier regions of early America (Kentucky and Tennessee) and with the start of the Second Great

---

11. Henry Smith, *Recollections and Reflections of an Old Itinerant* (New York: Lane & Tippett, 1848), 257.

12. Joseph Frye to Thomas McCormick, 8 July 1813. For more information on the tensions, see Taves, *Fits, Trances, & Visions*, 90-98.

Awakening there. The selections below have been chosen partly to show how widespread these phenomena were among Methodists before the beginning of the Awakening in the nineteenth century.

SHOUTING AND GETTING "HAPPY"

Various degrees of ecstasy were common in Methodist experience, especially in public worship. One itinerant preacher, Philip Bruce, describes such scenes in 1788 southern Virginia.

In many places in this circuit, as soon as the preacher begins to speak, the power of God appears to be present, which is attended with trembling among the people, and falling down; some lie void of motion or breath, others are in strong convulsions: and thus they continue, till the Lord raises them up, which is attended with emotions of joy and rapture. When one gets happy, it spreads like a flame: so that one after another, they arise to join in the praises of their loving Redeemer.

But the greatest work in many parts of this circuit is among the blacks.... A few nights past we held a night-meeting for the Negroes in the Isle of Wight county. Soon after preaching began, there arose a cry among the poor slaves (of which there was a great number present) which in a short time drowned the preaching: a number were on the floor crying for mercy, but soon one and another arose praising GOD. Those who were happy would surround those who were careless, with such alarming exhortations, as appeared sufficient to soften the hardest hearts. If they could get them to hang down their heads, they would begin to shout and praise GOD, and the others would soon begin to tremble and sink. I saw a number (some who at first appeared to be most stubborn) brought to the floor, and there lie crying till most of them got happy.[13]

The shouting could occur spontaneously, even as Methodists traveled together, as seen in this account from John Jeremiah Jacob, a preacher from western Maryland.

---

13. "An extract of a letter from Philip Bruce, elder of the Methodist Episcopal Church, to Bishop Coke, dated Portsmouth, Virginia, March 25, 1788," *Arminian Magazine* (Philadelphia) 2 (1790): 563-64.

The next day (Sunday) we had meeting at Brother Poole's. On our way, about 20 of us being together, some were sweetly singing the songs of Zion.[14] My wife just behind began to shout and praise the Lord. I felt greatly the presence and power of the highest and cried out, "The Lord is here!" And an old man, who had joined us the night before [and] was riding by my side, exclaimed with transport, "Yes! Glory to God! I know the Lord is here! Oh, that all the world knew how good the Lord is! O, God is a God of love. I love every body, etc. Oh, this is the best day I ever saw, etc."[15]

Shouting became a common aspect of Methodist identity. As such, references to shouting find their way into early Methodist hymnody. The following three examples are pulled from a much larger body of such material.

#1

The way to praise the God above
Is first to feel his pardoning love.
Then time and talents always give
To God while he shall let us live.

Seek not the form but feel the power;
Stand always, catch the streaming shower
of grace and glory from above.
Drink, praise, and shout redeeming love.[16]

#2

My Savior's name I'll gladly sing-*Halle-hallelujah.*
He is my Captain, friend and King-*Halle-hallelujah.*
Where'er I go his name I'll bless-*Halle-hallelujah.*
And shout among the Methodist-*O glory Hallelujah.*

The Devil's camps I'll bid adieu,
And Zion's pleasant way pursue;

---

14. "Zion" is used typologically to refer to the church.
15. Marjorie Moran Holmes, "The Life and Diary of the Reverend John Jeremiah Jacob (1757–1839)" (M.A. Thesis, Duke University, 1941), 161-62.
16. Nathaniel Mills, Journal, 1 February 1806.

O sinners turn, repent and list,
And fight like valiant Methodist.

I'm not ashamed to own the Lord,
Nor to defend his holy word;
My soul has often been refreshed
Among the shouting Methodist.

As good a church, as can be found,
Their doctrine is so pure and sound,
One reason which I give for this,
The Devil hates the Methodist.

The world, the Devil, and Tom Paine,[17]
Have tried their force, but all in vain,
They can't prevail—the reason is,
The Lord defends the Methodist.

If Satan could them all destroy,
The troops of hell would shout for joy;
I'll pray that God would them increase
And fill the world with Methodist.

They pray, they sing, they preach the best,
And do the Devil most molest;
If Satan had his cursed way,
He'd kill and damn them all to-day.

They are despised by Satan's train,
Because they shout and preach so plain;
I'm bound to march to endless bliss,
And die a shouting Methodist.

The saints of every sect I love,
And hope to meet their souls above;

---

17. An influential Enlightenment writer in the late-eighteenth century who championed
Deism over classical trinitarian Christianity.

But yet for all, I must confess,
I do prefer the Methodist.

There's many of a different name,
That's followers of the bleeding Lamb;
But most of them were brought to peace,
By the despised Methodist.

We shout too much for sinners here,
But when in heaven we do appear,
Our shouts shall make the heavens ring,
When all the saints shall join to sing.[18]

#3
My God my heart with love inflamed
That I may in thy holy name
Aloud with songs of praise rejoice
while I have breath to raise my voice.
Then will I shout, then will I sing
And make the heavenly arches ring.
I'll sing and shout forevermore
On that eternal happy shore.

O hope of glory Jesus come
And make my heart thy constant home.
For the short remnant of my days
I want to sing and shout thy praise.
Incessantly I want to pray,
And live rejoicing every day
And to give thanks in every thing
And sing and shout and shout and sing.

When on my dying bed I lay,
Lord, give me strength to sing and pray

---

18. Henry Bradford, Hymnbook. Another version can be found in Mead, *Hymns and Spiritual Songs* (1807).

And praise thee with my latest breath
Until my tongue is stilled by death.
Then brothers, sisters shouting come
My body follow to the tomb.
And as you march the solemn road
Loud sing and shout the praise of God.

Then you below and I above
We'll sing and shout the God we love
Until that great tremendous day
When he shall call our slumbering clay.
Then from our dusty beds we'll spring
And shout "O death! where is thy sting?"
"O grave, where is thy victory?"
We'll shout through all eternity.[19]

A common aspect of early Methodist spiritual ecstasy was falling and loss of bodily power. Several itinerant preachers describe the phenomenon on different occasions, the last showing how he struggles to understand and accept the practice.

Glory to Jesus on high! We have what is the most inviting among us, that is, the Lord in power converting sinners; and the saints feel as if they were swimming in the ocean of redeeming love, overwhelmed with the glorious billows. Some fall motionless, and lay, some for minutes, others for hours, and some for a great part of the night, without the use of their limbs or speech; and then they spring up, with heaven in their eyes, and music on their tongues, and praise the Lord, overwhelmed with love divine.[20]

We had a watch night. The Lord was with us of a truth. My wife was so overpowered she sank in praises to God. As we returned to Father Hinton's that night she sank again under the power of God

---

19. A hymn entitled "Christian Shouting," ca. 1790–1800, possibly written by William Colbert, an itinerant Methodist preacher, in Spiritual Songs (Edward Dromgoole papers), 17.

20. Undated Letter from William Colbert to Ezekiel Cooper, reproduced by Cooper in his letter dated 7 September 1801 from Philadelphia to Thomas Coke, which is printed in *Methodist Magazine* (London) 25 (1802): 425.

and asked me if I did not see the light that surrounded us. I asked, "What light?" She said, "A most beautiful light that circled all round us and we were in it." Oh, God, may we ever walk in the light of the Lord.[21]

On Monday morning after the meeting, several persons joining in prayer, one of them fell to the floor. Some of the neighbors coming in, the meetings continued till ten o'clock in the evening. This was the most remarkable day I ever knew. In the course of the day, numbers who were opposed to religion came in, and as soon as the Christians joined in prayer for any one of them, that one would fall as if he was shot through the heart. Sometimes before they were in the house the space of one minute they would be brought to the floor, even while they were exclaiming against the proceedings of the meeting. Once they all joined in prayer for a revival of religion in the neighborhood, and at the very same hour the people in their own houses and fields were slain by the power of God. I then began to conclude that this could not be the work of imagination for these people a mile off, who knew nothing of the meeting, were slain as they were about their work on the very time when those persons prayed for them. In short, I don't remember that the people who were assembled, prayed for anything in the course of the day, but their prayers were answered; and a great revival of religion took place from that time. In the evening I was more sensibly convinced that it was the work of God. I concluded that by reasoning on the subject I became more miserable, and that I would let them enjoy their way of worship, and I would look to God for myself; and while I was attempting to pray for myself, on a sudden my mind was powerfully exercised about indwelling sin, and the great distance I was from the fountain of purity. I found enough then to employ my thoughts without judging others, so that I paid no attention to what was doing in the house, but prayed the Lord to bring me to a closer union with himself. While in that exercise of mind, I lost the use of my bodily powers and fell to the floor. I did not know at what time I fell, for my mind was so exercised about eternal things that I knew but little about the body. I lay in that state

---

21. Benjamin Lakin, Journal, 22 March 1802.

about an hour and a half, as I was informed by those who were present. While I lay on the floor my mind was active, and I had the greatest sense of eternal things that I ever had. At length I arose filled with such peace and comfort, as I can never describe.[22]

RAPTURE IN GOD'S PRESENCE

Sarah Jones, a Virginia Methodist, describes rapturous ecstasy in a hymn entitled "A Rapture."

> Bright scenes of glory strike my sense
> And all my passions capture.
> Eternal beauties round me shine
> Infusing warmest rapture.
> All earth in deepest sack cloth lies
> While Christ my only treasure
> Inflames my heart with countless joys
> And fills my days with pleasure.
>
> The bliss that rolls through those above,
> Through those in glory seated,
> Which cause them loudest songs to sing
> Then thousand times repeated,
> Dart thro' my breast in radiant flames
> Constraining loudest praises
> O'erwhelming all my powers with joy
> Till all within me blazes.
>
> I feast on honey, milk, and wine.
> I drink perpetual sweetness.
> Mount Zion's odors through me roll
> While Christ unfolds his greatness.
> No mortal tongue can show my joys
> Nor can an angel tell them,

---

22. Keith, *Experience of William Keith*, 17-19.

Ten thousand times surpassing all
Terrestrial words or emblems.

When earth and seas shall be no more.
And all their glories perish.
When sun and moon shall cease to shine
And stars in midnight languish.
My joys refined shall higher rise
Mount heaven's radiant glory
And tell through all immortal day
Love's all immortal story.

Engulfed in pleasures here I roll
In swelling waves of glory.
I dive in pleasures deep and full
And groan to tell my story.
I rise in pure seraphic bliss
Overwhelmed in thanks and praises
In all the heights of love caressed
Surround the throne in blazes.

My captivated spirits fly
Through shining worlds of beauty.
Dissolved in blushes loud I cry
His praises strong and mighty.
And here I'll sing and swell the strain
Of harmony delighted,
And with the millions learn the notes
Of saints in Christ united.[23]

In a letter, Sarah Jones describes a similar rapture in prose.

When the blaze of ecstasy slacks in my soul, there stands the
Devil with ten thousand darts but he gets nothing by it. I flew to
God and his word, and got a search, and found the serpent's haunt,
twisted him out, and he flew like lightning from me, and I was caught

---

23. Spiritual Songs (Edward Dromgoole papers), 8-9.

up into the third Heaven, and was wrapped in such flames of dying love, I can by no means express it. This was while in my room at work, Mr. Jones[24] and family [close] by. Such seas of busting glory came rolling from Heaven, I screamed out—weakness overpowered my limbs—my dear companion smiled in pleasing wonder, and joy and pleasure filled my room. I grasped happiness and gazed in admiration and swam in the full rivers that issued from the throne of God.[25]

Catherine Garrettson describes similar raptures on two occasions in her diary.

At family duty [family prayer], [I] found unusual liberty in prayer and continued at this exercise longer than usual. When the family was dismissed, [I] went to my private devotions, and after prayer found a quiet waiting upon God. I leaned myself against the post of [the] bed, and found myself so swallowed up in God, as I have never before experienced. Oh! What moments were these! A divine sweetness thrilled through my whole frame. I can compare myself to nothing more aptly than a blank sheet of paper, not a thought, not an idea that I can trace passed through my mind. It was that stillness which cries, "Speak, Lord, thy servant heareth" (1 Samuel 3:9). Perhaps an half hour I was thus waiting upon God in speechless adoration, which dared hardly breathe....I have never before experienced anything like this. I have felt joy. My soul has been melted with gratitude; I have laid in the dust of the earth before my God: But such a peace I never knew before. At length tears flowed down my cheeks. I groaned my thanks; and then prostrating myself on the floor, I found great liberty in interceding for others. I forgot none that had before at any time laid on my mind, for I prayed for the whole world. Thus I believe passed another half hour. I then prepared for bed. And [I] fell asleep like an infant.[26]

For eight days past I have more or less communion with my God. But the exercises or rather manifestations of the last night exceeded anything I have ever yet passed through, scarcely had I bent my knees before my God, that his love was shed abroad in my

---

24. Her husband.
25. Minter, ed., *Devout Letters*, 9-10.
26. Catherine Garrettson, Diary, 3 June 1792.

heart in a powerful manner. I prayed for a dear saint very near to me that the Lord would be pleased to visit him as he did me. And this prayer seemed to mount on the wings of love to heaven. I now had such a sense and sight of the purity of God as drew me back into an attitude of fixed astonishment. I gazed intently and saw nothing but immaculate purity. I then adored and worshiped in spirit and in truth. Next was presented to me the love of [the] God-Man.[27] Joy sprang up in my heart and I involuntarily broke out in these words:

> Love divine, all loves excelling,
>   Joy of heaven to earth come down.
> Fix in us thy humble dwelling
>   All thy tender mercies crown.
> Jesus thou art all compassion
>   Pure unbounded love thou art.[28]

My mouth was opened to praise the God of love and mercy. I sang hallelujahs out of a full heart. I now was led to see the height and breadth, the length and depth of my Redeemer's love. I worshiped, adored, and loved in a powerful manner. I was left as a drop in the ocean of unexampled love. I was then sunk in the depths of humility. I lay before the Lord with my hand on my mouth, and my mouth in the dust. Again how was my view of God's condescension enlarged. I was now made to see that I came naked into the world, that I should carry nothing with me when I departed. That everything I did possess or hope for was the immediate gift of God and to be returned to him the moment he demanded them. I then passed through an act of perfect resignation; I gave up everything freely to him, who at the time commanded the surrender. I was then drawn gently down in silent waiting on the Lord. Lord, what wouldst thou have me do? I then submissively gave myself into his hands to be disposed of in all things. I then requested to eat the body and drink the blood of Jesus, that I might be a partaker of his divine nature and assimilated to his blessed likeness. The Lord heard me. A divine sweetness

---

27. I.e., Jesus Christ.
28. A well-known hymn by Charles Wesley.

penetrated my soul, and made the tears of gratitude and love abundantly flow down my cheeks.[29]

VISIONS AND DREAMS

One of the first generation of itinerant preachers, John Littlejohn, relates an account of a visionary stupor. The phenomenon was a common one for early Methodists. See the additional accounts in the chapter on heaven and hell.

The following was told me today: A boy who for sometime past has enjoyed the love of God lay as in a trance for 24 hours. His brother with whom he lived did all he could to rouse him in vain. He was bled in the arm. Water was poured into his mouth and other things were tried but in vain. When he awoke he said Christ took him by the hand and led him to heaven. He saw but one person that he knew. He wished to stay. Christ said not yet. He then led him to hell. He saw more persons here than he had seen in heaven and many he knew. And [he] spoke to a brother of his who told him to let his oldest brother know that if he did not repent he would go there. Also [there was] a son of Mr. Faulkner who told him to tell his father the same. But what surprised him most was [that] he saw a man there who everybody thought was in heaven. He asked him what he came there for. He told him, "For lightness and trifling." Many soldiers were there and he saw one from that neighborhood there. Some who heard this said it was a lie. Others said, "Whip him." His brother said he said so that he might use him better. Some said the last man he spoke of was alive. The boy said, "Well, if he is alive, I have told a lie but if he is dead I have spoke the truth." He told his brother he should not stay with him long. He should die soon. About a week after, news arrived that the man he spoke of was dead and the boy is now expected to die. Those things do not move me. I state the facts as I heard them. They may be of God or of Satan. I cannot tell. Be this as it may, I pray good may come out of it.[30]

---

29. Catherine Garrettson, Diary, 7 March 1793.
30. John Littlejohn, Journal, 37-38.

Littlejohn relates an earlier dream that sparked a renewed commitment to preach the gospel in the midst of the opposition that early Methodism often encountered. Methodists often relied on dreams for guidance, comfort, and discernment of God's hand in their circumstances, and Littlejohn defends this practice by appeal to scripture.

My dreams were a terror to me. I often dreamed of preaching the Gospel and when I awoke my eyes were drowned with tears and I longed for morning. One of my dreams was forcibly fixed in my memory and having been afterwards almost literally fulfilled, I here transcribe it. I dreamed that I was at preaching in Norfolk [Virginia]. Mr. Wm. [William] Watters[31] was preaching when several man-of-wars men[32] came with swords to persecute the Methodists and disturbed the people. Mr. Wm. Watters exhorted them not to fear but in vain I got into the pulpit and cried, "Blessed are they who are persecuted for righteousness' sake for theirs is the Kingdom of heaven" [Matthew 5:10]. A servant cut off Mr. Busky's fingers. I was then left alone in the pulpit. I went out and was surprised to see no persons in the street. I felt sorry so many were afraid to suffer. Walking home (thinking I lived in Norfolk), not in the least afraid, I saw the servant with his sword drawn in the street. Looking back, I saw Mr. Armatt taking Mrs. A. [Armatt] out of the way. I cried, "Take care or your wife will carry you to hell." I went on my way passing the servant without the least fear and got home. And to my surprise [I] found two candles burning on the floor with two pillows lying near them. Taking up the pillows, I blew out the lights and went to see a neighbor. Here I saw Betsy Crawley laying over a table weeping bitterly. I asked, "What are you crying for." She answered, "I feared you would be killed." I scolded her sharply and left the home. My business calling me up [the] street, it occurred [to me], "You ought not to run in the way of your enemies." I said, "My business calls. Therefore I will go not fearing what man can do." I had not got far before many pursued, throwing mud, stones, etc., but none fell upon me. This enraged them the more, seeing their labor lost. I was surrounded on every side. I saw no way to escape yet, without fear, I looked up, saw a

---

31. Another itinerant preacher.
32. Presumably sailors or marines.

piece of timber projecting from a house. I got upon it. One of the mob took hold. I looked up a third time, saw another, but could only sit on it with my legs hanging down. The man pursued but could only touch the soles of my shoes. Those below [were] still pelting me with dirt and stones. Finding their labor lost, they left me sitting on the timber. I awoke and beheld it was a dream. This dream was a great blessing to me; its interpretation to me was easy: "For God speaketh once, yea twice, yet man perceiveth it not. In a dream, in a vision of the night, when deep sleep falleth upon men, in slumberings upon the bed; then he openth the ears of men, and sealeth their instruction." Job 33:14-16. This dream made a great impression upon my mind and caused me to pray that God would send me to preach his word.[33]

Zilpha Elaw relates an appearing of Christ that seems much more than just a vision. This encounter with Christ was part of her gradual conversion to salvation.

But as the darkness was gradually dispelled, the light dawned upon my mind, and I increased in knowledge daily, yet I possessed no assurance of my acceptance before God although I enjoyed a greater peace of mind in waiting upon my heavenly Father than at any previous time. My prayer was daily for the Lord to assure me of the forgiveness of my sins, and I at length proved the verification of the promise, "They that seek shall find" for, one evening, whilst singing one of the songs of Zion, I distinctly saw the Lord Jesus approach me with open arms, and a most divine and heavenly smile upon his countenance. As He advanced towards me, I felt that his very looks spoke, and said, "Thy prayer is accepted. I own thy name." From that day to the present, I have never entertained a doubt of the manifestation of his love to my soul.

Yes, I may say further than this because, at the time when this occurrence took place, I was milking in the cow stall. And the manifestation of his presence was so clearly apparent that even the beast of the stall turned her head and bowed herself upon the ground.[34]

---

33. John Littlejohn, Journal, 7-9.

34. Zilpha Elaw, *Memoirs of the Life, Religious Experience, Ministerial Travels, and Labours of Mrs. Zilpha Elaw, An American Female of Colour* (London: published by the author, 1846), 5-7.

In this dream sequence, a New York itinerant preacher, William Keith, tells about his childhood dreams that eventually led to his conversion. Keith is sure that his subsequent experiences with the Methodists fulfilled what he had dreamt as a child.

I saw that all the evils I had done were sins against my Maker. One evening I went to bed greatly distressed on account of my sins. I saw no way to make an atonement for them, and had no knowledge of the way of salvation by Christ. I thought that the Son of God had power while on earth, in human flesh, to save such as came to him with a sincere heart, but how a guilty sinner could now be brought into favor with God was a mystery beyond my reach. At length I fell asleep and fancied that I saw the enemy of souls coming to take me away. Being unable to make any resistance, I became an easy prey. He bound my hands and feet and hurried me with all speed to a lake of fire, where I saw thousands of miserable beings rolling in the liquid flames with tortures inexpressible. While he was preparing to throw me in, I saw one coming whose form was like the Son of God, at whose presence the enemy fled. He took me up in his arms, unbound my hands and feet, and carried me to a pleasant field, where I saw six men in the air, clothed in white and sitting on white horses: each one had a trumpet in his hand, which filled the air with the most melodious sounds I ever heard. Charmed with such uncommon music, I said in a rapture, "Let me go with them!" My guide said, "Not now, but remember this." He then vanished, and I awoke.

In the month of May, 1794, there was a quarterly meeting[35] held among the Methodists in New Hartford settlement. Thomas Ware presided at the meeting. He was the sixth Methodist preacher I had seen, and when I saw them, I well recollected that they bore an exact resemblance to those six men whom I saw in a dream when I was eight years of age. On Saturday in time of meeting, the glory of the Lord seemed so to fill the house, that it greatly increased my sense of guilt.[36]

---

35. Quarterly meetings were the administrative meeting for a circuit. In early Methodism they also served as extended occasions for worship; cf. Ruth, *A Little Heaven Below*.
36. Keith, *Experience of William Keith*, 6-7, 11.

Early Methodists had a deep concern for salvation, both their own and that of others. They were eager to notice and relate accounts of dreams where there were admonitions to heed the gospel. Here are two accounts of persons delivering such messages.

While we were exercised in singing and prayer with him (a man under conviction of sin), C. Noble, a young woman that lived in the house, appeared to be affected considerably. Some time after, as she was asleep in a room, she dreamed that her mother that had been dead for several years came to her and laid her hand upon her cheek and advised her to embrace the offer of mercy and to tell her sister the same. She then awoke and thought she saw her mother go out the room. The next day she was relating her dream to some of the family who looked at her cheek and saw the mark of three fingers which continued for several days.[37]

Thursday, March 1 [1798] I rode from Mount Hope to Hopewell and preached at Silvanius Maberies' [Mayberry's?] on Matthew 7:13-14. Here is a young man by the name of David Brian that says he went home from work one evening, and went to bed, and that he lay as he thought: half awake and half asleep. He dreams something appeared to him all in white like a child about as high as a table, and told if he did not repent and turn to God he would be lost or go to hell. It affected him much for he set out to seek the salvation of his soul, I am told. And I conversed with him myself and have reason to believe he has [sought salvation]. Whatever some may think of this, all that fear God must acknowledge that he has many ways to bring sinners to repentance.[38]

Here is a similar dream with an additional twist. The preacher who records the dream, Myles Greene, seems eager to frame it in such a way that it serves to warn against a practice Methodists opposed: attending dances and balls.

Mr. Caleb Evans of Bristol called to visit. One of his hearers saw a young lady in the parlor who came to the hot wells for her health

---

37. Noah Fidler, Journal, 8 July 1802.
38. William Colbert, Journal, 3:39.

and lodged with them. Observing her unusually pensive, Mr. Evans took the liberty to inquire the reason. She answered, "Sir, I will think no more of it; it was only a dream." And [she] said she would not be so childish as to be alarmed at a dream. "But sir," said she, "I will tell you my dream, and then I will think no more of it." She then repeated as follows: "I dreamed I was at the ball where I intend to go tonight. Soon after I was in the room I was taken very ill and they gave me a smelling bottle. And then [I] was brought home into this room, and I was put in that chair (pointing at an elbow chair), fainted and died. I then thought I was carried to a place where [there] were angels and holy people singing hymns and praises to God. [At] that I found myself very unhappy and desired to go [away] from them. My conductor said if I did I should never come there again. With that he violently whirled me and I fell down, down [through] this darkness and thundering and sulphorous [hell] into flames. And when the flames began to scorch me I was alarmed with hideous cries and awoke." Mr. Evans made some serious remarks on the dream and desired the young lady not to go the ball that night. She said she would for she was more of a woman than to mind dreams. She went to the ball [and] was taken ill. A smelling bottle was given her according to her dream. She was brought home and put into the chair above mentioned, fainted, and died.[39]

OTHER SUPERNATURAL PHENOMENA

The early Methodist world was a supernatural world. They expected to find traces of God's activity and communication throughout. They were quick to discern God's hand in unusual phenomena. Here Philip Gatch, an itinerant preacher, relates his interpretation of signs and wonders in the heavens during the American Revolution. A more modern reader might wonder if Gatch had seen a UFO.

Those awful appearances in the sky were very present about this time and many undertook to account for them. I had and still have my thoughts concerning them, I believe it was the fulfilling of the

---

39. Myles Greene, *Journal*, 19 August 1789.

prophecy of the prophet Joel [in the] second chapter and in the 28th and 29th verses [where] the Lord promises to pour out his Spirit upon all flesh and the effect it shall have and in the 30th verse [where it says] "And I will show wonders in the heaven and in the earth blood and fire and pillars of smoke." The first appearance I saw was the summer I got religion. It was in the east. A light appeared to break through the sky about as big as a common house. It appeared somewhat changeable. I saw it again the same summer. It was more changeable. And as time rolled on it became more common and more awful. There appeared to be a pillar of cloud of smoke beneath it. And sometimes the appearance of awful flames would rise to a great height and extend to a great distance. And at times it would appear like streaming blood descending in showers. It must be acknowledged that it was of God and demands our attention. Wonderful are his works and his ways past finding out.[40]

William Jessop, another itinerant preacher, relates a heavenly sign (likely a meteor) seen by other Methodists.

Last Sunday night a number of friends saw a great light like unto a flame of fire a little above the tops of the trees, going towards this house, which they construed to be an omen of this work [being saved from sin] of God among the people.[41]

In a combination of phenomena, Catherine Garrettson, a New York Methodist, dreams of heavenly signs.

On Friday I spent the night in my sister Montgomery's in that room where some years ago God had wonderfully blessed my soul and enabled me to rejoice for hours in his love. I dreamed I saw a glorious appearance in the sky. Something very bright surrounded with most luminous stars. I thought I called to Mr. G.____ [Garrettson, her husband] who was with me to look up saying at the same time, "and there shall be signs in the heavens." Underneath this a still more beautiful appearance shone forth, and

---

40. Philip Gatch, Autobiography.
41. William Jessop, Journal, 29 February 1788 (United Methodist Archives).

it was written in luminous letters the Tree of Life Whose Fruit is for the Healing of the Nations.[42] The first appearance I take to be a very glorious state of the church. The last, Christ's Second Coming.[43]

The supernatural entered early Methodist life in many ways. John Jea, an African American preacher, records how he miraculously learned to read with the aid of an angel.

The Lord heard my groans and cries at the end of six weeks, and sent the blessed angel of the covenant to my heart and soul, to release me from all my distress and troubles, and delivered me from all mine enemies, which were ready to destroy me. Thus the Lord was pleased in his infinite mercy, to send an angel, in a vision, in shining raiment, and his countenance shining as the sun, with a large Bible in his hands, and brought it unto me, and said, "I am come to bless thee, and to grant thee thy request," as you read in the Scriptures. Thus my eyes were opened at the end of six weeks, while I was praying, in the place where I slept. Although the place was as dark as a dungeon, I awoke, as the Scripture saith, and found it illuminated with the light of the glory of God, and the angel standing by me, with the large book open, which was the Holy Bible, and [the angel] said unto me, "Thou hast desired to read and understand this book, and to speak the language of it both in English and in Dutch; I will therefore teach thee, and now read"; and then he taught me to read the first chapter of the Gospel according to St. John; and when I had read the whole chapter, the angel and the book were both gone in the twinkling of an eye, which astonished me very much, for the place was dark immediately, being about four o'clock in the morning in the winter season. After my astonishment had a little subsided, I began to think whether it was a fact that an angel had taught me to read, or only a dream for I was in such a straight, like Peter was in prison, when the angel smote him on the side, and said unto Peter, "Arise, Peter, and take thy garment, and spread it around thee, and follow me." [Acts 12:8] And Peter knew not whether it was a dream or not and when the angel touched him the second time, Peter arose, took his

---

42. Revelation 22:2.
43. Catherine Garrettson, Diary, 5 December 1797.

garment, folded it around him, and followed the angel, and the gates opened unto him of their own accord. So it was with me when the room was darkened again, that I wondered within myself whether I could read or not, but the Spirit of the Lord convinced me that I could. I then went out of the house to a secret place and there rendered thanksgiving and praises unto God's holy name for his goodness in showing me to read his holy word, to understand it, and to speak it, both in the English and Dutch languages. . . .

After I had finished my day's work I went to the minister's house, and told him that I could read, but he doubted greatly of it, and said to me, "How is it possible that you can read? For when you were a slave your master would not suffer any one, whatever, to come near you to teach you, nor any of the slaves, to read, and it is not long since you had your liberty, not long enough to learn to read." But I told him that the Lord had learnt [taught] me to read last night. He said it was impossible. I said, "Nothing is impossible with God, for all things are possible with him; but the thing impossible with man is possible with God, for all things are possible with him; for he doth with the host of heaven, and with the inhabitants of the earth, as he pleaseth, and there is none that can withstay his hand, nor dare to say what dost thou? [Matthew 19:26] And so did the Lord with me as it pleased him, in showing me to read his word, and to speak it, and if you have a large Bible, as the Lord showed me last night, I can read it." But he said, "No, it is not possible that you can read." This grieved me greatly, which caused me to cry. His wife then spoke in my behalf and said to him, "You have a large Bible, fetch it, and let him try and see whether he can read it or not, and you will then be convinced." The minister then brought the Bible to me in order that I should read and, as he opened the Bible for me to read, it appeared to me that a person said, "That is the place, read it," which was the first chapter of the Gospel of St. John, the same the Lord had taught me to read. So I read to the minister, and he said to me, "You read very well and very distinct" and asked me who had taught me. I said that the Lord himself had taught me last night. He said that it was impossible, but, if it were so, he should find it out. On saying this he went and got other books to see whether I could read them. I tried but could not. He then brought a spelling book to see if I could spell, but he found to his great astonishment that I could not. This convinced him and his wife that it was the Lord's work, and it was marvelous in their eyes.[44]

Early Methodists expected healing miracles too. Here two itinerant preachers, Noah Fidler and Henry Boehm, record healings experienced in the early nineteenth century.

I preached at Edward Teal's on 2 Peter 2:9. The power of God came down. P. Linder was awakened who soon after took sick, which caused her convictions to deepen through the affliction of her body and distress of mind. She was confined to bed for several days. She began to fear that hell must shortly be her portion. In her distress she sent for Brother Hammon, a local preacher, to come and pray with her. While he was praying the Lord set both her soul and body at liberty. She immediately got up and told the people she was well, praised God for her deliverance, and exhorted others to turn to the Lord.[45]

Our quarterly meeting began.... The Lord was powerfully [present?] through the course of our meeting. In the evening there were meetings at two places. The Lord worked like himself. One of my brother's little daughters had been very ill so that she was confined to her bed. After meeting began the people earnestly prayed to the Lord for a blessing. Their prayers were answered. Many rejoiced in the Lord [that] the Savior of them would take notice of her. The pains she had were removed in a moment so that she could leap and praise God. See, the Lord has still power to heal soul and body. I feel thankful that I lived to see this night. My aged father[46] and mother were present. Their souls were filled with joy to see their children and children's children shouting the praises of God. [It] was heaven in my soul and glory all round.[47]

In the following passage, itinerant preacher Nathan Bangs describes the release of a demon-possessed man at an 1805 camp meeting.

44. John Jea, *The Life, History, and Unparalleled Sufferings of John Jea, The African Preacher* (Portsea, England, 1811?), 34-37. Jea's narrative is reprinted in Hodges, *Black Itinerants of the Gospel.*

45. Noah Fidler, Journal, 2 June 1802.

46. This was Martin Boehm, who with William Otterbein cofounded the United Brethren Church.

47. Henry Boehm, Journal, 2 August 1800.

A young man who had received the spirit of adoption not long since had got into despair by giving away to the suggestion of Satan that he had since sinned against the Holy Ghost. His distress was so great that he was delirious. He was brought into the camp so much against his will that we were obliged to hold him in order to keep him there. His case was opened to us by Brother Dunham, and his actions plainly indicated that he was possessed for as soon as prayer was mentioned he would struggle with all his might to get away which seemed to be similar to that recorded by the evangelist "let us alone; trouble us not before the time."[48] The wicked children of the devil were so enraged because he was brought there that they came upon us and would have taken him away with violence had we not formed a ring round him of five or six deep in order to keep them off. We first besought God for Christ's sake to restore him to his right mind which was done. He then began to pray for himself and though he did not immediately obtain the faith of assurance yet he was delivered from despair and before the meeting broke up obtained the peace of God to his soul. Glory be to God who hears prayer.[49]

COMPLAINTS AND QUESTIONS

Not all early Methodists were pleased with the demonstrative, ecstatic nature of Methodist piety. Beginning in the late-eighteenth century and increasingly through the nineteenth century, voices for moderation spoke out. One such voice was John Fanning Watson, a Philadelphia Methodist, who published his sentiments in the 1810s. Watson attacks ecstasy in several ways, especially in how regular and systematic it seems to have become in worship.

I believe in the fact, that sinners do sometimes cry for mercy under the "sense of the weight and burden of sins (as the church service expresses it) too intolerable to be borne"; and I believe, when some convictions are thus powerful, they will be proportionably expressive of their joy at deliverance. But I do not believe that

---

48. Compare Matthew 8:29.
49. Nathan Bangs, Journal, 5 October 1805.

these, or any other people, will be graciously led into the like excessive feelings and outward signs, in all their future ordinary meetings.... They (proponents of ecstasy) aim to affect irregular meetings as most affecting their feelings, not considering that where there are no extraordinary convicted persons, there is no cause to make the effect they seek. Such persons, in my opinion, learn a habit of vehemence; they see example, and they sometimes hear of precept from those who should be their teachers of better things....

If we inspect them closely, we discern that they (the loudest, most exuberant Methodists) are mostly persons of credulous, uninformed minds; who, before their change to grace, had been of rude education and careless of those prescribed forms of good manners and refinement, of which polite education is never divested—and which indeed, religion ought to cherish....

From a careful perusal of the whole New Testament, after the ascension, we can, I think, boldly challenge any sober reader, or candid critic, to produce even a solitary instance of screaming, jumping up and down in the same place (when not walking I mean), or shouting, in any meeting assembled for religious worship. On the contrary, the quiet attention, and the inculcation of "sobriety, gravity, decency, and order," and acting to edification, is very remarkably enjoined.[50]

---

50. [John Fanning Watson], *Methodist Error; Or, Friendly, Christian Advice, To those Methodists, Who indulge in extravagant emotions and bodily exercises*, 2nd ed. (Trenton: D. & E. Fenton, 1819), 15-17, 86.

CHAPTER 6
WORSHIP AND PREACHING

"Church of Englandism felt." In the introduction, I suggested this phrase as one of the better definitions for early Methodism's character. Take the orthodox Christianity represented by the Church of England, move it into the affective realm of the heart, and you have a basic sense of the essence of early Methodism.

This generalization is particularly helpful for understanding the distinctive blend that came to characterize early Methodist worship. Services derived from the Church of England formed a central strand of this blend. John Wesley had been particularly concerned to ensure that this would be the case. When the American Methodists organized as a formal church in 1784, he adapted that Anglican *Book of Common Prayer* for their use. That adaptation, called the *Sunday Service of the Methodists in North America*, was fairly conservative in nature, retaining most of the structure and content of the original.[1] Although abbreviated in 1792 and sometimes ignored by preachers leading worship, the *Sunday Service* played a foundational role in shaping the practices and language of early Methodist worship, giving this worship an Anglican flavor.

Other major elements in the blend of early Methodist worship were derived from their Pietistic roots. These include some special services that became deeply ingrained in the early Methodist way

---

1. For more history on the *Sunday Service*, see Karen B. Westerfield Tucker, *American Methodist Worship* (New York: Oxford University Press, 2001), 4-11.

of life, like love feasts (services involving testimonies and the sharing of bread and water) and watch nights (extended nighttime services of preaching and praying). The Pietistic influence is also evident in fundamental Methodist convictions about worship: their preference for extemporaneous praying, a deep concern for having the heart moved in worship, and an emphasis on discerning inwardly the presence of God in worship.

As might be expected, the blending of these different strands created some tensions in Methodist spirituality. For example, the existence of set texts for many services (eventually codified as an addendum to the *Discipline*, the main governmental manual) sometimes sat uneasily with Methodist preferences for freedom and immediacy in worship.[2] There was a fear that the use of set prayer texts, a prescribed pattern of Scripture readings, and a tightly defined order of worship could lead to the kind of rote, monotone worship that failed to affect the heart, the arena for knowing God's saving touch. These same texts, however, had deep resonance in the Scriptures—Wesley had offered them for that reason—and could lead to a sense of unity in worship, a quality not to be underestimated in a church that valued its bonds of love.

The tensions can be summarized by looking at "formalism" and "enthusiasm." In the eighteenth century these terms were used to characterize opposite tendencies in worship. A "formalist" was someone who relied upon regular observance of the forms of worship. The emotional tone of a formalist's worship was usually rather quiet and orderly. Detractors assumed that it failed to address the heart, that such worshipers knew the form of godliness but not its inward power.[3] On the other side, an "enthusiast" was someone concerned with the direct power or inspiration of religion. Exuberant expression was the expected characteristic of an enthusiast's worship, and the loss of control or order was the perceived danger. Early Methodists were uncomfortable with either of these extremes. Of the two, however, a typical Methodist was most afraid of becoming a formalist.

To modern eyes the distinction between formalism and enthusiasm may look like it involves only the style of worship. It actually

---

2. See ibid., 11 and 272. Westerfield Tucker's book is the finest overview of the history of this subject. For a more intensive examination of worship in the first fifty years of American Methodism, see Ruth, *A Little Heaven Below*.

3. See 2 Timothy 3:5.

involves issues of spirituality that run much deeper than this, which is why formalism and enthusiasm have been topics of Methodist concern since the beginning.[4] Beneath the surface question of whether worship is orderly or disorderly, quiet or loud, is the question of how God's presence is conveyed to worshipers.[5] Does the Holy Spirit impress a sense of God's reality and love upon us directly, or is the transforming influence of God in our lives mediated through standard practices, rituals, and forms? When viewed as polar opposites, a pure enthusiast emphasizes exclusively the direct, immediate encounter with God in worship, while a pure formalist recognizes nothing that is not mediated by the standard forms of her or his church.

Early American Methodist spirituality leaned toward the enthusiast side of this spectrum. Several excerpts included below record how God had been encountered exuberantly (and rather directly) in Methodist worship. But these do not convey the whole story. From its founding, there was an emphasis in Methodism upon the use of the "means of grace." These are certain practices and occasions through which God was thought to convey grace. As such, the appreciation for mediation was also intrinsic to early Methodist spirituality. Indeed, the very name "Methodist" alluded to regular (or methodical) use of these means to experience the God who saves. The creative tension embodied here was one of Methodism's basic characteristics in worship.

Linked to the question about God's immediacy in worship is the important issue of how one can distinguish an experience of grace or discern God's presence in worship. On this issue early Methodists were less successful in sustaining a creative tension. As noted in earlier chapters, the primary—almost exclusive—manner in which they affirmed experiencing God's grace and presence was through the language of the heart. The importance they placed on inner assurance as the critical aspect of salvation probably locked

---

4. For an examination of these terms in John Wesley's thought, see Knight, *Presence of God*; and W. Stephen Gunter, *The Limits of "Love Divine": John Wesley's Response to Antinomianism and Enthusiasm* (Nashville: Kingswood Books, 1989). As Gunter notes (p. 271), opponents of Methodism who used "enthusiasm" as a derisive term often take for granted that the claimed experience of God conveyed false knowledge (see also Taves, *Fits, Trances, & Visions*, 16-17). Of course, no Methodist would accept such a definition as applicable to their worship.

5. Knight, *Presence of God*, 12.

them into this position. They had little way to describe God's presence and activity in worship outside the language of the heart. What they did have was a well-developed vocabulary that described the different emotional tones and affective states one could experience in worship.[6]

The weakness being suggested here was not necessarily a function of the emphasis on exuberant expression in early American Methodism. Although liturgical loudness is often associated with the enthusiasm, it need not be. As early British Methodist history shows, quiet forms of enthusiasm can also undercut the middle ground that Methodists were trying to maintain between the two extremes.[7] Methodists on both sides of the Atlantic did better in maintaining balance with respect to the immediacy of grace than they did with respect to the means of discerning it.

Something of the distinctive nature of early Methodist worship can be seen in the specific aspects of corporate worship that they valued most for mediating the experience of God. Over the course of Christian history the presence of God or Christ has been linked to several aspects of worship—such as the Word of God, the sacraments (particularly the Lord's Supper and baptism), fellowship, aesthetics and environment, music, and mission in the world. Different Christian groups tend to emphasize different combinations of these arenas. Usually one or two stand out as the primary venues through which a group expects to experience God's presence in worship. When considering early Methodism, three venues stand out in particular: the Word of God, the fellowship of the church, and mission in the world. Their worship focused on the Word of God, with an assumed backdrop of intense, countercultural fellowship, and strong grounding in a sense of God's active ministry to save sinners. Sacraments and music were occasionally mentioned by Methodists as other important settings where they expected to encounter God.[8] By contrast, they made little of worship aesthetics or environment.

---

6. See Ruth, *A Little Heaven Below*, 78-81.

7. Gunter's *Limits of "Love Divine"* is a fine work for showing how the root issue in enthusiasm was how one can know and experience God.

8. Considering how the Methodist movement caused an explosion of music in worship, it is notable how infrequently and how briefly early Methodists describe the role of music in their worship. They gave primacy to the ministry of the Word of God in worship, and one could suggest that they understood the use of music in these terms. What they had preached, testified to, and prayed—the Word of God—they also sang.

Before looking at Methodist accounts of worship, it is useful to review the typical kinds of Methodist services.[9] The most frequent service was a preaching service. At its simplest, this service consisted of a sermon and exhortation bracketed by hymns and extemporaneous prayers. Specific services of prayer, both in corporate settings and in families, were a second staple in Methodist practice. Both preaching and prayer services were typically open for nonmembers to attend.

Another set of services that early Methodists conducted regularly were designated "private," and access was restricted to members. The most important examples of this set were love feasts (testimonial services with the sharing of bread and water), administration of the Lord's Supper, and any worship components in gatherings of their discipleship groups (class meetings, band meetings, and society meetings).

Early Methodists also held a few specialized services like watch nights (a form of extended preaching/prayer vigil) and covenant services (where they renewed their self-dedication to God). On occasion, Methodists in a region gathered for protracted worship services, lasting several days. The original form of such gatherings was a quarterly meeting, which met four times a year for every circuit, usually over a weekend. Over time a longer style of gathering evolved from the quarterly meetings, which came to be called "camp meetings." Families came to camp meetings with provisions for housing and sustenance that allowed them to stay for a week or more and attend the numerous preaching and prayer services.

Finally, early Methodists practiced other occasional rites typical of any church, such as ordinations, funerals, weddings, and baptisms.

The entries collected below are intended to give a sense of early Methodist worship beyond what one could surmise from the official texts for worship services (none of which are included). They should provide some idea of basic Methodist worship practices, but the larger goal is to allow these Methodists to describe their experience of God in worship.

---

9. Extensive descriptions and bibliography for each of these services can be found in Westerfield Tucker, *American Methodist Worship*; and Ruth, *A Little Heaven Below*.

The first set of excerpts focus on the phenomenon that early Methodists called the "work of God." In continuity with the previous chapter, these descriptions show how Methodists valued ecstatic or exuberant experiences in worship. They also underline how Methodists considered corporate worship a prime venue for having a saving experience of God through Jesus Christ.

Because the preaching service was the mainstay of Methodist worship and ministry, the second set of selections focus on the act of preaching. These excerpts offer insight into both the Methodist conception of preaching and their characteristic practice of this means of grace.

The remaining sections in the chapter gather material on the different kinds of meetings and worship settings. They also look at specialized kinds of rites. Special attention is given to the rite of baptism because early Methodism was caught in the middle of debates over the legitimacy of infant baptism and the various ways of administering baptism. Methodist defense of infant baptism, and hesitancy to require baptism by immersion, placed them at odds with many in the wider world of heart-religion Christians in the late-eighteenth and early nineteenth centuries. In these selections Methodists seek to explain the reasonableness of their practices.

THE WORK OF GOD

The constant desire of early Methodist worship was for God to be present with power to save. They had a standard term for when they thought this occurred: the work of God. Methodists used the term to describe the scene within a single service as well as for the outbreak of an extended revival of religion. The following accounts show their excitement in seeing a new work. The first is by Henry Boehm, an itinerant preacher, who describes the response to his preaching.

The house could not contain all by one third. I endeavored to speak in the name of Jesus for "God so loved the world that he gave his only begotten Son, etc."[10] My soul was filled with the powers of the upper work.[11] Many felt the effects of the same: some

---

10. John 3:16.
11. Boehm's meaning is unclear. Perhaps he is suggesting that he felt the power of heaven.

fell to the flour, others leapt for joy, and mourners [were] crying for mercy.[12] After public meeting was over, we then set a bench for the mourners.[13] Between forty and fifty came forward and made a public acknowledgment. Others could not get forward by reason of the crowd. Some were enabled to shout redeeming love. God has done wonders for the peoples in this neighborhood.[14]

Here itinerant preacher William Jessop describes the scene when Christ arrives at a prayer meeting. Prayer services usually consisted of a sequence of several extemporaneous prayers, perhaps separated by hymns. Jessop's reference to a "shout of a king" is one of the most common expressions in Methodism to describe shouting in worship. Usually given as a "shout of a king in the camp," the image is based on 1 Samuel 4 where the arrival of the ark into the camp of the Israelites caused a shout to go up.[15]

I found the Lord good to me all the day long. In the evening [we] had a prayer meeting at Br[other]. Smith's. I did not feel right. At the beginning of the meeting, [I] sang and prayed, but it seemed like forced work. At the end of the meeting the blessed Samaritan[16] passed by and paid us a glorious visit. The Holy Ghost descended upon us [in] a mighty rushing wind, and the glory of God filled the house where we were. The shout of a king was in the midst, and many souls rejoiced in the Lord.[17]

The work of God sometimes involved an extended revival lasting over time and through several worship services. In the following account, itinerant preacher Ezekiel Cooper excitedly discusses a work that had begun in 1789 Baltimore, Maryland.

I think it is highly probable that you in the city of [New] York have heard various accounts of the very extraordinary work which

---

12. A "mourner" was a person under deep conviction for sin. The threefold division here is typical: those coming under conviction falling, those experiencing salvation leaping, and those mourning crying out in prayer.

13. This practice of having a "mourners' bench" was still a fairly new innovation.

14. Henry Boehm, Journal, 5 July 1801.

15. For more information see Ruth, *A Little Heaven Below*, 77; and Taves, *Fits, Trances, & Visions*, 115-17.

16. Jessop seems to be using an unusual biblical allusion to Christ in connecting him to the "Good Samaritan" in Luke 10:33.

17. William Jessop, Journal, 9 February 1788 (United Methodist Archives).

is among the Methodists in this town and other parts of this state.... The work, as you have heard, began many months ago and is still as lively as ever. God is pouring out his Spirit very wonderfully indeed to the admiration of all who see and hear. We have conversions every week and some times every day for days together. We have had from 1 to 30, 40, or 50 souls converted in a meeting. I have received from 1 to 20, 30, and 40 members in a day. Many stouthearted men and women have been brought to cry to God in bitter agonies for mercy until the Lord has filled them with peace and love. Some who had been obstinate [?] have felt the power to the salvation of their souls. The people of God rejoice and give glory to the Lord. The careless ungodly seem thunderstruck and a general panic arrests the astonished spectators.... Our quarterly meetings[18] in this town began last Saturday from which time there have been shoutings and conversions every day. We had a very glorious time Saturday. The love and power of God was like a fire among his people. Sunday morning at 8 o'clock love feast[19] began. O brother! In this my soul was ready to fly to the celestial world! How the love of heaven burned on the altars of our hearts! The place was truly awful because of God's presence! It appeared like the very suburbs of heaven. Souls were justified and sanctified by the power and virtue of grace. At 11 o'clock public[20] preaching began. The word was so accompanied by the energy of the Holy Ghost that few in the assembly but felt its power. The great deep of many hearts [was] broken thoroughly. At night we had a great outcry and several conversions to God. Glory to his name![21]

In 1798 Ezekiel Cooper received a similar description of an extended, city-wide work of God in Philadelphia. Richard Allen, future bishop of the African Methodist Episcopal Church, and Jupiter Gibson describe a worship-spawned revival, seemingly centered in Bethel, the African American congregation.

---

18. Quarterly meetings were the administrative meetings for a circuit or, in this case, a city station. The business session, called the quarterly meeting conference, was only a small part of the proceedings, however, as various worship services occupied most of the time. Typically they were held on a two-day, weekend format as in this case.

19. A love feast was a testimonial service with the sharing of bread and water. It typically was the first service on the second day of a quarterly meeting.

20. Access to the love feast was restricted. A preaching service, in contrast, was open to all and thus was "public."

21. Ezekiel Cooper to "Dear Brother," 14 August 1789, Ezekiel Cooper papers (vol. 16, ms. 8).

Knowing it to be our duty to write to you and ought to have done it before but know not how to convey it to you, we take the present opportunity to inform you that there has a very great revival taken place in our churches and is still ... spreading. Our evening meetings mostly continue until 10 or 12 o'clock and from 4 to 8 [people are] convinced[22] and converted of a night, Whites and Blacks. Our churches are crowded, particularly Bethel.[23] ... It is at Bethel the work is in general for at prayer meetings the house is crowded and persons under conviction for weeks come there to get converted. The Lord meets them in the manes [?] and they return to their houses rejoicing. Such a revival[24] has never taken place in this city before. Many backsliders are reclaimed, and the old believers [are] getting more zeal for the glory of God and salvation of souls. At our love feast on the 16th instant [16 February 1798] the house was crowded and [the love feast] continued until after 12 o'clock. Such a time of the power of the Almighty has not been seen there [in] twenty years.... He has greatly blessed the labors of his servants. Our class meetings[25] are crowded and remarkably lively. In short, we have no barren meetings. We have the pleasure of informing you that there is a great revival in all the churches in the city. Many [are] convinced and converted and many added to the number of the Whites.[26] May the glory rebound to his great Name.... Our congregations nearly consist of as many Whites as Blacks. Many that never attended any place of worship come. Some [come] through curiosity, and many of them are awakened and join the society[27] so that nearly as many Whites as Black are convinced and converted to the Lord.... Many of the official members are very useful in our prayer meetings, in particular, Henry Manly. His labors and pleadings with the Lord at such times are indescribable for when the meetings are almost broke up he often

---

22. Meaning that these people come under conviction for sin.

23. Bethel is the original black congregation founded by Richard Allen and others. It eventually became the "mother" church of the African Methodist Episcopal Church. At this time, however, it is still a congregation within the Methodist Episcopal Church.

24. At this time "revival" refers to a "work of God" that has happened spontaneously, not to a series of revival meetings scheduled in hope of a work happening.

25. The required weekly small group meetings for Methodist members.

26. In other words, the revival is not restricted to Bethel, a black congregation, but is present also in the white Methodist congregations in Philadelphia.

27. Being "awakened" refers to coming to a new initial sensibility of God's grace. Society is the original Methodist term for a congregation.

renews them when there are souls in distress. And at his pleadings the Lord sends the blessing down. We must conclude our imperfect account of the work amongst us trusting that he who has begun the work will carry it on to perfection and that you, Reverend Sir, may have the happiness of often hearing good news from Zion and you [may] stand often strengthened in seeing the work flourish on the right and left.

Your unworthy servants in Jesus

Signed by Order of the Board   Richard Allen

Jupiter Gibson[28]

PREACHING

It should be no surprise that the main term used for an early Methodist minister is preacher, given the importance of preaching to early Methodist worship. One does not hold a funeral, for instance—one "preaches" a funeral. Preaching is the mainstay of Methodist worship. In the following essay entitled "The Art of Preaching," the goal of good preaching is highlighted: the preacher must explore the human heart and win a lasting response to the gospel. The essay is found in the papers of Edward Dromgoole, a man who began preaching in the 1770s. It is not clear if it is his work.

That preacher that would speak home to the consciences of men, must lay open the human heart, and trace its windings, its disguises, and corruptions. He must unfold the principles and springs of human conduct, remove from actions their false colorings, and distinguish appearances from realities. He must detest the various biases of self-love and self-deceit, expose the struggles of interfering passions, paint the several virtues and vices, in all the beauty of the one, and deformity of the other....In short, [he must] draw voice and passion from the heart of man, so that every one shall hear, see, and recognize himself and stand acquitted and condemned in his own breast, according as he deserves one or the other....A facility immediately subordinated to this (the conscience or the mind), and which must be employed as a main instru-

---

28. Richard Allen and Jupiter Gibson to Ezekiel Cooper, Philadelphia, 22 February 1798.

ment to work upon it, is the imagination, that active and wonderful power, which presents to us the various images of things, and invests them with the mighty force they have to charm or frighten, to attract our admiration or excite our aversion. It must therefore be no mean part of the preacher's business to apply himself to this noble faculty and bring distant objects almost present to the mind by a lively representation. But how is this to be done?...It is through material and animated pictures of Good and Evil, Virtue and Vice, Heaven and Hell, and all those other awful and momentous topics which religion affords that the imagination is to be roused and the various affections of our nature interested. Upon the whole the judgment must be informed, and the passions moved in order to do lasting good.[29]

Listeners to early Methodist preachers and exhorters[30] often spoke with amazement of how the speaker seemed to know exactly what the listener was thinking and feeling. Partly that is so because of the close social affinity between speaker and listener, and partly because it is often a short time between conversion and the beginning of a speaking ministry. In the following outline, which can form the basis for either a sermon or exhortation, Ezekiel Cooper shows the kind of insight that left many amazed at Methodist preaching. One can imagine a listener feeling like the thoughts of his or her heart are laid bare.

The arguments of Satan in temptation and they obviated[31]
1. This is a pleasant sin. Who can withhold himself from such delights?
Answer: Be it so but are the gripes of consciences and pains of hell so [pleasant], too?
2. Here is a secret sin. This will never bring you into disgrace abroad. None shall know it.
[Answer:] But can you find a place void of divine presence?
3. Come. Here is a profitable sin. Stretch thy conscience a little and make yourself [profit]. Now is the time.
[Answer:] But what profit to gain the world and lose your soul?[32]

---

29. The Art of Preaching (Edward Dromgoole papers), 5-9.
30. Exhorters spoke in worship without basing their talk on a specific Bible verse.
31. Obviated means disposed of.
32. See Matthew 16:26, Mark 8:36, and Luke 9:25.

4. This is a small sin, a trifle.

[Answers:] 1. But is the majesty [of God] against whom I sin too small? 2. Is there a small hell? 3. The less you sin the less the inducement. 4. Shall I offend God for a trifle?

5. Come. God is merciful. He will pass by this sin as an infirmity.

[Answer:] But where is a promise to resumption (presumptuous?) sinners.[33]

6. Why, good men have sinned and been restored, therefore you may yet be safe.

[Answer:] Is this recorded for my imitation or my warning?[34]

Early Methodist preachers are concerned that they speak with God's power. Itinerant preacher William Spencer reveals in this diary entry some of the inward turmoil that a preacher could feel. Here Spencer describes how he inwardly felt God's help to be able to "speak with liberty," the standard Methodist phrase for finding ease and power in speaking.

This day I preached to a vast congregation at Brother Atkinson's. And, glory be to God, it was a most heavenly time to my poor soul and to the souls of many more. I found the cross to be heavy this day indeed. I had a deep sense of my weakness and if ever I felt my dependence upon God, I felt it this day, and when I got up into the pulpit, my knees (as it were) smote[35] over against the other. O! how did I beg of God to assist me, and blessed be his dear name, he did assist me wonderfully. I no sooner began to speak, but the fear of men and devils vanished, and I felt Jesus in my soul. Glory to God, I felt the joys of heaven, and never had better liberty in speaking, I believe, in all my life.[36]

Among the longest-lasting practices that emerged in early Methodism were altar calls and mourners' benches. Both began to be used in the 1790s. Prior to that time mourners were left in place. Preachers, exhorters, and other praying Christians spread through the space to minister to

---

33. It is unclear what Cooper wrote and unclear what he means. See Psalm 19:13 if he meant presumptuous sinners.

34. Ezekiel Cooper, "His Book," 13.

35. That is, his knees struck each other.

36. William Spencer, Diary, 25 April 1790.

them wherever they might be. In the following passage, itinerant preacher James Meacham describes a very early altar call. The scene is the worship services at a quarterly meeting in southern Virginia in 1797.

The sacramental feast[37] began at 9 o'clock. It was a sweet time. During love feast my soul was deeply humiliated. I wept many tears, probably more than I had shed for 2 years. The Lord was very precious to my Bro[ther] Whatcoat[38] [who] preached from Revelation 11:18. I think [it was] a great subject. After him I exhorted a few minutes but to no purpose. Bro[ther]. Easter gave an exhortation, [and] the power of the Lord attended the Word. He begged the company to unite with [each other] for about 5 minutes in silent prayer. They did so, and in a little time the power of the Lord came down upon the people. Many were crying out for mercy. The mourners were then called together and prayer made for them. First one and then another would pray for them until several were delivered. I left the meeting after staying about six hours and one half. But there was but little appearance of its breaking when I left it. How long it continued or how many found the Lord after I went away I know not. I tarried at bro[ther]. Dromgoole's again. My soul is happy but not enough. God is love. O may I love him more and more until I love him with all my heart.[39]

Early Methodists preached and exhorted in waves, one after another. One can see this phenomenon in the following information summarized from the journal of William Colbert, an itinerant preacher. Colbert records the data while describing the services at a camp meeting[40] that began on Thursday, 19 September 1805.

Date	Service#	(P)reaching/ (E)xhorting	Length	Text
19	First	Solomon Sharp (P)	1:38	Joshua 3:5
19	First	Joseph Stephens (E)	0:22	—
19	Second	Asa Smith (P)	0:38	Daniel 2:34-5
19	Second	James Moore (P)	0:25	—

---

37. Meacham is referring to the common practice of combining the sacrament of the Lord's Supper with a love feast.

38. Richard Whatcoat, an itinerant preacher sent over by John Wesley in 1784 and later elected bishop.

39. James Meacham, Journal, 19 February 1797.

40. See the description of camp meetings below.

19	Third	William Colbert (P)	?	2 Timothy 6:2
19	Third	Asa Smith (E)	?	—
19	Third	Solomon Sharp (E)	?	—
20	First	John Woolson (E)	0:10	—
20	Second	Joseph Stephens (P)	0:40	Isaiah 60:1
20	Second	William Fisher (E)	0:15	—
20	Second	Asa Smith (E)	0:32	—
20	Third	Matthew Greentree (P)	1:08	John 14:11
20	Third	James Moore (E)	0:20	—
20	Fourth	Solomon Sharp (P)	1:22	John 1:29
20	Fourth	Asa Smith (E)	0:10	—
20	Fourth	William Colbert (E)	?	—
21	First	Isaac Anderson (E)	?	—
21	Second	William Hunger (P)	1:03	1 John 1:9
21	Second	Richard Sneath (E)	0:25	—
22	First	Richard Sneath (P)	?	Philippians 3:3
22	First	William Hunter (E)	?	—
22	First	Solomon Sharp (E)	?	—
22	First	Michael Coate (P)	1:10	Revelation 20:12
22	First	Solomon Sharp (E)	0:20	—
22	First	Asa Smith (E)	0:15	—
22	Second	James Smith (P)	0:15	Zechariah 14:6-8
22	Second	Solomon Sharp (E)	?	—[41]

Despite its power, early Methodist preaching was sometimes not a well-thought-out, well-prepared discourse. Kentucky itinerant Benjamin Lakin describes a time in 1802 when he selected his biblical text by chance as he stood in the pulpit.

[I] Had to preach in the evening. My mind was fluttering from one text to another and could not fix on a text. The people had collected, and my mind was distressed not knowing how or what to speak from. I concluded to open my Bible and [preach from] the first text that struck my eye, if I could see anything in it to speak

---

41. William Colbert, Journal, 5:110-12.

from it. I opened to James 1:5. I had considerable liberty in speaking. The next day a man told me (in substance) that the sermon had an uncommon effect upon him. Oh Lord, how unsearchable are thy judgments and thy ways past finding out.[42]

At an informal, unscheduled level, women often spoke in early Methodist worship. Occasionally, it seems an appointment was made for women preachers. In the following journal entry, William Colbert, the itinerant preacher mainly responsible for the station of Philadelphia, describes his scheduling of a traveling woman preacher, a British Quaker, in that city's main Methodist church in November, 1805.

I attended the funeral of a friend by the name of Jackson from Southwark to Crown Street. After I had done speaking at the grave, the female itinerant spoke and prayed. Her name is Dorothy Ripley. She, with an old friend who appears to be a man of a very loving spirit, came home with me and drank tea. I was pleased with their conversation and gave the little woman liberty to preach in St. George's.[43] I have preached at Kensington tonight from 1 Thessalonians 5:19 and gave out for her to hold meeting in St. George's on Friday evening....

I have felt very heavy at heart. At night after drinking tea at Alexander Cooke's I heard the female itinerant, Dorothy Ripley, preach in her way. She began with "O Death, where is thy sting? O Grave, where is thy victory?"[44] It looked very strange to see two women get up into the high pulpit at St. George's. How prevalent is the love of novelty. This house was crowded with people to hear this [sic] women talk.[45]

If early Methodist preachers were fiery speakers, early Methodist congregations were lively too. Intentional disruptions were not unusual. Itinerant preacher Benjamin Lakin describes one disruptive young man and his judgment on such "persecutors of religion."

I had been here once before, and, while I was preaching from Luke 2:9 and enforcing the latter part of the text ("it shall be hewn

---

42. See Romans 11:33. Benjamin Lakin, Journal, 7 August 1802.
43. St. George's was the oldest Methodist congregation in Philadelphia.
44. 1 Corinthians 15:55.
45. William Colbert, Journal, 5:124-25.

down and cast into the fire"), a young man walked out of the house and began to crack nuts by the house's side. I cried out, "It may be God will soon hew down that young man that is cracking nuts and cast him into the fire." I now received an account that God has called him to give an account of his conduct.[46] In this place there were five or six men that were bitter persecutors of religion. Lately one of them running off his horse broke his leg and had it cut off, one is dead, and another is at the point of death. Surely these are the judgments of God.[47]

"PROTRACTED" MEETINGS

One of the practices that early Methodists shared with other Christians of their time was the holding of multi-day worship meetings, "protracted meetings" to use their term. In the eighteenth century the most important of these was the quarterly meeting.[48] Eventually quarterly meetings evolved into camp meetings and were supplanted by the latter.[49] The following account by Daniel Asbury shows a quarterly meeting on the verge of becoming a camp meeting. Asbury describes the meeting in a letter to his bishop.

Yadkin Circuit, North Carolina, Aug. 20, 1802

A great and glorious work has taken place in this circuit since conference. The number converted I cannot tell. I have seen and felt more since I saw you than ever before. Many stout-hearted sinners have turned to the Lord, and at our common meetings loud cries and shouts of praise are heard. It is not uncommon for meetings to last from twelve o'clock in the day to twelve at night. At a quarterly meeting held in Iredell county, which began the 30th of July and continued four days, the power of the Lord began on Friday about sun-set, under an exhortation, and continued till Monday twelve o'clock without intermission. The groans of the distressed went up on Friday night from all parts of the camp and increased till ten o'clock the next day, when many found the Lord precious in the pardon of their sins.

---

46. Lakin likely means that the young man died.
47. Benjamin Lakin, Journal, 5 January 1803.
48. See Ruth, *A Little Heaven Below*.
49. See Ruth, "Reconsidering the Emergence of the Second Great Awakening," 334-55.

On Saturday afternoon, while brother Douthit[50] was at prayer, the mighty power of the Lord came down: many hard-hearted sinners fell to the ground, and cried to the Lord for mercy, as from the belly of hell. The slain of the Lord were many, and numbers that fell, rose again with the new song. The next morning was an awful time: some shouting praise to God, others screaming for mercy, and the whole congregation seemed thunder-struck.

On Sunday evening, after brother Ormond's[51] sermon, under prayer, the Lord displayed his power in an increasing manner. The heavens were black with clouds, the thunder and lightning was awful, and the ground seemed covered with sinners. The wounded were taken to the tents, but some stayed at the stand in the hardest rain, and pleaded with the Lord, and about midnight they were delivered. The storm of rain was so powerful, that the wicked were obliged to keep close to the tents, and the Lord mowed them down on every hand. Mr. Hall, Mr. King, and myself continued the whole night in prayer for the mourners. Next morning I preached, and notwithstanding the rain, they heard with the greatest attention. Among the subjects of this work was a doctor, who came with salts of Hart's-horn to apply to those who fell, but the Lord brought him down, and many others with him, who went home praising God. This is a little of what I had seen in Yadkin circuit. I am more than ever bound for glory.

Yours,

Daniel Asbury[52]

Quarterly meetings (by that name) were soon supplanted by camp meetings, which became a standard feature of Methodist life in the nineteenth century. In the following diary entry, itinerant preacher Nathan Bangs describes an 1805 camp meeting in Canada. The account is repeated in such length because much Methodist worship was like what Bangs describes here.

Agreeable to appointment our Camp Meeting began at the Bay of Quinte in Adolphustown on the 27th of September 1805 at

---

50. James Douthet, the presiding elder.
51. William Ormond, whose materials are found throughout this book.
52. *Extracts of Letters*, 57-59.

1 o'clock.[53] It was held in an open field. In the center of which a stage was erected, and about 10 or 12 rods from the stage the tents were pitched in a direct line forming a right angle.

At the hour appointed we judged there were about 2,500 people on the ground. The worship was introduced with singing and prayer, and a short sermon delivered by Br[other]. Case on "Brethren, pray."[54] A number of exhortations followed but with little movement among the people. After an intermission of 20 minutes, a second sermon was delivered by N.B.[55] on "Christ our Wisdom, Righteousness, Sanctification and Redemption,"[56] after which some exhorted and the Spirit of the Lord began to move on the minds of the people. [After] An intermission of one hour and an half, a prayer meeting was held by the whole congregation at the stage. At first it seemed dull, but an exhortation being given by one of the preachers and then prayer again, [and] the power of God descended upon the camp, which soon raised songs of praise to God for salvation found. This continued till about 10 o'clock at night when a sermon was delivered by Br[other]. Madden on "We love him, because he first loved us."[57] The night was now clear and still, and one who exhorted observed [that] he believed God had driven away the clouds from the sky in answer to prayer. Several exhortations were given much to the purpose, and a solemn awe rested upon our minds while the Spirit of God powerfully operated upon our hearts. The exercise continued till past 12 o'clock when the majority retired to their tents. During this time 4 sinners were justified and 2 backsliders reclaimed.[58]

At 5 o'clock [the] next morning, Saturday September 28, prayer meeting was held against the stage and continued until 8. Then a sermon was preached by Br[other]. Shedon on "And he preached Christ unto them,"[59] which was applied with power. Exhortations followed in the demonstration of the Spirit. At 12 o'clock Br[other]

---

53. In Ontario Province, west of Kingston.
54. Probably on either 1 Thessalonians 5:25 or 2 Thessalonians 3:1.
55. Nathan Bangs is referring to himself.
56. 1 Corinthians 1:30.
57. 1 John 4:19.
58. To be justified was the first experience of salvation. It refers to a forgiveness of sins. Backsliders were those who had once been religious but had fallen away from their commitment.
59. Probably Acts 8:5 or 9:20.

Myon (?) addressed us in the Name of the Lord on "My people are destroyed for lack of knowledge,"[60] at the application of which God made bare his potent arm, for the windows of heaven were opened and the bursting power of God descended upon the congregation in such an awful manner that it raised a general outcry among the people who began to be numerous. The traveling and local preachers[61] descended from the stage and ran among the crowd, exhorting the impenitent, comforting the distressed and encouraging the faithful, [and] calling out men and brethren to help. The word of command was instantly obeyed for old and young, male and female were now employed in carrying on the work of God.

The people of God were chiefly in a bunch by themselves when the camp took fire and the wicked formed a circle round about where they stood with astonishment.... As soon as any were wounded by the Spirit of God, they were immediately surrounded by a group of men and women who were earnestly engaged with God for their deliverance, and such faith had they that few were left before they were enabled to sing the song of redeeming love. It might now be said of a truth the God of the Hebrews is come into the camp[62] for the noise was heard afar off. The groans and cries of the wounded, the shouts of the delivered, the prayers of the faithful, the exhortations of the courageous penetrated the very heavens and reverberated through the neighborhood. This exercise continued till about sunset... [after which] Br[other]. Steel preached on "Behold he cometh with clouds, etc."[63] After several exhortations, the exercise[64] ran into a prayer meeting which continued all night without intermission, during which time 5 souls were justified, 8 backsliders reclaimed, and 25 sanctified. Our grateful hearts could not but return thanks to our gracious Sovereign for so manifesting to them of his loving kindness. Therefore we sang, "Glory to God in the highest."[65]

---

60. Hosea 4:6.
61. These were the two kinds of preachers in early Methodism: itinerant/traveling and local. Itinerants earned their living by preaching and actively traveled. Locals did neither. It seems that all the preachers were on the stage together while one was preaching.
62. The image is based on 1 Samuel 4 where the arrival of the ark into the camp of the Israelites caused a shout to go up.
63. Revelation 1:7.
64. "Religious exercises" is a phrase they use to describe the activity of worship.
65. It is not clear whether Bangs is referring to a specific musical text or is just saying that they sang praises.

On Sabbath morning as the material sun rose and darted its luminous rays into our tents we presented ourselves before the Lord of all the earth and besought the Sun of Righteousness[66] to rise and shine upon our minds. And glory be to God our prayer gained access in the court of heaven, for the exhilarating streams of divine light illuminated our souls and the balmy drops of Jesus' love gladdened our hearts. O what a glorious morning was this to us all to find [that] the sun still continued to rise and bear up the ark of God.[67] At about 7 o'clock love feast began. We ranged the people in square body together[68] and after the bread and water, the lovers of God and man spoke feelingly and powerfully of the goodness of God to their souls especially since they had assembled in that place, and so expressed their gratitude to God for the introduction of camp meeting among them. It was now that God showed himself again by smiting the wicked with conviction [for sins] which again employed God's dear people in prayer on their behalf. The people flocked together from different quarters until we judged there were at least 2,000. Some supposed there were 2,500. As the prayers of the faithful were so loud and incessant around the stage that preaching could not be heard, we withdrew to a wagon where N.B. [Nathan Bangs] spoke on "Yea doubtless and I count all things but loss for the excellency of the knowledge of Jesus Christ my God."[69] After this, the noise ceased so that the congregated assembly gathered around the stand from whence Brother Pryer (?) spoke on "Many are called but few are chosen."[70] But even while he was speaking, the cries of the distressed in some of the neighboring tents was such that it occasioned much disorder and irregularity, as some would be running to and foe and from place to place....

There was not however such a terrible outcry now as yesterday, yet the Lord was still at work. Some exhortations followed the sermon, and then preparation was made for administering the supper

---

66. An allusion to Malachi 4:2.

67. Bangs is mixing popular Old Testament allusions. His point is that they found Christ present in their worship on Sunday morning.

68. That is, the people were formed into a square.

69. Philippians 3:8.

70. Matthew 22:14.

of the Lord. The disciples of Jesus came forward with boldness and owned their divine Teacher in this holy ordinance whilst hundreds of spectators were looking on with amazement to see the mighty display of God's power,[71] for many were overwhelmed with the loving presence of God during this season of commemorating one of the greatest events ever exhibited to human view. After the sacrament, the meeting was carried on with exhortation, prayer, and singing, shouting, and praising without any intermission until [the] next morning. We shall notice some things remarkable during this awful period. Just after the sacrament a young woman of high rank was struck by the power of God, and her sister, seeing her weeping, came and took her away by some from the multitude. Some of the daughters of Jerusalem[72] seeing the daughters of pride running away with one of Christ's lambs pursued after them, retook the broken-hearted sinner, and brought her back. The wolf who stole away the lamb followed back, and was soon shot with an arrow from the Almighty, which constrained her to cry aloud for mercy. And it was not long before God heard her cry and changed her ferocious nature into the lamb-like nature of Christ. Anon [immediately] the retaken captive was enabled to say, "The Lord has become my salvation, therefore will I praise him."[73] A little boy of 11 years old was struck under conviction in the camp and converted on the spot. I saw them carry him away to the tent whilst his tongue was employed in lifting forth the praises of his Redeemer. . . .

There is one circumstance more we would not neglect to mention and so much the more as it shows the entire union which the instruments of this work felt one with another. Just at the close, after a majority of the people were dispersed, and the oil of God's grace still continuing to circulate through our hearts, a local Elder,[74] who had been an instrument in converting many souls in this province, began to feel the happy effects of it yet more powerfully in his soul whilst himself and others were interceding on the behalf

---

71. Bangs's description reflects early Methodist practice: not all who were in attendance would have communed.
72. That is, some Christian women.
73. Compare Exodus 15:2.
74. That is, a local preacher who had also received ordination as an elder. Early Methodism had two classes of preachers (itinerant and local) and two orders of ministry (elder and deacon). One could be a preacher without being ordained.

of a broken hearted sinner. The traveling ministers together with the local preachers formed in a cluster together around said elder with their hands clasped around each other's necks. Tears streaming from many of their eyes and hearts uplifted to God, [they] broke out in such expressions of gratitude to God and for one another [while] the presence of him who filleth all in all,[75] [so] filled our hearts with raptures of divine joy that it drew tears of thankfulness from almost every bystander. Whilst our souls were thus expanded and filled with the pure stream of the water of life,[76] we seemed to be absent from the body and present with the Lord,[77] anticipating that pure and perennial bliss where the saints of the most high shall eternally bathe in the bright beams of the smiling countenance of God. Thus our congenial souls were mingling together with the rest of our dear brethren who were standing round in the praise of their God and our God. Surely heaven smiled at this hour and we doubt not but if the curtain had been drawn aside we should have beheld a multitude of the heavenly host praising God and saying, "Glory, honor, praise and power be unto God and the lamb forever,"[78] whose loving Spirit inspires such reciprocal love in the souls of men.

The number brought into liberty during the last 24 hours were 21 justified, 18 backsliders reclaimed, and 14 sanctified. The sum total [was] 30 justified, 28 backsliders reclaimed, and 33 sanctified, 91 in all. To conclude, the hour came that we must part but even after we had been about 3 days and nights upon the ground and had taken very little sleep and rest yet there seemed to be an unwillingness in the minds of some to leave the spot. And even after we started, we cast a longing lingering look behind, fueling a regret at evacuating the place where God had so richly blessed us and given us such a signal victory over our [spiritual] enemies....

Finally, we have every reason to praise God for the introduction of camp meetings among us as we have proved it to be powerful means of awakening and converting souls. O that this blessed work may be carried on till the ends of the earth shall see the sal-

---

75. Compare Ephesians 1:23. It is interesting and typical that when Bangs needs to describe important moments that he tends to use biblical allusions.

76. Compare Revelation 22:1.

77. Compare 2 Corinthians 5:8.

78. Compare Revelation 5:12-13.

vation of our God and his knowledge cover the earth as the waters cover the great deep.[79] Let all that love God say, "Amen. Amen."[80]

OTHER SPECIAL SERVICES

Early Methodists also had other distinctive worship practices. Itinerant preacher Seely Bunn describes two such practices in an 1805 letter. The first is a Christmas sunrise service.[81] The other is a watch night service held on New Year's Eve.[82] Watch nights are long, vigil-like services. Bunn's service includes a covenant renewal, another Methodist distinctive.[83]

The last Christmas was the happiest that many here ever experienced. On Christmas morning we met about two hours before day, and it was a very blessed opportunity to many souls. And as I was desirous to close the old year in devotional exercises, I appointed a Watch night on New Year's eve. After a sermon was preached, several exhortations were given, and a few minutes before 12 o'clock, brother John Chalmers, junior, stood up to exhort, and after speaking a little, he paused, pulled out his watch, and said, "The old year—the year 1804, is gone: it is forever gone." He then proposed to the serious part of the congregation to renew their covenant with God, holding up his hand, and proposing to all who were resolved to be faithful to God to do the same. Immediately a number arose, and, I believe, with hearts devoutly lifted up to God, held up their hands in token of their determination to be his. And at that instant a copious shower of blessings descended on the congregation. A heavenly flame ran from heart to heart. Sinners were struck, and some constrained to cry for mercy. It was a glorious time indeed. None but those who know the love of God can form a just idea of it.[84]

---

79. Compare Isaiah 52:10.

80. Nathan Bangs, Journal, 5 October 1805. See also Abel Stevens, *Life and Times of Nathan Bangs, D.D.* (New York: Carlton & Porter, 1863), 148-49.

81. For additional examples of early morning Christmas sermons, see Benjamin Lakin, Journal, 25 December 1803; and Nathaniel Mills, Journal, 25 December 1787.

82. For more information, see Ruth, *A Little Heaven Below*, 93-97; and Leigh E. Schmidt, "Time, Celebration, and the Christian Year in Eighteenth-Century Evangelicalism," in *Evangelicalism: Comparative Studies of Popular Protestantism in North America, the British Isles, and Beyond, 1700–1990*, ed. Mark A. Noll, et al. (New York: Oxford University Press, 1994), 101.

83. See David H. Tripp, *The Renewal of the Covenant in the Methodist Tradition* (London: Epworth Press, 1969).

84. [Seely Bunn], "From Seely Bunn, to the Rev. Dr. Coke. George-Town and City Washington, March 6, 1805," *Methodist Magazine* (London) 28 (1805): 474.

The itinerant preachers call for a day of fasting in 1796.

It is recommended by the general traveling ministry[85] of the Methodist Episcopal Church, that the first Friday in March, 1796, should be held as a most solemn day of fasting, humiliation, prayer, and supplication. It is desired, that it should be attended to in all our societies and congregations, with sabbatical strictness that we should bewail our manifold sins and iniquities: our growing idolatry, which is covetousness, and the prevailing love of the world; our shameful breach of promises, and irreligious habits of making contracts, even without the attention of honest heathens to fulfill them; our superstition, the trusting in ceremonial and legal righteousness, and substituting means[86] and opinions for religion; the profanation of the name of the Lord; the contempt of the Sabbath, even by those who acknowledge the obligation we are under to keep it holy, for many make no distinction between this and a common day, and others make a very bad distinction by sleeping, walking, visiting, talking about the world, and taking their pleasure; too many also, in many parts of the country, profane the sacred day, by running their land and water stages, wagons, etc.; disobedience to parents, various debaucheries, drunkenness, and such like. [Let us fast] To lament the deep rooted vassalage that still reigns in many parts of these free, independent, United States [and] to call upon the Lord to direct our rulers and teach our senators wisdom [so] that the Lord would teach our people a just and lawful submission to their rulers [and so] that America may not commit abominations with other corrupt nations of the earth, and partake of their sins and their plagues [and so] that the gospel may be preached with more purity, and be heard with more affection and that he would stop the growing infidelity of this age, by calling out men who shall preach and live the gospel [to the end] that the professors may believe the truths, feel the power, partake of the blessings, breathe the spirit, and obey the precepts of this glorious gospel dispensation [and] that Africans and Indians may help to fill the pure church of God.[87]

---

85. The itinerant preachers as a group.
86. That is, outward religious activity.
87. *Minutes of the Methodist Conferences* (1813), 162-63.

LOVE FEAST AND THE LORD'S SUPPER

One of the most important services in the early Methodist worship repertoire was the love feast, a service consisting of the sharing of bread, water, and testimonies of Christian experience.[88] *Generally, Methodists closed these services to nonmembers. In his handwritten hymnal New York Methodist Ebenezer Hills includes the following hymn, which shows the importance of love feasts.*

> Come, Jesus, crown our feast of love.
> We come to meet thee here.
> Send down thy Spirit from above
> And drooping souls to cheer.

> We come from far to taste thy love
> And Brethren here to meet,
> To raise our notes to God above,
> To fall beneath his feet.

> Lord, thou will hear us when we pray
> And praise thy holy name.
> To us thy goodness, Lord, display.
> Send down the sacred flame.

> Here, Lord, thy children thou dost meet,
> To feed the hungry child
> The bread of life divinely sweet,
> Through Jesus reconciled.

> Here, Lord, on earth we speak thy praise.
> Thy goodness we adore.
> Lord, make us perfect in thy ways
> That we may praise thee more.

> Glory to God, come, taste his love,
> Brethren and sisters all.

88. See Ruth, *A Little Heaven Below*, 104-18.

In streams of blessing from above
From heaven now may it fall.

Here, Lord, we cast our burdens down
Beneath the Savior's cross,
In raptures all our sorrows drown,
Of sin consume the dross.

O wondrous grace, o boundless love,
Our tongues begin to sing,
But when we rise to worlds above
To praise our God and King,

A feast of love we then shall keep
Of perfect love professed,
At God's right hand then take a seat
And reign among the blest.[89]

Like many other eighteenth- and early-nineteenth-century evangelicals, Methodists evidenced a real desire for the Lord's Supper. In 1806 Francis Ward speaks of how New York Methodists encountered Christ as the sacrament was administered in a camp meeting.

The Lord spread a table for his people in the wilderness, and hundreds partook of the sacramental bread and wine, the symbols of the Redeemer's passion. There they commemorated his dreadful sufferings, and covenanted with him anew, and there they received fresh effusions of his love.[90]

Thomas Sargent paints a similar scene at an 1804 camp meeting outside Baltimore. Since early Methodists restricted access to the Lord's Supper, the ratio between the number of communicants and total worshipers is not surprising.

---

89. Ebenezer Hills hymnal, Hymn 46, Ezekiel Cooper papers (vol. 24).

90. Francis Ward, *An Account of Three Camp-Meetings held by the Methodists, at Sharon, Litchfield County, Connecticut; at Rhinebeck, in Dutchess County; and at Petersburgh, In Rensselaer County, New-York State* (Brooklyn: Robinson & Little, 1806), 19.

But the Sabbath, I believe, was generally considered as the greatest day. We met the rising sun by administering the sacrament to about one thousand communicants, all of who were in ecstasies of joy. By ten o'clock we had at the lowest calculation eight thousand souls on the campground.... Our strong-lunged men exerted themselves until the whole forest echoed, and all the trees of the woods clapped their hands.[91] God came near, sinners fell in abundance, Christians rejoiced and shouted, and a glorious sacrifice of praise ascended to God.... I am reconciled to camp meetings fully, but it was what I saw and felt of the great things of God's power [in camp meetings] that reconciled me.[92]

Itinerant Ezekiel Cooper outlines his understanding of the meaning of the Lord's Supper and how one should prepare to receive it.

[The] Sacrament 1 Corinthians 11:26[93]
I. The end of it.
  1. Renewal of our baptismal covenant.
  2. A solemn remembrance of Christ in his passion and death.
  3. To fortify against sin and temptation.
  4. To unite Christians as the grains of wheat or flour in the loaf and the grapes and drops in the wine.
II. Our obligations to it as a duty.
  1. From command.
  2. Example.
  3. Interest.
III. A necessary preparation.
  1. Close examination 1 Corinthians 11:28.[94]
  2. Confession and humiliation.
  3. Love and charity with all men.
  4. A fixed resolution to lead a new life.[95]

---

91. Compare Isaiah 55:12.

92. *Extracts of Letters*, 110-11.

93. "For as often as ye eat this bread, and drink this cup, ye do shew the Lord's death till he come."

94. "But let a man examine himself, and so let him eat of *that* bread, and drink of *that* cup."

95. In the last three elements of preparation Cooper is probably drawing from the part of the communion service which reads "Ye that do truly and earnestly repent of your sins, and are in love and charity with your neighbors, and intend to lead a new life, following the commandments of God, and walking from henceforth in his holy ways; draw near with faith, and take this holy sacrament to your comfort: and make your humble confession to Almighty God, meekly kneeling upon your knees."

IV. Answer objections.
   1. Some believe it right yet have doubts they are unworthy.
   2. Some have doubts whether it was to be continued in the church.[96]
V. How we are to behave after it.[97]

Bishops Thomas Coke and Francis Asbury speak on the propriety of the Methodist practice of kneeling to receive Communion, reflecting Methodism's Anglican roots. The issue of appropriate posture was a long-standing issue among Protestants. The bishops also give a rationale for closed Communion.

As the Scripture is silent about the posture of the communicants, we prefer the most humble, whatever our Savior might have permitted when he instituted the sacred ordinance. Besides, as we always receive the elements in prayer, we for that reason also prefer the kneeling posture.[98] We must also observe, that our elders should be very cautious how they admit to the communion persons who are not in our society.[99] It would be highly injurious to our brethren, if we suffered any to partake of the Lord's Supper with them, whom we would not readily admit into our society on application made to us. Those whom we judge unfit to partake of our profitable, prudential[100] means of grace, we should most certainly think improper to be partakers of an ordinance which has been expressly instituted by Christ himself.[101]

BAPTISM

Fanny Newell describes her experience of baptism in the early nineteenth century.

---

96. Some Quakers would hold this position. It is not clear whom else Cooper would have in mind.

97. Ezekiel Cooper, "His Book," 47.

98. Kneeling was the standard position for Methodists to pray.

99. In this early period, "society" is the standard Methodist word for church.

100. This distinction between prudential and instituted means of grace was an important one in early Methodism. See Knight, *Presence of God*, 2-5. Means of grace are those ways in which people most commonly experience God's grace and thus grow in Christian maturity. Prudential means are those which God providentially has provided to Methodists as a distinctive people like small accountability groups (class and band meetings) and special worship services (e.g., love feasts). Instituted means, on the other hand, are those which Christ expressly instituted for all Christians like the Lord's Supper.

101. *Doctrines and Discipline of the Methodist Episcopal Church* (1798), 119-20.

My soul was happy, and I longed to embrace the holy ordinance of baptism, and thus [give] evidence to the world that I had put off the old man and his deeds, and had put on the new man, which is Christ the Lord,[102] resolving by his grace to come out and be separated from the wicked world, its habits, maxims, and wrong customs. This was a most memorable day to me and also to many others.

On my way to the meeting I breathed out my heart in constant prayer to God for strength to raise me above the fear of man, and give me that faith that overcomes, and holds the promise fast. After a short discourse, I arose and told my desire and intention and related my experience in some of the most important parts. And when the necessary preparation was made, we repaired to the water, and I could say truly, "We are marching through Immanuel's land to fairer worlds on high."[103] The language of my heart was poured out in the following hymn, which I repeated as I passed down to the water. I could not recollect from whence it came, yet I was able to repeat it then and to retain it in my memory ever since. Afterwards I found it in the Methodist hymnbook.

> Happy soul! Thy days are ended
> All thy mourning days below.
> Go, by angel guards attended
> To the sight of Jesus, go.
> Waiting to receive thy spirit,
> Lo! The Savior stands above,
> Shows the purchase of his merit,
> Reaches out the crown of love.
>
> Struggle through thy latest passion,
> To thy great Redeemer's breast,
> To his uttermost salvation,
> To his everlasting rest.
> For the joy he sets before thee,
> Bear a momentary pain.

102. See Ephesians 4:22 and Colossians 3:9.
103. From an Isaac Watts hymn, "Come, ye that love the Lord."

Die to live a life of glory.
Suffer with thy Lord to reign.[104]

Eight persons were baptized before myself, I being the youngest. When it came to my turn, my heart leaped for joy, and I cried out as I moved along "farewell, vain world, I am going home"[105] and stepped down into the water, and thought that I could have gone across the pond as easily as I did three rods. I kneeled down and was plunged forward, and when I arose, I stood some time in the water and exhorted the numerous congregation which crowded round the shore. And I praised the Lord with loud strains. O the raptures! In which my soul was held! Caught up as it were to the third heaven,[106] I had renewed my strength to travel the celestial road heavenward. We went to the place appointed for prayer meeting, shouting and singing, and a most glorious time it was.[107]

One of the points of contention in worship was the practice of infant baptism.[108] Early Methodists uniformly defended the practice. In the following passage, Fanny Newell describes the baptism of her son (notice the language of baptism as an act of devotion/dedication) and how the sense of God's presence changed the opinion of some about the propriety of baptizing children.

At a quarterly meeting held in Cabot, we devoted our son to God in the holy ordinance of baptism. And so manifest was the approbation of that God, to whom we set him apart by this sacred seal, that error stood back, and one of the most rigid said, "Let them who think it their duty to baptize infants do it, and the Lord bless them." A young woman, who had waited to be baptized by immersion on this occasion, rose in a distant part of the crowded assembly, and said with a loud and quick voice, "Let me go to heaven with little children" [and] rushed through the crowd, kneeled

---

104. See the American Methodist standard: *A Pocket Hymn-Book, Designed as a Constant Companion for the Pious*, 18th edition (Philadelphia: Parry Hall, 1793), 172-73.

105. Possibly a reference to the hymn "Traveling Pilgrim."

106. 2 Corinthians 12:2.

107. Fanny Newell, *Memoirs*, 38-39.

108. See Gayle Carlton Felton, *This Gift of Water: The Practice and Theology of Baptism Among Methodists in America* (Nashville: Abingdon, 1992).

down, and was baptized by pouring. This gave such a shock to the people, and the glory of God was so manifest that all appeared to be satisfied that God owned this ordinance. My soul felt a blessing in giving myself afresh to him with all I have and am. O that we may have grace to bring this child up for God. Amen.[109]

Itinerant preacher Freeborn Garrettson supports the practice of infant baptism by a typology comparing baptism and circumcision.

I was dedicated to God in the ordinance of baptism in infancy and in the Name of the Father, Son, and Holy Ghost I have baptized thousands. And I feel it to be my duty to assign to this congregation and the citizens at large reasons why I baptize little children as well as grown persons and, secondly, give my sentiments concerning the mode the most congenial to my sentiment and practices....

We can substantiate that the covenant entered into with Abraham in which the sign of circumcision was given was a gracious one and renewed under the gospel dispensation....Under the Jewish dispensation infants had a right to the seal of the covenant and who is he that is hardy enough to deny infants the same right under our glorious dispensation?...Now take a view of the nature of Christian baptism. It is the entering seal of the new covenant and water is applied to the subject, representing an application of that precious blood which has been shed for the cleansing of the soul. "I will sprinkle clean water upon you, etc."[110] "I will pour out my spirit upon you, etc."[111] Infants, as well as grown persons, are subjects of this ordinance. I know of no objection to infant baptism that would not lay with the same weight against admitting infants into covenant among the Jews.[112]

Two hymns in Henry Bradford's handwritten hymnal makes arguments for infant baptism based on comparison with Old Testament practices.

---

109. Fanny Newell, *Memoirs*, 122.
110. Ezekiel 36:25.
111. Compare Joel 2:28 and Acts 2:17 (quoting Joel).
112. Freeborn Garrettson, untitled sermon on Mark 16:15-16, Garrettson Family papers (box 1, folder 19).

Thus did the sons of Abraham pass
Under the bloody seals of grace.
The young disciples bore the yoke
Till Christ the painful bondage broke.

By milder ways does Jesus prove
His Father's covenant and his love,
He seals to saints his glorious grace
And not forbids their infant race.

Their seed is sprinkled with his blood,
Their children set apart for God.
His spirit on their offspring shed
Like water poured upon the head.

Let every saint with cheerful voice
In this large covenant rejoice.
Young children in their early day
Shall give the God of Abram praise.[113]

The second hymn also calls upon some New Testament examples.

Thus saith the mercy of the Lord:
"I'll be a God to thee.
I'll bless thy num'rous race and they
Shall be a seed to me."

Abraham believed the promised grace
And gave his son to God.
But water seals the blessing now
That once was sealed with blood.

Thus Lydia[114] sanctified her house
When she received the word.

---

113. Henry Bradford, Hymnbook, 30.
114. Referring to Acts 16:15, where Lydia and her entire household were baptized.

Thus the believing jailor[115] gave
His household to the Lord.

Thus later saints, Eternal King,
Thine ancient truth embrace,
To thee their infant offspring bring
And humbly claim the grace.[116]

Another early Methodist hymn defending infant baptism has Jesus himself commanding the practice.

1. Come, let us unto Jesus go
And ask him if it can be so
That babes can have in Christ no part
Who once embraced them to his heart?

2. Has heav'n decreed that infants must
In cruel flames be ever curst?
Must they forever burn in hell
Because their Father Adam fell?

3. "No," Jesus says, "I am their friend;
Upon my truth they may depend.
In Matthew, Mark, and Luke you'll find,
I have not left one babe behind.

4. "You need not think I'll bear the blame.
Baptize them all in my great name.
The seal imparts to infants giv'n
They are my blood-bought heirs[117] of heav'n."[118]

High theological motives are not the only reasons people brought their children for baptism. For many, the most important aspect of the service

---

115. Referring to Acts 16:33, where a jailor and his entire household were baptized.
116. Henry Bradford, Hymnbook, 30.
117. Compare Romans 8:17 and Galatians 3:29.
118. Stith Mead, *Hymns and Spiritual Songs*, 97.

is the naming of the child. North Carolinian itinerant preacher William Ormond describes a scene in 1797 almost worthy of tabloid coverage.

... then [I] came to Sister Overstreet's. And in the evening one Mr. Joiner and his wife came. The woman brought up a child in her arms, and desired me to baptize him. I thought the child was theirs, and baptized him by the name of Chancy King. They went off, and in a short time one widow Smith came with a child in her arms, crying. And it seemed her heart would break with distress, [she] informing me that those people [i.e., the previous couple] had got her child and had him baptized by a wrong name. I then found out the secret. The widow Smith charged her bastard child to [Mr.] Joiner.[119] Mrs. Joiner was much disturbed, and, as one Anthony King was supposed to be the father, she slyly and cunningly had him baptized by that name. The widow Smith desired to have the child baptized over again and [to] give him another name. This I refused until she had proven herself to be the mother, [and thus] the proper person to name her child, and brought a certificate from a Justice of the Peace living in Halifax County. This she did not do. Therefore I came [went] away....

[When Ormond returns in the next month, Smith accomplishes her purpose.]

The widow Smith presented me a certificate from Major Haywood, and I baptized her child by the name of Lunsford Joiner.[120]

For other early Methodists the desire was simpler: safeguarding their children in case of death. This motivation has been shared by Christian parents since at least the early Middle Ages. It is hard to tell if itinerant preacher Nathaniel Mills disapproves.

I stopped on the way to baptize a sick child. Some people appear as much concerned lest their children should die before they are baptized, as if it would endanger their salvation.[121]

Another common point of dispute about baptism is the proper mode of administering it. Early Methodists allowed a variety of modes, as Ezekiel Cooper shows in 1788.

---

119. That is, she accused Joiner of being the father.
120. William Ormond, Journal, 3 July 1797 and 15 August 1797.
121. Nathaniel Mills, Journal, 28 August 1811.

I had liberty in the forenoon, but in the afternoon I was in a degree shut up.[122] After the last sermon, I had to baptize two young men: one by pouring [and] the other by immersion. I went down to the water where I performed the ordinance, and, having a mixed congregation,[123] I was led to speak largely in vindication of baptizing both ways according to the desire of the people. Insisting that the apostolic mode of baptizing could not be proved to be altogether one way or the other, I told them if any would show me Scripture to condemn my mode I would then give it up. I found much satisfaction while speaking upon the subject.[124]

Methodists contended with several groups who insisted that immersion was the biblical standard for baptizing. The following anonymous hymn seeks to counter that argument.

1. You say, "Go read the scriptures
And in them we shall find
The ordinance immersion
Upon us all enjoined."
How can you be immersed?
The word we cannot find.
And if it's in your bible
I'm sure it's not in mine.

2. We've read the third of Matthew.[125]
We've read the scriptures through.
We cannot find immersion
With all that we can do.
You call us "antichristians."
We wish that you could see
The precious blood of Jesus
Shed on mount Calvary.

---

122. Cooper means that he preached easily in the morning but had difficulty in the afternoon.

123. Cooper probably means that he had both Methodists and non-Methodists in attendance.

124. Ezekiel Cooper, Journal, 6 July 1788.

125. Referring to the story of John baptizing Jesus and others in the Jordan River.

3. But when you do immerse them,
Which we do think is wrong,
It makes my heart to tremble
They think the work is done.
You say my Lord's a Baptist.
How do you realize
For there never was a Baptist
But one who did baptize?[126]

4. You seem to rage vehemently
About the word "into."[127]
But that is not immersion
You cannot make it so.
When Philip baptized the eunuch,[128]
They both went down into.
But which one went the deepest,
I'm sure you do not know.

5. It's true John[129] was a Baptist
As we may plainly see.
But the least that's in the kingdom
Is greater now than he.[130]
Your charity is scanty
And that the world can see.
If you do not quit immersion
We cannot all agree.[131]

---

126. That is, Jesus cannot be called a "Baptist" because he never actually baptized anyone in water.

127. In other words, the Baptist position is that immersion is necessarily implied in biblical accounts of baptism where the people went *into* the water.

128. See Acts 8:38.

129. John the Baptist. See Matthew 3, Mark 1, Luke 3, and John 1.

130. See Matthew 11:11 and Luke 7:28.

131. Collection of Spiritual Songs (Winchester, Ky.), 15-16.

CHAPTER 7

ETHOS

Deep desire and longing were central to early Methodist spirituality. The affective dimension of their lives was fully engaged, but not in a way that undercut the ethical dimension. Desire, whether to avoid the coming wrath of God or to seek the eternal enjoyment of God, was to be demonstrated in a certain way of living. Love for God, for instance, was expected to result in abhorrence of the "vice and criminal amusement of the world" on the one hand and in a grasping of righteousness on the other.[1] While early Methodists expressed much of their ethos as the avoidance of certain behaviors, avoiding evil was only part of the story. The goal was not just to avoid hell, it was to be made fit to enjoy the God of heaven. This meant the reshaping of lives.

This ethos was not just a matter of individual behavior. The Methodist vision was for a holy *people*. This communal vision stood behind the rigorous Methodist ethos. Methodists assumed their distinctive way of life as part of their communal identity, particularly as it marked them as different from the surrounding culture. There was no witness—and no path to heaven—in conformity. Individual Methodists identified with the group by accepting this communal ethos and desiring to live by it. The ethos provided a boundary that marked the group, distinguishing it from the surrounding culture.

---

1. *Doctrines and Discipline of the Methodist Episcopal Church* (1798), 137.

The most succinct summary of early Methodist ethos is the document John Wesley crafted at the beginning of the movement—the "General Rules." These rules were read regularly in Methodist worship, and they served as a standard for new members. According to bishops Coke and Asbury, they constituted "one of the completest systems of Christian ethics or morals, for its size, which ever was published by an uninspired [i.e., non-scriptural] writer."[2] As such, they provide a helpful sketch of the basic ethos of early Methodism on this side of the Atlantic as well.

While there was no prerequisite of Christian faith or ethos prior to joining the Methodists, the General Rules sketched the expectations that members took on at the time of joining, as an evidence of their continuing desire to seek salvation. These expectations were gathered in sets under three main headings. The first set listed behaviors that expressed resistance to the typical evils of the world "by doing no harm, by avoiding evil of every kind: especially that which is most generally practised." The second set gathered expectations for how Methodists would go beyond simple "purity," demonstrating a righteousness that the world did not have "by doing good, by being in every kind merciful after their power, as they have opportunity, doing good of every possible sort, and as far as is possible, to all men." The third set of guidelines focused on the methodical use of the means of grace, the "attending upon all the ordinances of God," including worship, interaction with the Scriptures, fasting, prayer, and the Lord's Supper.[3] The specifics gathered under these three categories formed the heart of the Methodist ethos.

In its historical context the early Methodist ethos was radical and rigorous. When Methodism entered New England in the late-1790s, for instance, it faced the same reception that it had drawn in England: the elite feared it as a challenge to the social order, and the middle class feared its challenge to local traditions and family institutions.[4] The values Methodists embodied clashed with the prevailing culture. Their prohibitions struck at popular activities: fine clothing, dancing, and drinking. Their worship could be loud, boisterous, and seemingly full of disorder. Their itinerant preachers

---

2. Ibid., 135.
3. Ibid., 133-35.
4. See Richard D. Shiels, "The Methodist Invasion of Congregational New England," in Hatch & Wigger, eds., *Methodism and the Shaping of American Culture*, 272.

lacked formal theological education and avoided the markers of high status within society like fine clothing, unlike the typical Congregational minister.

The contrast of Methodist ethos with the culture of the South in the early republic was particularly striking, and has drawn the attention of much recent study. Scholars describe the prevailing culture in the South during this period as a "culture of honor."[5] It was hierarchical in structure, built on the honor that one cultivated in relation to their social and economic status. The upper classes displayed their visible markers of wealth, position, and honor in a regular rhythm of communal events—some social, some political, some religious, and some recreational. Even events like dances were opportunities for "competitive display" in which alliances and match-making among the well-to-do were accomplished.[6] Behind the culture of honor was an "ethos of honor," in which "external appearance and performance and the judgments of others formed the center of personal identity and self-worth."[7] Wealth, connections, and status were all important. Knowing one's place—and having others know one's place—in that hierarchy of wealth and status were equally crucial.

Into that environment came the Methodists with their General Rules, a sobriety toward high culture, and a spirituality of free grace that equalized people's standing before God. The combination was combustible. Methodists condemned both the activities that constituted the heart of this culture and the worldview that lay behind them. It was not just the drinking, dancing, fancy dress, and slave-owning themselves that Methodists condemned but the self-indulgence, self-assertion, pride, and willfulness that these activities revealed. The same was true for those lower-class activities that showed these sinful dispositions.

The Methodist stance on any single ethical issue inevitably connected to broader themes in their overall ethos. Consider their insistence on keeping Sunday as a day of Sabbath rest. The broader roots for this concern trace to the Puritans of the sixteenth and

---

5. Three of the most detailed accounts are Heyrman, *Southern Cross*, 15-26; Lyerly, *Methodism and the Southern Mind*, 39-42; and Schneider, *Way of the Cross*, 23-27.

6. Schneider, *Way of the Cross*, 9.

7. A. Gregory Schneider, "The Ritual of Happy Dying among Early American Methodists," *Church History* 56 (1987): 350.

seventeenth centuries and, behind them, continental Reformed theology. Wesley mediated this commitment by including it in the General Rules. The notion was reinforced by the similar commitment of contemporaneous Baptists and by the sabbatarian ethos of New England. In the upper South, Sabbath-keeping Protestants valued observation of the day of rest, free from work and frivolous amusements, as a countercultural break from the broad practice in "sinful society" of devoting Sunday to "sport, merriment, and dissipation."[8] While sharing this conviction, bishops Coke and Asbury offered Methodists another reason for strict observation of the Sabbath. Against the Enlightenment tendency to downplay special revelation in preference for only "universal" moral norms, the bishops suggested that keeping the Sabbath was a way to maintain a testimony to Christianity as divine revelation.[9]

Similar accounts of complex rationales and meanings could be given for the Methodist positions on extravagant dress and alcohol.[10] The aspect of early Methodist ethos that merits most attention, however, is their stance on slavery.[11] Over time a variety of factors eroded the earliest, strict opposition to owning slaves. While Methodists in the period we have been considering never fully embraced slavery as an institution, they did increasingly accommodate slave-owning even by their own members. There were varying levels of agreement and compliance with the initial strict rejection of slavery among rank-and-file members and (eventually) among the preachers. This divergence was created in part by the fact that laws in some states prevented what the Methodists would have liked to achieve.

Thus the history of early Methodist activity with regard to slavery was one of growing accommodation. The "high water mark" came in 1784 with the creation of The Methodist Episcopal Church.

---

8. Ibid.

9. *Doctrines and Discipline of the Methodist Episcopal Church* (1798), 138.

10. For an exploration of the prohibitions against extravagant dress in Wesley and early Methodism, see Leigh Eric Schmidt, "'A Church-going People are a Dress-loving People': Clothes, Communication, and Religious Culture in Early America," *Church History* 58 (1989): 36-51. Concerning alcohol, see Ivan Burnett Jr., "Methodist Origins: John Wesley and Alcohol," *Methodist History* 13, 4 (July 1975): 3-17.

11. The most useful treatments of this issue include Donald G. Mathews, *Slavery and Methodism: A Chapter in American Morality 1780–1845* (Princeton: Princeton University Press, 1965); Wigger, *Taking Heaven by Storm*, 125-50; Lyerly, *Methodism and the Southern Mind*, 119-45; and Andrews, *The Methodists and Revolutionary America*, 123-54.

The legislation adopted at this founding rigorously sought to curtail slave-owning by members: Any Methodists who owned slaves were given a year to execute a legal document to free them. Back in the circuits, Methodists responded immediately and harshly. Within six months the policy was indefinitely suspended. The same failure faced the 1785 Methodist-led drive in Virginia to petition the state legislature to abolish slavery.[12] These reversals led to a period of relative official silence on the issue. When the issue was picked up again, the general trend was an easing of the original rigorous stance, despite the objections of some.

Why was slavery such a mixed bag in the Methodist ethos? For one thing, many of the preachers who initially opposed slavery in a hard-line fashion found that it raised barriers to their mission of aggressive evangelistic outreach to all people.[13] Not only were slave owners less responsive to evangelistic overtures from those trying to increase public opposition to slavery, the owners cut off the preachers' access to the slaves as well. Another factor that undercut the initial opposition was the self-authenticating nature of "experimental religion." Slave ownership did not seem to prevent someone from having the sorts of crisis experiences accompanied by inward assurance that Methodists saw as the essence of salvation. How could they discredit a slave owner who testified of that experience?

In hindsight, the typical Methodist appeal to motivate its membership to free their slaves can also be considered naive. Exhortations relied upon affective terms reminiscent of Methodists' experience of God's heart in converting them (compassion, mercy, pity) to create a feeling of empathy for their slaves. This approach underestimated the countering values of profit and self-interest that undergirded slavery.[14] Similarly, many Methodists, including some of the preachers, failed to see the interdependence of racism and slavery.[15] At the same time that they were taking public stances against slavery, they were less than comfortable welcoming blacks fully into Methodist life and ministry. It is hard to reshape the tree if one does not strike at the root.

---

12. See Richard K. MacMaster, "Liberty or Property? The Methodists Petition for Emancipation in Virginia, 1785," *Methodist History* 10, 1 (October 1971): 44-55.

13. Lyerly, *Methodism and the Southern Mind*, 143.

14. Ibid., 130, 135.

15. Ibid., 120.

An interesting aspect of the Methodist ethos on slavery was the intentional push for members to manumit their slaves. Eventually a formal procedure was created in which members brought the details of their purchase of slaves to the administrative meeting for the circuit, the quarterly meeting conference. (This became official policy after 1796.) Weighing the various factors (age of the slave, gender, purchase price), the quarterly meeting conference determined the length of slavery and required the slave owner to execute a legal document freeing the slave at the end of that time period. Failure to obey was grounds for expulsion.

The backdrop to this practice seems to have been a kind of gradation in the kinds of evils possible in slave owning. The worst evils were slavery in perpetuity and refusal to allow slaves to hear the gospel. The fear of perpetual slavery was the reason that selling slaves was very much looked down upon. Harsh treatment, like beating, of slaves was also condemned. Less troublesome was purchasing a slave to free her or him, even after a period of slavery. The extent to which this internal drive for manumission succeeded varied by region.[16]

The following excerpts survey the ethical stance and internal tensions of early Methodism. The first section gives a sense of the typical rigorousness and countercultural stance of the movement. This ethical tone was not just a matter of preachers chastising laity. It was commonly shared. Accordingly, two examples of Methodist laywomen complaining about moral laxity (including among the preachers!) have been included. The subsequent sections touch on what early Methodists considered the most critical ethical issues. Unlike previous chapters, there is more repetition of sources. This degree of repetition between sections allows the reader to see how stances on single issues were part of a general ethical suspicion toward the world. The reader should note that, although there was a typical ethos, there was not uniformity across early Methodism. This is best seen in the section on the struggles surrounding slavery.

---

16. See Kenneth L. Carroll, "Religious Influences on the Manumission of Slaves in Caroline, Dorchester, and Talbot Counties," *Maryland Historical Magazine* 56 (1961): 191-95. T. Stephen Whitman, *The Price of Freedom: Slavery and Manumission in Baltimore and Early National Maryland* (Lexington: University Press of Kentucky, 1997), 97, 204 note 19.

THE ETHICAL TONE OF METHODISM

After itinerant preacher William Spencer catches himself in unnecessary lightness, he describes in the 1790 journal entry the desired tone for Methodist life: solemnity.

Thursday, May 20th after preaching, I was troubled with a light and trifling spirit. O! How sensibly did I feel the need of a deeper work of grace in my soul. O! That my God may deepen his work in me every hour of my life. Solemnity is the very life of religion. O, Lord Jesus, make me more and more solemn every day. Death is solemn. Judgment is solemn. God is solemn. Christ is solemn. Angels are solemn. O! how can I be trifling? May God Almighty make me solemn and deeply pious and faithful for the Lord Jesus' sake. Amen.[17]

In his list of various kinds of devils, Ezekiel Cooper summarizes the kinds of vices and sins against which Methodists stood.

There are various kinds of devils besetting the human heart; understand [the source to be] Beelzebub, the Prince of Devils.

1) A proud devil; 2) An obstinate one; 3) A swearing one; 4) A lying one; 5) A covetous or mammon one; 6) A drunken one; 7) An envying one; 8) A passionate one; 9) An adulterous one; 10) [A] peevish one; 11) [A] malicious one; 12) [A] revengeful [one]; 13) A discontented one; 14) An infidel one; 15) A cruel one; 16) A slothful one; 17) An ungrateful one; 18) [A] hardhearted one; 19) A dumb one; 20) A flattering one; 21) A disputing one; 22) A laughing, trifling one; 23) A prejudiced one; 24) [A] bigoted one; 25) [A] boasting one; 26) A deceitful one; 27) A shameful one; 28) A persecuting one; 29) A gaming one; 30) A pleasureful one; 31) A mischief-making one; 32) A tattling one; 33) A dishonest one; 34) A quarrelling one; 35) A disdaining, scornful one; 36) A gluttonous one; 37) A murdering one; 38) A man-fearing one; 39) A man-pleasing one; 40) A hypocritical one; 41) A self-righteous [one]; 42) A false-hoping one; 43) A high minded [one]; 44) A conceited one; 45) [A] presumptuous one; 46) A vain-glorying one; 47) A Sabbath-breaking

---

17. William Spencer, Diary, 20 May 1790.

one; 48) A dancing one; 49) [A] playhouse one; 49) [A] horse racing one;[18] 50) Many more, [and] Beelzebub is the prince of all.[19]

In a similar list Cooper points to such sins as the reason God's judgments pervade the world. Such judgments have a redemptive purpose—to bring people to repentance.

I. [The] Causes of God's judgments being abroad
  1. The great neglect of religion
  2. The great contempt: profanation of God's word, ordinances and Sabbath
  3. The existing reproach of religion
  4. The great profaneness or wickedness of the people, all kinds of sin
  5. The idolatry of men
  6. The vainness and ungodliness of the priests
  7. The iniquities of rulers, the heads of the land
  8. The pride of the land
  9. Injustice
  10. The great infidelity: Deism,[20] etc.
II. What end God has in view in sending his judgments abroad
  1. To humble the people
  2. To reform them from their evil
  3. To bring them to real penitence
  4. To bring them to Christ and faith in him
  5. To bring us to obedience in life
  6. To [bring us to] holiness in heart.
III. What are we to do when the judgments are abroad
  1. As above 1 humble [ourselves] 2 reform [ourselves], etc.
  2. Fast and afflict ourselves
  3. To learn righteousness in heart and life: civil, religious and domestic[21]

---

18. The author's numbering is off in the original.
19. Ezekiel Cooper, "His Book," 19-20.
20. Deism affirmed belief in a Supreme Creator who was not actively involved with creation. It also downplayed any supernatural, special revelation in the Christian faith.
21. Ezekiel Cooper, "His Book," 106.

In a 1792 letter to preacher Enoch George, Virginian Methodist Sarah Jones complains about what she sees as the growing moral laxness among Methodists. Jones is familiar with the growing tensions between James O'Kelly, a prominent Virginia preacher, and bishop Francis Asbury during this period.

Were there ever such trying grievous times upon the earth? Where is the love, the former love among brethren?[22] Where is the unanimity of sentiment and oneness of mind? Do the preachers agree as once they did? Some of them slight each other much, jealousies rise, and love waxes colder and colder, and the private members[23] are afraid to make known their exercises to their brethren. A strangeness takes place, and mourning follows. Then I fly as the turtle[dove] to the clefts of Christ's side, and hide me in the secret of his presence. If we don't take care, Methodism will feel judgment without mercy! Pride, that accursed wedge, is hid in our camp and I awfully fear [that] popularity and conformity to the world will sink some of our preachers and people. O brother, answer me, is there not much more effeminacy and worldly delicacy among both preachers and people, than formerly? Not in all, but generally. Has not dress, etc. crept in with trifling conversation? Yes, frothy, idle speaking, to little or no purpose, with but little solemn exhorting one another. [There is] little prayer, few tears, little lowliness and meekness, with long suffering, and forbearing one another in love, keeping the unity of the Spirit in the bond of peace.[24] But O, there are yet a "few names in Sardis"[25] that love holiness, and as little children, love to be talking of Jesus but, alas, these are pointed at and persecuted. I could say much more but you see and feel it so, I believe.[26]

In this 1791 journal entry, itinerant preacher James Meacham describes an exhortation delivered by an old woman identified only as "Sister Whitehead" to a large collection of Methodists gathered in Virginia. Like Sarah Jones above, Whitehead is concerned that Methodists' original

---

22. "Brethren" in this context refers to other Methodists.
23. "Private members" refers to rank-and-file Methodists. Within "private" occasions like the weekly small group meeting (class meetings) or testimonial services (love feasts), Methodists discussed their religious experiences with each other.
24. See Ephesians 4:3.
25. See Revelation 3:4.
26. Jeremiah Minter, ed., *Devout Letters*, 123-24.

strictness is slipping away to the detriment of the church's power and fellowship. For Whitehead, general worldliness, concern with fashion, and a growing hypocrisy on slavery are related aspects of this communal backsliding.

[I] rode very early to the conference[27] to hear the experiences of the dear preachers, but it was nearly over before I got there. There were six deacons ordained, three traveling and three local. Mr. Asbury preached from John 4:14. [It was] a very great sermon, indeed I believe it had the powerful effect upon the congregation. Brother Marvel gave a warm exhortation. Likewise after him Brother O'Kelly [exhorted]. The Lord let down his awful power, and soon I could not hear him speak, being drowned with the cries and shouts of the people. Then came on the communion. Fifty preachers I saw surround the Lord's Table. In this time a precious dear woman, Sister Whitehead, rose up and begged the preachers to excuse her, she was weak and a poor woman, but she was awfully impressed with grief and that was almost more than she could bear up under. She said when she turned her eyes upon the young sisters and saw them catching after the modes of fashion of this world which passes away, backsliding from God and wounding his cause, she could scarcely bear up under her grief. And what was worse than all her poor dear young preachers, some of them would be following the fashions of the wicked world that ought to be examples of the flock.... They would stand in the pulpit and explode the cursed practice of slavery, and then they themselves would marry a young woman who held slaves and keep them fast in bloody slavery. Members who have been professors of religion of Jesus Christ for ten or twelve years would come to me and apparently be as happy as saints in heaven, and follow them home and you will see their slaves in the field and kitchens cruelly oppressed, half starved, and nearly naked. "O! my Lord," [she said], "is this the religion of my adorable master Jesus? How can I keep grieving over these cruel oppressions [oppressors?] who are in error. And I fear they will be slaves to the devil in hell forever." So the dear woman swooned away, being greatly exhausted. I hope this lecture may never be forgotten.[28]

---

27. The Annual Conference held at Lane's Chapel in Sussex County, Virginia, at the end of December, 1791. An annual conference was the administrative meeting for a region. Itinerant preachers attended the business sessions, and many others attended the worship services.

28. William K. Boyd, "A Journal and Travel of James Meacham," *Annual Publication of Historical Papers of the Historical Society of Trinity College* 10 (1914): 92-93.

*Eccentric and popular Methodist evangelist Lorenzo Dow describes the
kind of cultural spheres suspect to early Methodists. Dow uses the image
of these spheres being "schools of Babylon" where people learn the way of
sinfulness. Babylon, the place of Israelite exile, has been a common
metaphor for a place of idolatry and abomination since biblical times.*

There were also certain associations, which may well be denom-
inated the "Schools of Babylon" so great [is] the influence of their
example and the progress of their pupils!

Men of ability and spirit, being intoxicated with the wine of
Bacchus,[29] volunteer their services, pleased with the idea of becoming masters in those schools, which by the [many] is considered as
an important distinction, and constituting them great and mighty
men!

The first is the "Military School." Here is taught the art of war. Its
object is fame and glory. Although it is attended with such horrors
as tend to harden the heart, yet many weak men are so infatuated
as to be delighted at the sight.

The second is the "Dancing School." Here is taught the important art of hopping and jumping about, at a signal made by a Black
man, who, as their captain, with his noisy instruments directs their
movements, whilst they turn back and face to and fro, without
either sense or reason except indeed, it may serve to show fine
shapes and clothes. But consumptions are dated, and serious
impressions are driven away!

The third is the School of Lawyers. The nature of this association
will be discovered by the following lines:

"Should I be a lawyer, I must lie and cheat:

For honest lawyers have no bread to eat;

'Tis rogues and villains see the lawyers high,

And see the men, who gold and silver buy."

The fourth is the School of Music, intending to divert the mind
and touch the passions. And [it] is admirably calculated to be a
substitute for penitence, and the prologue to forgiven indulgences.

In the fifth is taught the Art of Dress. This is intended to hide
deformity, and please the eye, to gain a fanciful pre-eminence and
wear the bell, as first in fashion, glorying in their shame. For dress

---

29. Bacchus was a god from Greek mythology associated with wine and levity.

was ordained in consequence of Sin and may be considered as a badge of fallen nature.

The sixth is the School of Quacks. They have had success in imposing on the ignorant by high sounding words. But the poor deceived sufferers at length detect the imposition and die to warn their survivors not to partake of their follies.

In the seventh is taught the fascinating art of Theatric representation. This is called a very moral institution by its advocates, who affect to consider it very corrective of every species of vice. But matter of fact sufficiently proves that the theater is best supported when vice most abounds.

The eighth is an establishment for the promotion of Polite Literature. Here lectures are given upon the barbarity and folly displayed by the writers of the Old and New Testament[30] and on the sublimity, beauty, elegance, taste, and morality, which are everywhere found in a choice collection of Romances and Novels. This establishment is exclusively intended for privileged orders. Such as have been distinguished by wealth and idleness, and such as had rather feel than think.

The ninth is a very extensive institution, having many united colleges, in which are taught the various arts of picking pockets, picking locks, stealing, highway robbery, house-breaking, etc. And the progress of those pupils who are instructed in these various branches is really prodigious.

There is also a department, an appendage to the former, where is taught the art of preparing and using false weights and measures, the method of raising false charges, of managing extortion, the excellent art of over-bearing and over-reaching in bargains, and the making of other's extremity their own opportunity to be well served at their expense.

The eleventh is furnished with male and female instructors for the improvement of tattling, back-biting, lying, etc. Here also astonishing progress I made by all the pupils of both sexes.

The twelfth is a School for Match-making. And considering the motives which seem to govern most people on the subject of marriage and the many unhappy families which are formed, it would appear that the "wine" of Bacchus furnished the stimulus, and

---

30. Dow means that those who read "polite literature" are offended by the earthiness of the Bible.

Cupid and Hymen the only bands of union. But this is a private establishment, and their lessons are secretly given.

The thirteenth is the University of Grandeur. Here pompous show, empty titles, impudent flatteries, haughty oppression, vain ignorance, pampering luxury and wanton reveling, are effectually taught. This establishment is the most popular, and scarcely a family can be found in all the precincts of Babylon, which is not ambitious to obtain a finishing touch to the education of their children in this grand university.[31]

KEEPING THE SABBATH

In this 1798 passage, Methodist bishops Thomas Coke and Francis Asbury speak on how violating the Sabbath is the source for much evil. For Coke and Asbury, keeping the Sabbath serves as a buffer to prevent those who want to destroy Christianity.

Sabbath breaking is a vice which may be committed under various specious pretences, though it is the forerunner of all evil. In this day especially it is a vice inexcusable in those who make the least profession of Christianity, when the entire rejection of the Sabbath is looked upon by the enemies of revealed religion, in general, as the most effectual means to destroy Christianity itself. O let us all come out to the help of the Lord against the mighty (Judges 5:23) and love the Sabbath for the sake of its Divine Founder and the inestimable blessings flowing from the due observance of it. It has been already honored by the divine rest from creation, and is an emblem of that spiritual and eternal rest which remains for the people of God (Hebrews 4:9).[32]

In this sermon on the Sabbath from the 1790s, Daniel Fidler discusses his understanding of why keeping the Sabbath holy is so important. For him, it is not simply a matter of abstaining from work but of honoring God and anticipating the ultimate day of rest. The text for Fidler's sermon is Exodus 20:8 ("Remember the Sabbath day, to keep it holy"). Fidler begins

---

31. Lorenzo Dow, "Journey from Babylon to Jerusalem," in *All the Polemical Works of Lorenzo Dow* (New York: J. C. Totten, 1814), 250-53.

32. *Doctrines and Discipline of the Methodist Episcopal Church* (1798), 138-39.

by explaining how Sunday, seemingly the first day of the week, is the orig-inal Sabbath (the seventh day of the week).

I make some observations on the Sabbath day.

[I.] The Jews were told what day they were to keep, the seventh after six days labor. Whether this was the seventh by computation from the first [day of the week] or seventh from the day of their coming out of Egypt or both is not certain.

A late pious writer seems to prove that the Sabbath was changed when Israel came out of Egypt, which change continued till our Lord rose again but that then the original Sabbath was restored. And he makes it highly probable at least that the one we observe is the Seventh from Creation.

II. How the Sabbath must be observed.

1. As a day of rest, you must do no manner of work in all your dwellings.

2. As a holy day set apart to the honor of the holy God, [who] by his blessing it had made it holy. You by solemnly blessing him must keep it holy and not alienate it to any other purpose than that for which the difference between it and other days were instituted.

3. Who must observe? You, your son and your daughter. The wife is not mentioned because she is supposed to be one with the husband and present with him.

4. And the servant and strangers within your gate. So masters of families should take care not only to keep this day holy themselves but that their households should also observe it to keep it holy to the Lord.

III. What we are forbid to do on the Sabbath

1. The omission or careless performance of the duties required.[33]

2. And the profaning of the day by idleness, or doing that which is in itself sinful or unnecessary: thoughts, words, or works about worldly employment.

3. Also keep all under our charge from profaning the holy day.

Conclusion. [As] the Sabbath began in the finishing [of] the work of creation, so will the everlasting Sabbath [be] in finishing the work of providence and redemption. We remember the weekly Sabbath in expectation of eternal rest.[34]

---

33. Fidler presumably means worship and attentiveness to God.
34. Daniel Fidler, Sermon notebook, 14-16.

Itinerant preacher Nathaniel Mills expresses his reservations about performing a wedding on a Sabbath. He dislikes both the extra work that is created for servants and women as well as how the festive occasion might contradict the day's desired solemnity.

Immediately after (a class) meeting [I] rode near[ly] 2 miles to join a couple in holy wedlock, which I'm not fond of doing on the Sabbath, as it causes so much work for the servants or the women on the Sabbath and collects a good many people who are apt to have a good deal of trifling conversation at such times.[35]

Keeping the Sabbath was not just a theoretical matter for early Methodists. Consider the action that an 1806 meeting of the quarterly meeting conference for the Hockhocking circuit in Ohio took against a local preacher, John Williams, for returning home from a grain mill on a Sunday.

A charge was [brought] against John Williams for breaking the Sabbath. . . . The question was asked John Williams his reason for returning from [the] mill on the Sabbath day. His reply was his state of debility and that they could be better accommodated at home and that his wife's horse food was out.[36]

Seven years later, the Hockhocking circuit is still concerned with Sabbath violations.

After hearing the accused as well as the accuser, it was determined by vote
1st) That this [quarterly meeting] conference fully disapproves of Brother S. Jones's conduct in making sugar on the Sabbath;
2nd) That owing to certain palliating [i.e., moderating] circumstances that the presiding elder[37] give Brother Jones a reproof for his conduct and that he retain his standing in society [with] he acknowledging that under similar circumstances he would not do it again.[38]

---

35. Nathaniel Mills, Journal, 25 October 1812.
36. Hockhocking Circuit, Book of Records, 8-11 August, 1806. Unfortunately, the page is torn at this point in the manuscript and it is difficult to know the outcome of Williams's trial.
37. A presiding elder was the itinerant preacher responsible for a district, which included several circuits. Presiding elders presided at quarterly meeting conferences.
38. Hockhocking Circuit, Book of Records, 13 February 1813.

DRESS

In this 1798 passage, bishops Thomas Coke and Francis Asbury continue their commentary on an appropriate Methodist lifestyle. By experience and by Scripture, they see elaborate, expensive dress as a stumbling block to holiness.

As our one aim, in all our economy and ministerial labors, is to raise a holy people, crucified to the world, and alive to God, we cannot allow of anything which has an immediate tendency to defeat our main design, and to strengthen and puff up the carnal mind. Few things, perhaps, have a greater tendency to this than gay apparel, which is expressly and repeatedly forbidden by the scriptures. We endeavor to follow the Word of God and whilst we have that on our side, we must go on, and leave all consequences to the Lord.[39]

Lucy Watson follows these precepts. In various places she discusses her commitment to simplicity of dress. In the first passage, Watson discusses how attachment to fancy dress (and dancing) under peer pressure was a struggle in her progress toward conversion.

After a few years, I was drawn into [fancy] company and soon became attached to it and of its accompaniment, dress and dancing. The latter, was called harmless and genteel mirth, [by] even the professedly religious, both in (New) Jersey and in New England. But although no one told me it was sinful yet I could feel it so with the reproaches of an awakened conscience after my return from such amusements. Often, in the time of a thunder gust, I have felt like a criminal and would greatly tremble with fear. All I dared to say, was, "Oh God, be merciful to me a sinner." And this I was impelled to repeat perpetually. I would then make solemn promises that if God would spare me, I would break off youthful folly and serve him. And for a while, [I] would betake myself to reading and prayer. But again my gay companions would entice me away and I would soon forget my good resolutions.[40]

---

39. *Doctrines and Discipline of the Methodist Episcopal Church* (1798), 159.
40. Lucy Fanning Watson, Experiences, 11-12.

In a letter written after her conversion, Lucy Watson relates an incident that gave her the conviction to give up fancy dress.

I pity those who are imperceptibly drawn into the vortex of fashion and vainglory. In my young days I was told of a Miss Emlin, a young woman of wealth. As she was walking the street of Philadelphia she met with William Lavery who said to her, "Well, call her by name Satin without and Satan within." She was struck with conviction from those words and went home and laid aside all her rich clothing and dressed herself in a suit of brown Holland. Even her bonnet was of the same. This is the way our Savior taught us to deny ourselves and take up the cross and follow Him who was meek and lowly. This was a seasonable lesson for me at that time. I had conflicts in my mind whether I should follow my own inclination or conform to the gospel plan but by this I was decided in my mind.[41]

The issue of dress was one in which Sarah Jones was willing to take on the realm of evil. Deeply absorbing Methodist prohibitions against fancy dress, she applied their standards to her children, so that they were out of step with the surrounding culture. Restricted by her desire to be obedient to her husband and stung by the criticism of fellow Christians, Jones exhibits a defiant tone nonetheless. This and similar passages reveals that degree to which Sarah Jones's zeal ran beyond the normal Methodist standard, which, in comparison to the surrounding society, was strict enough in itself.

Sister Williams, many of the dear people of God are grieved with poor me about my children's dress, when if they knew the real truth, they would rather weep for me. I have openly talked it over with Mr. Jones and brother S————l,[42] and Mr. Jones is my head, my dear, and he positively commands my children to dress as others do. O my dear, it is my grief. I can witness it by my class [meeting] and neighbors. I cannot help it. Bear me up in prayer. I abhor dress and fashion, more than necessary decency, and this may be

---

41. Lucy Fanning Watson, undated letter to "My Friend Logan," Watson Family papers (box 2, folder 5).

42. Another convention for disguising the identity was to include only the first and last initials.

opened in proof thereof. I abhor it. But, O, the dear Christians are so easy [easily] tried with me, a poor fighting, conquering, prevailing soul, who feels like climbing mountains and facing hell with every foe. God is on my side, and no weapon of war that ever was formed against me prospered.... Hell is angry, and wants to divide the army. Stand your ground, and march. Jesus Christ is in the front. In his name I dare devils. Hell stoops. Satan has tried his best to kill me, yet I live, and am more than conqueror.[43]

Not all Methodists are committed equally to abstaining from fancy clothing. Itinerant preacher James Meacham complains in his journal about Methodists too enamored in his opinion with the devilish practice that works against a Christlike character.

My Soul is burdened and grieved with our sisters' manner of putting on their apparel, some with their rings and ruffles, others with their necklaces and laces, which is pointed by against the power of truth and humility [i.e., this practice works against the power of truth and humility]....

I hope Satan's rings, ruffles, necklaces, and laces begin to fall. O Lord, keep me humble and give me faith for sinners. Lord, I wonder how I should feel if I was to see every sinner in Hanover circuit born again?[44]

Another itinerant preacher, William Colbert, describes how a word to backsliders caused one woman to simplify her dress in the midst of an 1802 worship service.

Brother Jonathan Newman...faithfully warned backsliders. He called on one young woman by name, which so mortified her that she replied in the congregation. But there was such a display of the power of God, after the administration of the Lord's Supper, that this young woman came forward and took her gold beads off her neck and her tinsel off her hat, and was brought on her knees before the Lord. Among many who were crying for mercy, several

---

43. Minter, ed., *Devout Letters*, 87-88.
44. James Meacham, Journal, 6 November 1788 and 14 December 1788. Meacham was traveling the Hanover circuit in Virginia.

found the Lord, several backsliders professed to be restored, and several to experience holiness of heart.[45]

Itinerant preacher Seth Crowell connects a strict stance on dress to an 1811 revival in his New York circuit among the various societies (congregations). Crowell began his first large worship and business meeting for the circuit with a reading of the official Methodist standards on dress. He enforced Methodist discipline: the lack of compliance meant no admission to the testimonial service called the love feast.

There has been a great revival of religion in the society at China Hill: upwards of twenty have joined society, and there is a prospect of many more joining. Some few have got religion in other societies and there is a prospect of much good on the circuit at large. Our first quarterly meeting commenced the 11th of August, in Chatham. On Saturday we had a good and gracious time. I read the rules of our societies, and particularly the rules on dress, and informed our members that we were determined to enforce all our rules on our societies, and we hoped that all our official members would concur with us in this work, and every other member who felt zealous for the cause of God, would join with us in this important work. And we informed them that all who would not conform to the rules concerning dress could not be admitted into [the] love feast. Our official members promised us all the assistance in their power and I can truly say that I never received the aid of the official characters on any circuit more generally than I did on Chatham circuit. And the consequence was that we had a great revival of religion, both in and out of the societies.[46]

DRUNKENNESS AND ALCOHOL

Continuing their 1798 commentary, bishops Thomas Coke and Francis Asbury discuss the dangers of excessive drinking.

The sin of drunkenness should be particularly guarded against in a country where the materials for distilled liquors so much

---

45. William Colbert, Journal, 4:93-94.
46. Seth Crowell, *The Journal of Seth Crowell; containing an Account of His Travels as a Methodist Preacher for Twelve Years* (New York: J. C. Totten, 1813), 104-5.

abound. Sensuality, alas! of every kind, but particularly that which arises from intemperance in the use of distilled liquors, soils and defiles the soul, fills it full of impure desires, and turns the human nature, capable of the image of God, into a loathsome beast.[47]

Itinerant preacher Ezekiel Cooper can find no positive aspect to drinking as he details all the dangers to society, church, home, and individual persons.

Evils of spirituous liquors

I. To a nation in civil society
  1. The great consumption of wealth: too much sunk in the immense expense of importing
  2. The loss of time among the citizens in drinking in their assembling, etc.
  3. The corruption of morals, etc.
  4. The broils and contests which originate in the intemperate use of it
  5. The disqualification of men for their various duties in different offices—judiciary, legislative and executive—also as physicians, also in maritime employ, and military

II. The religious society
  1. Prevents many from religion
  2. Turns many from the ways of piety
  3. Ruins many souls

III. In domestic society
  1. Brings families to waste
  2. [Brings persons] To disgrace often
  3. Creates distress and variance and brings on a chain of family disturbances between husbands and wives, parents and children

IV. Personal or bodily evils
  1. Ruins the health of many
  2. Transmits chronic diseases
  3. Entails pains, gouts, etc.
  4. Shortens the days of many
  5. Strips the senses and degrades the human creature to brutality[48]

---

47. *Doctrines and Discipline of the Methodist Episcopal Church* (1798), 138.
48. Ezekiel Cooper, "His Book," 104-5.

As with other ethical stances, Methodists showed their distrust of alcohol by concrete actions. In the following passage an Ohio circuit makes a specific rule about drinking on July 4. The passage is an example of Methodist suspicion about all sorts of common partying.

We the members of Quarterly Meeting Conference[49] held at Tilmon Luese's the 19th day of August 1809 do unanimously agree that the attending of barbecues and drinking of toasts on the 4th of July is contrary to the Spirit of Christianity and cannot be done to the glory of God.[50]

In the following records, a Delaware circuit disciplines ones of its members for drunkenness, suspending him from preaching for three months. Such instances were common. Later that year the circuit passes a rule against daily drinking.

Journal of the Quarterly Conference Held at Thoroughfare Neck 2 February 1805

In the case of Isaiah Rigs [there is] an accusation for swearing and drunkenness.

He denied the charge, and [after] an investigation he was found guilty of such impropriety as to suspend his official office for 3 months.[51]

Journal of Quarterly Conference Held at D[uck] Creek Crossroads 23 July 1805

Resolved that the Conference oppose by precept and example the daily use of spirituous liquors.[52]

SLAVERY AND MANUMMISSION

The history of early American Methodists' response to slavery is a difficult story. Over time there was a gradual lessening of the initially rigorous

---

49. The quarterly meeting conference was the administrative body for the circuit. It consisted of both clergy and laity.

50. Hockhocking Circuit, Book of Records, 19 August 1809.

51. Smyrna Circuit and Old Union Church, Quarterly Meeting Conference Record Book, 2 February 1805.

52. Ibid., 23 July 1805.

stance against slavery. Nonetheless, in the first fifty years of American Methodism, there remained a strong presumption against slavery, particularly in cruel and unrestricted forms. The following reflects some of the reasons some Methodists thought slavery a harsh injustice. It is a hymn exhorting slave owners to understand the institution from their slaves' perspective by listening to their prayer.

1 Slave holders, stop awhile, forbear,
And listen to the Negroes' prayer:
"Lord, if thou in equality
View all the sons of Adam die,

2 Why do thou hide thy face from slaves,
Here bound by fate to serve the knaves,
First stole away from Africa,
Transported to America,

3 Like hogs or sheep at market sold,
To stand exposed to heat and cold,
And after all the tedious round,
At night to stretch upon the ground,

4 To work all day and half the night,
And rise before the morning light,
Sustain the lash, endure the pain,
Exposed to storms of wind and rain?

5 Although our skins be black as jet,
Our hair all curled, our noses flat,
Shall we from this no freedom have
Until we find it in the grave?

6 When will Jehovah hear our cries?
When will the son of freedom rise?
When will a Moses for us stand
And free us all from Pharaoh's hand?"[53]

In a 1791 essay published in The Maryland Journal, *itinerant preacher Ezekiel Cooper responds to an earlier essay published in the same*

---

53. Collection of Spiritual Songs (Winchester, Ky.), 17.

journal under the pseudonym "Lawyer." Whereas "Lawyer" had argued for slavery, Cooper argues vehemently against it. For Cooper, slavery violates Scripture in several ways, not the least of which is that it contradicts the Golden Rule. Cooper insists that using biblical examples of slavery to condone American slavery overlooks that a new gospel dispensation has begun in Christ.

I am surprised at Lawyer, that he should fly to the Holy Scriptures (the very book, which teaches us the eternal rule of justice) in order to vindicate the violation of the law of God in nature and, thereby, strive to justify men in their arbitrary despotism over the rights and liberties of their fellow creatures. This is the very book, gentlemen, that teaches us to "do unto all men, as we would wish, they should do unto us."[54] It teaches us to let the oppressed go free and shows unto us the danger of oppression. (See Ecclesiastes 4:1, Isaiah 1:17, Proverbs 22:31. Numerous texts could readily be brought in favor of this cause.) But to return to Lawyer's arguments. He certainly did not reflect that, since bond servants were allowed of as slaves in Scripture, the dispensation of God's people is changed.... Would Lawyer presume to vindicate the customs of ancient times as justifiable now? Would he say, that the laws, or rules, of the Jews in the letter should be enforced now? Then we must have a king as well as a slave. God allowed them to have monarchs—not that monarchy or slavery was providentially intended from the beginning.[55]

Twenty years later Daniel Coker, an African American preacher in Baltimore, takes Cooper's scriptural argument to a higher level. Arguing against the suggestion of a Virginian proponent of slavery that the Apostle Paul condoned slavery, Coker (the "Minister") insists not only that "perpetual, unconditional slavery" contradicts the Golden Rule, but that this kind of slavery cannot abide with broader scriptural principles of justice.

Minister: No sir, for I would observe, that, although the apostle [Paul] acted with this prudent reserve the unreasonableness of

---

54. This is Cooper's version of the Golden Rule. See Matthew 7:12 and Luke 6:31.
55. Ezekiel Cooper to Mrs. Goddard and Angell, "To the Maryland Journal &c," 18 April 1791, Ezekiel Cooper papers (vol. 20, ms. 9).

perpetual, unconditional slavery, may be easily inferred from the righteous and benevolent doctrines and duties taught in the New Testament. It is very evident that slavery is contrary to the spirit and nature of the Christian religion. It is contrary to that most excellent precept laid down by the Divine Author of the Christian establishment, that is, "Whatsoever ye would that men should do to you, do ye even so to them; for this is the law and the prophets." Matthew 7:12... is a precept that is finely calculated to teach the duties of justice, to enforce their obligations, and [to] persuade the mind to obedience so that nothing can excel it. No man, when he views the hardships and misery, the boundless labors, the unreasonable punishments, the separation between loving husbands and wives, between affectionate parents and children, can say, in truth, [that] "Were I in their place, I should be contented" [or] that would say, "I so far approve of such usage as to believe [that] the law that subjects me to it is perfectly right [and] that I and my offspring should be denied the protection of law and yet by the same law be bound to suffer all these calamities although I never forfeited my freedom nor merited such cruel treatment more than others." No sir. There is a viceregent in our breasts that bears testimony against this, as unreasonable and wicked: "He hath shewed thee, O man, what is good; and what doth the Lord require of thee, but to do justly, and love mercy, and to walk humbly with thy God" Micah 6:8.[56]

Some of the more zealous preachers who critiqued slavery must have become frustrated at times. In the following journal entry, itinerant preacher William Jessop seems almost satisfied that a slave buyer suddenly died while bidding on a slave in 1790. Jessop hopes this served as a warning to others.

This evening brother C. informed me of a remarkable circumstance that happened lately in the neighborhood. A certain old gentleman was at a venue where there were a number of poor black people set up for sale. There were some men present who were friends to freedom. [They] found their hearts much tendered by rea-

---

56. Daniel Coker, *A Dialogue Between a Virginian and an African Minister* (Baltimore: Benjamin Edes, 1810), 24-26. See Lyerly, *Methodism and the Southern Mind*, 70-71 for the historical context of this publication.

son of the cries and lamentations of the distressed beings [and] were engaged in fixing upon certain measures to procure the freedom of those distressed mortals. But the old gentleman above mentioned greatly opposed them and, while standing in the door of the house bidding for one of the Negroes ... was in a moment struck speechless, fell down, was taken up, and carried to a bed. And the same night [he] was a breathless corpse. It is hoped this circumstance will be a warning to those who are great advocates for slavery.[57]

Similarly, in this December 1801 passage, itinerant preacher William Colbert is very harsh in his opinion of a woman slave owner who deceived her slaves. Tricking them into thinking they were being moved, she intended instead to sell them. Colbert thinks the women slaves' desire to drown with their children rather than be sold is heroic. In his mind, the wrong resides with the slave owner, not the slaves.

I preached at Curtis' meetinghouse, with a degree of freedom from Luke 16:9. Here, thank God, I was enabled to scourge the sons and daughters of oppression, those infernal drovers of the human race. May we not suppose that clouds of vengeance are collecting over the heads of the inhabitants of this country for their cruelty [to] the poor distressed Africans? I have been informed of a number of the poor blacks being sold by one who is called a young "lady," but may be considered a young devil, dressed in a garment of flesh and blood.... [She sent her slaves] to an island in the Chesapeake Bay, where they could be taken by the Negro buyer at a signal being given, who was to deceive them by telling them they were to be taken to Baltimore. But, when they were shipped, they found they were going down the Bay instead of sailing up [to Baltimore], at which some of the women heroically ... with their children in their arms, leapt into the Bay and became eternally free from their oppressors. "O earth and seas cover not their blood."[58]

Earlier Colbert reflects on some criticism he received for including black Methodists under the common terms all Methodists usually held for each other: brother and sister. Colbert attributes to sinful pride the refusal by some 1796 white Methodists to address blacks with these terms.

---

57. William Jessop, Journal, 20 January 1790 (St. George's).
58. William Colbert, Journal, 4:48.

My feelings have been hurt in this place, when I ... was spoken to for calling the Black people "Brethren" and "Sisters" here and in Milford, although I do not remember that I did call them "Brethren" and "Sisters" but when I spoke to them collectively. And I know not what objection can be brought to speaking to them in this manner, seeing that, God "has made of one blood all nations of men, for to dwell on all the face of the earth."[59] And, although it is urged that calling them "Brother" and "Sister" will make them proud, I fear their [i.e., the complainers] unwillingness to call them Brother and Sister springs from pride. I know that from their [the black Methodists] education that care ought to be taken to keep them humble, but, at the same time, it ought not be forgotten that they are men of like passions with ourselves. And, as men and Christians, they ought not to be spoken to like brutes or slaves. The great Apostle Paul thought not himself too good to own Onesimus, whom he had begotten in his bonds, and call him his son. And, when he sent him back to his master Philemon, Philemon was exhorted to receive him not as a servant, but as a brother.[60] And why should we from the color of our skin look upon ourselves too good to call one of the sable[61] race "Brother" or "Sister"?[62]

Colbert had seen such obstinacy by some white Methodists before. In the following journal passage, recorded as he rode the Harford circuit (Maryland) in 1791, Colbert tells about the attitude of one Methodist slave owner.

I preached at Thomas Hill's on Proverbs 29:16 [and] met the class.[63] And, as there was one that held slaves, I spoke to him about it, but he said that, "God Almighty gave them to him, and he intended to keep them." But [I] told him that God Almighty never gave them to him. In the afternoon I met a class at Gunpowder Chapel and spoke to some there on the impropriety of slave holding, but they do not appear to be willing to give them up.[64]

---

59. Acts 17:26.
60. Colbert is referring to the story behind the biblical book Philemon.
61. Sable is the color black.
62. William Colbert, Journal, 2:84.
63. Colbert is referring to meeting with a class meeting. Itinerants met with classes in order to discover the quality of faith and piety among Methodists.
64. William Colbert, Journal, 1:45.

During this period Methodists who purchased slaves were required to bring the details of the purchase to his or her quarterly meeting conference. These conferences considered the sex and age of the slave, his or her physical condition, and the amount paid. The conference then ruled on how long the slave had to serve. The Methodist slave owner was required to draft a writ of manumission allowing for the slave's freedom at the end of that period and to show it to the quarterly meeting conference. His or her failure to abide by the decision of the quarterly meeting conference could result in expulsion or other punishment. The following are minutes of such determinations by various quarterly meeting conferences, starting with the Harford circuit where Colbert had had such trouble.

At a quarterly meeting conference held at the Fork meeting house on the 24th day of November 1800. The business then settled by said conference is as follows, namely:

1st) James Deaver's Negro man be liberated in seven years from the above date;

2nd) Joshua Durlanger's Negro woman be liberated in five years from the above date;

3rd) Thomas Bond produced a certificate that he had liberated his Negro woman according to the determination of a quarterly conference held at the Fork meeting house in August 1799.[65]

Perhaps reflecting the stubbornness about slavery that Colbert had earlier experienced on this circuit, it took the quarterly meeting conference over a year to gain the compliance of Jesse Jarrett concerning manumission of a nine-year-old slave named only as Tom.

[Quarterly Conference held at Bush Chapel July 2, 1803.]

Resolved that Jesse Jarrett manumit his Negro boy, Tom (which he bought of Patience Watters) to be free when he arrives at 27 years of age, he the said boy being at this time about nine years old.

[At the next quarterly meeting held at Abingdon Chapel on 8 October 1803.]

William Smith (a steward) [is] appointed to inquire of Jesse Jarrett the cause why he has not complied with the rule and resolve of [the] last quarterly conference respecting the manumission of his boy called Tom.

---

65. Harford Circuit Quarterly Meeting Conference Records, 24 November 1800.

[Finally, Jarrett complies in November 1804.]

At a quarterly meeting held November 3 and 4, 1804, Jesse Jarrett presented a [writ of] manumission liberating his boy Tom agreeably to the foregoing resolve.[66]

The same procedure was followed in other circuits. Note these examples from a variety of quarterly meeting conferences.

On the application of Benjamin Bowen, a local preacher of our church, to adjudge the time of a Negro woman named Nan, purchased by him for the sum of forty pounds, this conference, after considering the matter fully, are of [the] opinion that the said woman shall serve the time of eight years from the time of purchase.[67]

Q[uestion] 4. Are there any slaves lately purchased to be submitted to the judgment of this conference?

A[nswer]. Brother John Bloodgood purchased a black woman named Rachel, aged twenty three years, and a child named Nicholas, aged two years [for the] price [of] three hundred dollars. The Conference adjudged the woman to serve twelve years from the time of purchase and the child until he is thirty years of age.[68]

James L. Higgins bought a black man named Isaac, age about nineteen years and cost him four hundred dollars. The determination of the conference was that Isaac should serve eighteen years.[69]

[Concerning] James Raymond in the purchase of a Negro named Benjamin, aged 21-22 years old, for which he paid 80 pounds, submitted to this conference to determine what time he shall serve. And it is agreed that he shall serve 6 years and 6 months from time of purchase.

[Concerning] Isaiah Rigs in the purchase of [a] Negro [named] Joseph, age 16 years old in May 1804. [It is determined that he is] to serve 10 years from [the] time of purchase.

---

66. Ibid., 6-7.

67. Baltimore Circuit Steward's Book 1794–1815, 20 June 1801 (pp. 53-54).

68. Great Falls (Maryland) Circuit Quarterly Meeting Conference Minutes, 16-17 December 1809.

69. Frederick (Maryland) Circuit, Proceedings of the Quarterly Conferences, 7 June 1806.

Ditto [Concerning Isaiah Rigs' purchase of] William Davis, a Black man, aged 17 the first of last March. [It is determined that he is] to serve 10 years from [the] time of purchase.

Resolved that every person produce a certificate of emancipation in all the cases determined by this conference in 3 months from such determination.[70]

In the case of George Wesket and Negroes, Bridget and [her] child George. The conference resolved that Bridget shall be free 1 January 1817 and that George, her child, [shall] serve until 1 January 1840 and that George Wesket lay before the next Quarterly Meeting Conference a certificate of said Negroes' emancipation.[71]

It is further determined that James Deems do emancipate the Negro woman aged thirty-eight years, for which he gave one hundred and seventy-five dollars at the expiration of twelve years, provided the said woman have no children, but, if she should have any, they shall be liberated agreeable to the rules of the Methodist Church, and the above obligations shall be void.[72]

Sometimes civil law restrained the power of quarterly meeting conference to ensure set times were established for manumission of slaves, as in this 1807 case in the Baltimore circuit.

Stone Chapel, 26 and 27 December 1807. William Stevenson applied to have adjudged the time of two slaves he has purchased both above the age of 45 years for the sum of $111, one of them named Abel, the other called Maria. This Conference considering the law [that] prohibits their being set free after the above age have left a discretionary power with him to act agreeable to the rules and regulations of our Church.[73]

Occasionally the administrative records of the quarterly meeting conferences provide evidence of Methodists granting manumission of slaves—

---

70. Smyrna Circuit (Delaware) and Old Union Church Quarterly Meeting Conference Record Book, 20 December 1805.

71. Accomack (Virginia) Circuit Quarterly Meeting Conference records, 31 August and 1 September 1816.

72. Tar River (North Carolina) Circuit Quarterly Meeting Conference records, 6-7 July 1800.

73. Baltimore Circuit Steward's Book 1794–1815, 111.

either at the end of their agreed service or on purchase. The following comes from the records of the Berkley circuit.

Jefferson County, Virginia. I, Thomas Keyes, do hereby release and discharge the following slave, Dinah, who was give by David Osborne to my wife Margaret Keyes, from all manner of servitude or bondage of servitude and that as fully and clearly as myself might or could have held her in bondage or slavery. Given under my hand and seal this twenty-second day of February in the year of our Lord one thousand eight hundred and fourteen.[74]

Quarterly meeting records can also evidence disciplinary action taken by the conference against members who violate certain ethical norms about slavery. A good example comes from the Baltimore circuit.

Stone Chapel, 12 and 13 February 1803. Thomas Bennet was excluded from society at this quarterly meeting for selling a Negro man for life.

Gatch's Chapel, 12 and 13 November 1803. Benjamin Bowen, a local preacher and class leader, was suspended from all official duties in the church at this quarterly meeting for six months for whipping a Negro man immoderately.[75]

The prominence of—and tensions over—the issue of slavery among early Methodists grew over time. A sense of matters toward the end of the period of our focus can be gleaned from the records of the Madison circuit in Kentucky. By 1812 the quarterly meeting conference could routinely ratify the purchase of slaves for the seemingly humane motive of making possible their eventual emancipation.

At a Quarterly Meeting Conference for Madison Circuit at Matthew Markland's on Saturday February 13, 1812.

1st) The Case of Brother Reuben Hatton's buying a Negro came before the Conference. And a large majority of them [i.e., the quarterly meeting conference] are of [the] opinion that Brother Hatton has bought the Negro through motives of mercy and humanity.

---

74. Berkley Circuit Steward's Book 1807–1820, 50.
75. Ibid., 67.

2nd) Brother Bennett's case came before the Conference concerning his buying three Negroes, to wit, a woman and her two children. And, as Brother Bennett says his intention is to set her children free after they make him compensation, the majority is of the opinion that his motives were humane and merciful.[76]

The Madison circuit records also reveal that the conference was faced with Methodist slave owners who resisted the expectation of eventual manumission. Consider the case of Nathaniel Tevis, dealt with in fall 1813 through spring 1814.

Presley Morris gave information to the conference that Nathaniel Tevis has purchased a Negro, and he has not been cited to appear before this conference. Therefore the conference lays it over till the next Quarterly Conference....

The case of Nathaniel Tevis respecting his purchasing a slave was at the last quarterly meeting conference laid over until this conference and said Tevis has not attended to the same. And, furthermore, Brother James McMahon has stated to the conference that in a conversation with Brother Tevis he indicated to him that he meant to retain the slave in servitude, in consequence of which the Conference determines that the preacher who has the charge of the circuit deal with him according to the rule respecting slavery.[77]

Similarly, in 1815 the quarterly meeting conference had to vote to expel J. Bennett from membership in the church before he was willing to comply with Methodist guidelines on slavery.

Again the report of the Committee referred from the last to the present Quarterly Meeting Conference in the case of Brother J. Bennett. And the said committee reports that he has purchased a Negro girl and the Conference has confirmed the report of the committee. And, in consequence of his refusing to comply with the rule on slavery, [he] is expelled [from] the society. Brother J. Pace in behalf of J. Bennett signifies to the conference that brother J. Bennett means to appeal his case to the Annual Conference....

76. Madison Circuit Quarterly Meeting Conference records 1810–1825, 3.
77. Ibid., 11-12, 14.

Brother Bennett, who was expelled from society for refusing to comply with the rule on slavery, submitted his case to the Quarterly Meeting Conference [concerning] a Negro girl named Sarah of 18 years of age for which he gave 370 dollars. He proposed that the said girl should serve 20 years and the Conference thinks the proposal reasonable, and, in consequence of this compliance, the Conference agrees to restore him to his former privileges in the church.[78]

78. Ibid., 16, 19.

CHAPTER 8

CHURCH FELLOWSHIP, DISCIPLINE, AND EXPULSION

Two of the most important terms in an early Methodist's vocabulary—connection and conference—hint at the importance of fellowship for Methodist spirituality. While both terms had technical meanings with respect to outward administrative structures, they also disclose the high view early Methodists had of how interacting with other Christians cultivated growth in God's grace. Methodists were connected to one another, and in so being sharpened and raised one another to new spiritual heights. They held conference with one another, and in so doing heard God speak a gracious word.

Methodists' experience of one another in the various ways they assembled reinforced the notion that Christian fellowship was an important arena for meeting God. God's grace was "social grace," to use the phrase from Charles Wesley, another of Methodism's founders.[1] In early Methodist understanding, spiritual power was directly tied to the quality of their fellowship. This conviction that had begun with Methodism's British founders carried over to early American Methodists, as their administrative manual inquired: "If

---

1. *A Collection of Hymns for the Use of the People called Methodists*, Hymn #507, st. 1, *Works of John Wesley* (Abingdon Press), 7:698.

we are united, what can stand before us? If we divide, we shall destroy ourselves, the work of God, and the souls of our people."[2]

Not surprisingly, early Methodists zealously dedicated time, energy, and resources to the development of structures that cultivated a unified, holy fellowship. In contrast to later forms of denominational structure, there were virtually no early Methodist programs or activities that did not relate directly to creation of community and its spiritual vitality in worship and evangelism.[3] Organization was for spiritual vitality.

The basic building blocks of Methodist fellowship were two kinds of small groups: class meetings and band meetings. Of the two, class meetings were the most prevalent and important.[4] Class meetings were required of all members. Ideally composed of around twelve members, they often reached much larger sizes. Their makeup varied. Sometimes they mixed genders and races, at other times members were separated by gender and race.[5] Classes also mixed people at various points of their spiritual experiences, an important part of their internal dynamic. Because an experience of conversion was not needed for Methodist membership (only a desire for salvation), serious seekers and inquirers were often grouped with members who could offer vivid testimony to justification and sanctification experiences. The presence of those further along in the Methodist order of salvation provided impetus and examples for those desiring the same experiences of grace. The extent of class meetings was quite large. By one historian's estimate, there might have been seven thousand class meetings in 1815.[6]

A class leader provided oversight. David Watson has suggested that the class leader was the "pivotal figure in early Methodist spirituality."[7] Class leaders supervised the weekly class meeting and visited its members' homes. An average Methodist received most

---

2. *Doctrines and Discipline of the Methodist Episcopal Church* (1798), 107.

3. For more on the spiritual vitality of early Methodist polity, see Richey, *Methodist Conference in America.*

4. An in-depth, recent study of American class meetings is Philip F. Hardt, *The Soul of Methodism: The Class Meeting in Early New York City Methodism* (Lanham: University Press of America, 2000).

5. Wigger, *Taking Heaven by Storm,* 84.

6. Ibid., 81.

7. David Lowes Watson, "Methodist Spirituality," in *Protestant Spiritual Traditions,* ed. Frank C. Senn (New York and Mahwah: Paulist Press, 1986), 232.

of her or his spiritual direction and pastoral care from the class leader, not the ever-traveling itinerant preacher. Although mainly men, some women served as class leaders.

Band meetings differed from class meetings in several respects. John Wesley's original purpose had been to gather small, tightly bound groups of "professors" to assist each other toward the goal of sanctification. The tone was more intense and confessional. Bands were either all men or all women. Participating in a band was optional for Methodists, and, it appears, most never belonged to one. By one estimate, fewer than 5 percent of the members in New York City in the 1790s belonged to a band.[8] This percentage was probably even lower for more rural circuits.

Early Methodists relied on several types of meetings to enhance the work of these small groups. Some of these were public meetings, open to all, and others were restricted to members except by permission. Class and band meetings were private in this manner, as were "society meetings," which gathered all the Methodists in a locale (that is, all the class and band members). Certain kinds of worship services were also restricted to members. The physical act of separating to meet added a visual dimension to the bounds of Methodist membership. It highlighted the notion of distinctiveness from the world, while still allowing the "world" to see clearly what Methodist community could be like. At its best, the dynamic between public and private meetings allowed Methodists to act out the grace-filled nature of a Christian people, offering the same as part of the gospel promise. As Russell Richey has put it, sometimes "their community was the message."[9]

The dynamics of Methodism's small groups—class meetings especially—were the seedbed for much of their spiritual vitality. The basic elements of discipline, separation, and boundary-setting, combined with testimony and intense communion, created a "sort of fusion reactor of the spirit."[10] Both meetings followed a common routine. In a class meeting, after an opening hymn and prayer, the class leader gave a statement on her or his spiritual condition and how she or he had fared during the previous week. The leader then

---

8. Hardt, *The Soul of Methodism*, 35.
9. Richey, *Early American Methodism*, 29. Richey's entire book describes the graced quality of early Methodist fellowship.
10. A. Gregory Schneider, *Way of the Cross*, xxvi.

examined each member in turn, asking how her or his "soul had prospered." The leader and class would offer direction, counsel, or encouragement as appropriate. The band meeting was marked by a more direct, confessional nature. These meetings explored the inward state of the member more deeply and intensely.

Affectionate Methodist fellowship was both appealing and countercultural. Given a context where honor and status were the building blocks of relationship (see chapter 7), the basing of human relationships on grace that moved the heart was striking, even contagious. Thus the embodying of a community of grace was part of the appeal of Methodism. As Russell Richey has noted, "For early Methodists, community was itself intensely spiritual, contagiously so, a spreading fire of love and holy zeal."[11] Since many of those drawn to Methodism had experienced disrupted ties in their previous social relationships, finding an affectionate fellowship was especially appealing.[12] A Methodist's experience of this fellowship was often connected directly to her or his experience of God.

Early Methodists had several ways for expressing how meaningful their fellowship was to their spiritual experience. One was the vocabulary they used to name each other. When speaking individually, they used family and friendship labels. The typical collective term for their fellowship, Zion, was likewise evocative. Pulled from Old Testament accounts of God's people, it suggested that Methodists saw their fellowship as part of the total scope of God's redemptive activity.[13] The direct relating of their fellowship to heaven was another way Methodists had of revealing the meaning of their common life (see chapter 4). In their estimation, the heart-bound fellowship of a holy people revealed heaven on earth.

Having a disciplined fellowship mediate their experience of God played an important role in maintaining balance in early Methodist spirituality. As noted in chapter 6, they tended to emphasize direct, unmediated experiences of God. The insistence on disciplined fellowship rooted Christian experience in a broader basis than just what one had inwardly felt. Without it, there was the danger of making feelings themselves the end of Christianity, a self-validat-

11. Richey, *Early American Methodism*, 3.
12. Heyrman, *Southern Cross*, 124 and 127.
13. Richey, *Early American Methodism*, 42-44.

ing measure of whether one had truly encountered God. At its best, early Methodist fellowship helped place direct inward experience in a broader context of remembrance and practices (the "means of grace" or the "ordinances of God," to use the language of the General Rules) that gave distinctive identity to the God they claimed to have experienced.[14] To make sure this occurred was the intent of discipline in Methodist fellowship. Of course, ultimate integrity depended on how closely the fellowship itself kept to those practices that revealed the distinctive identity of God and the broader history of God's saving work.[15] The same group dynamics could be used to create inward, affective experience apart from the classic content of the Christian faith. That was why it was crucial for early Methodist fellowship to be disciplined toward the classic means of Scripture, Lord's Supper, and a full diet of prayer in public worship centered on a broad remembrance of God.

Beyond the use of small groups, Methodists had other means of enforcing discipline in their fellowship. A probationary quality to membership was one means. Methodists accepted new members on probationary status (initially for a period of two months, changed in 1789 to a period of six months), after which a decision was made on whether to accept the probationer for full membership. Acceptance was not automatic. A kind of probationary status continued for all members in that every quarter the chief itinerant preacher in the circuit or station was to renew the membership ticket for each member. The ticket was necessary to gain admission to love feasts and other private meetings.

Church trials served as the most severe form of discipline. Such trials were not unique to Methodism, but the way that Methodists conducted them did reflect distinctive elements in their organization and ethos.[16] Cases were brought and people expelled for a variety of failures in conduct or in steadfastness with respect to attending class meetings, worship, and the Lord's Supper. The church's instructional manual seemed to make a difference between serious offenses seen as "expressly forbidden by the word

---

14. Knight, *Presence of God*, 11-15.

15. Compare Randy L. Maddox, "Social Grace: the Eclipse of the Church as a Means of Grace in American Methodism," in *Methodism in its Cultural Milieu*, ed. Timothy Macquiban (Oxford: Applied Theology Press, 1994), 132-39 to Knight, *Presence of God*.

16. James L. Lubach and Thomas L. Shanklin, "Abitrations and Trials of Members in the Methodist Episcopal Church: 1776–1860," *Methodist History* 9, 4 (July 1971): 36.

of God, [and] sufficient to exclude a person from the kingdom of grace and glory, and to make him [sic] a subject of wrath and hell"[17] and less serious offenses. They brought few trials on doctrinal matters.[18]

As with many issues in early Methodism, the reasons for conducting such trials seem connected to their concerns for salvation. In one way, such discipline was necessary for the salvation of individual members. Methodists thought that one could regress in grace as well as advance. There were no static states of grace in Methodist spirituality. Thus there needed to be disciplinary measures that could show the seriousness of how certain evil actions stalled advancement in grace.

In other ways, such rigorous discipline was needed for communal aspects of salvation. Since internal unity and harmony were such important qualities to early Methodists, an inability to rid the community of those who threatened the common ethos was potentially disastrous. They did not fear using measures that expelled those whose actions resulted in a schism of ethos. Surely they related this concern to how they understood their community as witness to the surrounding sinful world. "We will have a holy people, or none," exclaimed the bishops in their rationale for church trials.[19]

Methodism was not always at its best. There were problems in Methodist discipline. Different itinerant preachers enforced discipline inconsistently, even at the level of restricting access to class meetings and love feasts. At other times, despite their best intents, disciplinary actions and trials demonstrated the same characteristics of power, insult, and honor that belonged to the surrounding culture.[20]

The following excerpts show the ecstasy of Methodist fellowship as well as its moments of agony. The first two sets of material emphasize the former, under the headings of "the bonds of Christian love" and the "heavenly quality" of that fellowship. The remainder of the collection offers a sense of the rigorous discipline of Methodist fellowship, in part by consulting journal accounts and the administrative records from circuits.

---

17. *Doctrines and Discipline of the Methodist Episcopal Church* (1798), 161.
18. Kirby, et al., *The Methodists*, 167-68.
19. *Doctrines and Discipline of the Methodist Episcopal Church* (1798), 167.
20. Schneider, *Way of the Cross*, 86.

THE BONDS OF CHRISTIAN LOVE

This hymn, written by an anonymous author, celebrates the close sense of loving fellowship Methodists often experience among themselves. It raises a theme often recurring in early Methodist piety: a fellowship characterized by love here anticipates the life of heaven.

From whence doth this union arise
That hatred is conquered by love?
It fastens our souls in such ties
That nature nor time can remove.

It cannot in Eden be found
Nor yet in a paradise be lost.
It grows on Emanuel's ground
And Jesus' dear blood it did cost.

My friends are so dear unto me,
Our hearts so united in love.
Where Jesus is gone, we shall be
In yonder blest mansions above.

Oh! Then why so loath for to part
Since we shall ere long meet again?
Engraved on Emanuel's heart
At a distance we cannot remain.

Oh! When shall we see that bright day
And join with the angels above,
Leaving those vile bodies of clay,
United with Jesus in love?
With Jesus we ever shall reign
And all his sweet glory shall see.
Sing "Hallelujah, amen."
Amen, even so let it be.[21]

Writing to Bishop Asbury, presiding elder Shadrach Bostwick describes the loving unity experienced among Methodists in New England in 1799.

---

21. Henry Bradford, Hymnbook, 20.

Our quarterly meetings have been rendered singularly useful ...this year, and our friends seem much united, both to their preachers, discipline, one another, and to their Lord. I have the happiness to inform you that a spirit of love and union, both to doctrine, discipline, and each other subsists amongst all our preachers in this district. I have conversed freely and particularly with them, and I believe there is not a jarring string.[22]

Another anonymous hymn in Henry Bradford's manuscript hymnal exults in this sense of loving unity Methodists found in Jesus Christ. This hymn is also found in the manuscript hymnal collected by Edward Dromgoole, a prominent local preacher in southern Virginia. The lyrics as found in Dromgoole's hymnal are placed in parentheses.

Our hearts by love together knit
(Our hearts by love to Jesus knit),
Cemented, mixed in one (Cemented, joined in one).
One hope, one heart, one mind, one voice,
'Tis heaven on earth begun.
Our hearts did burn while tears spake
(Our hearts did burn while Jesus spake)
And glowed with sacred fire.
He stopped and talked and fed and blessed
And filled the enlarged desire.

Chorus
A Savior let creation sing
(O Savior, let creation sing).
A Savior let all heaven ring
(O Savior, let all heaven ring).
He's God with us, we feel him ours.
His fullness in our souls he pours.
'Tis almost done, 'tis almost o'er,
We are joining them that gone before
(We are joining those who are gone before).

---

22. *Extracts of Letters*, 9-10.

We then shall meet to part no more.
We then shall meet to part no more.

We are soldiers fighting for our God
(We're soldiers ...).
Let trembling cowards fly.
We'll stand unshaken firm and fixed
With Christ to live and die.
Let devils rage and hell assail.
We'll force our passage through
(We'll cut our passage through).
Let foes unite and friend desert.
We'll seize the crown our due.

Chorus

The little cloud increases still.
The heavens are big with rain.[23]
Well haste to catch the teaming showers
And all the moisture drain (And all the blessing gain).
Arise a stream, a torrent flows
But pour the mighty flood
O sweep the nations, shake the earth,
'Till all proclaim thee God.

Chorus

And when thou makes thy jewels up
And sets the starry crown (... thy starry crown),
When all thy sparkling gems shall shine
Proclaimed by thee thine own,
May we a little band of love,
Sinners saved by grace (Be sinners saved by grace),
From glory into glory shine
(From glory into glory changed),

---

23. Compare 1 Kings 18:44.

Proclaimed by thee thine own
(Behold thee face to face).[24]

One of the foundations for Methodist fellowship was the weekly class meeting. Here Methodists gathered for accountability and nurture, for prayer and spiritual guidance. The following hymn, simply entitled "Class Meeting" from New York Methodist Ebenezer Hill's manuscript hymnal rejoices in the sense of Jesus' presence in the midst of class meeting fellowship.

Ye children of the heavenly king
Before your Father bow.
With humble souls your off'rings bring
And pay your solemn vow.

He loves to hear his children pray,
To hear their songs of praise.
Come, he will feed your souls today
To him your voices raise.

From heaven to earth he comes to see,
To meet his children here,
With blessings all divinely free
Their drooping souls to cheer.

Temptations, darkness, fear, or doubt
All flee before his face.
His presence drives the tempter out
From this devoted place.
Make known your want of every kind
By prayer unlock the store.
A balm for every wound you'll find,
Wine, oil for every sore.

---

24. Henry Bradford, Hymnbook, 15; and Spiritual Songs (Edward Dromgoole papers), 15.

Refreshing dews of heavenly love
Fall round this little camp.
Come Holy Spirit, heavenly Dove,
Nor let yours joys be damp.

Celestial fire, consume the dross
And take away the tin.
Then will our longing souls rejoice
And triumph over sin.

Holy desires and heavenly peace
And consolation flow.
While faith and hope and love increase
Still more and more bestow.[25]

Despite the wonder many experienced in class meetings, not all Methodists were faithful in attendance. Itinerant preacher John Littlejohn threatens Methodists in 1778 to attend as the membership standards require.

I called the members together and told them plainly they must meet in class or be disowned. It were better to be without rule than not to keep rule.
[Four days later he adds:]
I called for the class papers[26] and find since April last some had only met 2, 3, 7, 8, [or] 9 times. [I] gave them a class paper, a faithful warning, and a serious admonition to beware of unfaithfulness.[27]

Methodist organizational rules required that new members join on a probationary status. Significantly, a saving experience was not required, only a desire "to flee from the wrath to come, and to be saved from their sins."[28] Thus "unconverted" seekers, who accepted the specific responsibilities

---

25. Ebenezer Hills hymnal, Hymn 44, Ezekiel Cooper papers (vol. 24).
26. Attendance was kept on class papers.
27. John Littlejohn, Journal, 121-22.
28. From the General Rules. See *Doctrines and Discipline of the Methodist Episcopal Church* (1798), 133.

of Methodist membership, also enjoyed Methodist fellowship. New York Methodist William Keith relates the complaints he heard about this practice, comparing them to the complaints leveled against Jesus for his fellowship practices. Keith explains how his doubts were eliminated by seeing how probationary fellowship can actually create deeper conversion experiences.

About this time there were some who strove to convince me that the Methodists were a deluded people. Their chief argument was, that we received people into our church who were unconverted or in other words: "This man receiveth sinners and eateth with them" (Luke 15:2). I pondered it in my mind until by vain reasoning I lost my comfortable exercises of grace.[29] But a circumstance occurred which removed my trials. Two young men joined our society, one of them was brought into liberty in such a manner that no person doubted his being born of God. The other could tell no other experience than this, that he had a desire to serve God. The one, however, whose experience was so great, soon fell into gross sins and was expelled; the other could daily tell of some exercises of grace which gave farther proof of his sincerity, until his experience became superior to the first. I then remembered the word of the Lord, which says, "him that is weak in the faith receive ye, but not to doubtful disputation" (Romans 14:1). And as we did not receive any into our church until we had seen their manner of life for six months, often speaking to them in class meeting and at other times, I concluded that a six months probation was a greater evidence than the relation of a great experience. My trials on this subject were therefore removed.[30]

Although "unsaved" persons could become members and participate in early Methodist fellowship, Methodists restricted access to certain kinds of meetings, particularly ones where fellowship is most important. Bishops Coke and Asbury explain the reason why access is denied to those who were spiritually "unawakened" and unwilling to abide by Methodist membership standards.

---

29. Keith means that he lost a sense of closeness to God and slipped away from his regular religious practices.

30. Keith, *Experience of William Keith*, 13.

The meeting of the society also, wherever practicable, is of considerable moment. There are various weighty subjects, peculiarly suitable to religious societies, which cannot be so well enlarged upon to a mixed congregation. Brotherly union and fellowship, Christian discipline in all its branches, and various other particulars may be enlarged upon and enforced with greater propriety and success on such occasions. At these times also we may enter more minutely into the different parts of the relative duties, than we can to unawakened souls, whose whole life is sin, and who are at the best only "like unto whited sepulchres, which indeed appear beautiful outward, but are within full of dead men's bones, and of all uncleanness."[31]

In another passage, Coke and Asbury again explain why keeping strangers from certain kinds of worship services and fellowship meetings is crucial to preserving Methodist fellowship as the occasion for revealing God's gracious presence.

It is manifestly our duty to fence in our society, and to preserve it from intruders, otherwise we should soon become a desolate waste. God would write Ichabod upon us, and the glory would be departed from Israel.[32] At the same time we should suffer those who are apparently sincere, if they request it, to see our order and discipline twice or thrice, that they themselves may judge whether it will be for their spiritual advantage to cast in their lot among us. But we should by no means exceed the indulgence here allowed, otherwise we should make our valuable meetings for Christian fellowship cheap and contemptible and bring a heavy burden on the minds of our brethren. Galatians 2:4-5, "Because of false brethren unawares brought in, who came in privily to spy out our liberty, which we have in Christ Jesus, that they might bring us into bondage: to whom we gave place by subjection, no, not for an hour." Ephesians 5:11, "have no fellowship with the unfruitful works of darkness."[33]

---

31. Matthew 23:27. *Doctrines and Discipline of the Methodist Episcopal Church* (1798), 121.
32. See 1 Samuel 4:21. "Ichabod" means "no glory." The biblical reference is to a time when the Philistines had captured the ark of God and thus God's glory had departed from Israel.
33. *Doctrines and Discipline of the Methodist Episcopal Church* (1798), 154.

Methodist itinerant preachers sometimes describe the difficulties in enforcing fellowship restrictions. In the following passage itinerant preacher William Ormond describes stubbornness of one disciplined member.

In class meeting (after preaching) a young woman by the name of Langly, who had been guilty of very bad acts, would intrude on us to stay in the room. I said much to her but it seemed to take but little effect. I then told Brother Watkins to put her out by force. After this was begun, she walked out and we had to shut the windows to prevent her peeping in.[34]

Itinerant preacher George Wells is determined to enforce restricted access to love feasts after his predecessors have been lax in the practice.

I feel poorly, but I determined to undertake and go through what lays before me through grace. The discipline of our church (respecting letting people into our love feasts) has been much relaxed within these three years. But now we are about to turn the tables and maintain our liberty as unspotted as we can well. I have to stand at the door so I took my place about half after 7 [a.m.] and maintained my post till 9. In the time one used violence and came in but Brother P, a local preacher, entreated him to go out peaceably. But he stood his ground until Brother P took of his great coat and intended to throw him out like a dog. He then went out peaceably. It was a good time. Several joined.[35]

Itinerant Ezekiel Cooper finds similar resistance at a 1785 meeting of the society in New York City.

I preached twice and met the society in the new church. I understood that some took offence at my requesting all but the members of society to withdraw. How very unreasonable are some men to be offended at what common sense tells us is right. It would be very unreasonable to let anybody and everybody stay, who would [stay], when we had something to say to the society only and alone.

---

34. William Ormond, Journal, 5 August 1791.
35. George Wells, Journal, 22 April 1792.

And, were we to admit one, then we must admit another. And where would we stop?[36]

Publicly expressing Methodist fellowship was not always so tension-filled. The following accounts describe a growing elaborateness to fellowship ceremonies at the end of camp meetings in 1806.

At length the last sermon was delivered and followed by exhortation, when the preachers, about twenty in number, drew up in a single line. And a procession was formed four deep, led by a preacher, in front of a number of little children singing hymns of praise and followed by hundreds who joined in the songs of Zion,[37] marching round the encampment. At first they passed behind the line of ministers, until the children headed by the preacher came up to it again, when every person formed in procession shook hands with all the ministers successively....

Souls filled with love are only parted in body, [since] their minds are united in one, [and] they cleave to one another in Jesus Christ, the common center of all true believers.[38]

The camp of Israel[39] had been a heaven from the preceding day; but now the rapture was heightened still more, all was joy and ecstasy of bliss, an emblem of the life of glory. Golden moments! ye are fled; for ye are not eternity. This feast of love, this heaven must end...refuses to stay; but arise, you who are bound to a heaven above the skies permanent and secure, and testify for God. Hundreds instantly arose, every hand was lifted up to heaven, and like the sound of many waters, the voice of the multitude broke forth; their violent bliss sent up to the listening skies the shouts of grateful praise....

The ministers, in number about thirty, formed in a line, and a vast multitude was arranged in procession four deep, the followers of the Lamb.[40] In their march, they encompassed once the

---

36. Ezekiel Cooper, Journal, 8 February 1785.
37. "Songs of Zion" refers to popular worship songs that reflect the people's piety.
38. Ward, *Account of Three Camp-Meetings*, 8.
39. "Camp of Israel" refers to the campground filled with the church, the New Israel.
40. That is, followers of Jesus Christ, the Lamb of God.

area within the tents, and then they all in rotation took their cordial farewell of the preachers, who parted from one another with most affectionate embraces. All beholders seemed struck with astonishment, their wondering eyes rapidly traversed the scene.[41]

At length the separation took place. Thrice the procession moved round the camp and the emotions of the people which formed it, and of the spectators also, were too powerful to be suppressed, above twenty preachers standing in a line to take their farewell of the people as they passed them; but when they began to embrace one another, a young woman who held out until then fell suddenly to the ground, and with two others persons was converted on the spot, after the dispersion of the multitude. Awakenings spread rapidly among those who remained. Numbers were crying for mercy, but few [remained] to pray with them. A messenger was dispatched for as many preachers as could return.[42]

CHRISTIAN FELLOWSHIP AS HEAVENLY

Describing the intense quality of their fellowship was often hard for early Methodists. A frequent approach was to characterize their fellowship here as an anticipation of heavenly fellowship, as we see in William Watters's description of a testimonial service.

Our love feast was one of the best I ever was in. We sat together in heavenly places, and, to express myself in the words which I immediately wrote down, I was as in a little Heaven below and believe Heaven above will differ more in quantity than in quality. Our eyes overflowed with tears and our hearts with love to God and each other. The holy fire, the heavenly flame, spread wider and wider, and rose higher and higher. O! happy people whose God is the Lord, may none of you ever weary in well doing. May we after having done the work allotted us, meet in our Father's Kingdom to tell the wonders of redeeming love and part no more.[43]

---

41. Ward, *Account of Three Camp-Meetings*, 15-16.
42. Ibid., 19.
43. William Watters, *Short Account*, 75-76.

The same sentiment can be sung. The following hymn describes the sweet bitterness Methodists often felt at the end of their meetings. It caused them to long for reunion in heaven where parting would be no more.

1. Come, saints, and help me sing
The praises of our God
For sending forth his only Son
To shed his precious blood.
To cleanse us from our sins,
When we were sunk in shame,
The Lamb of God he did appear
To take away our stain.

2. To Jesus Christ our king
Be glory ever given
By every Christian here below
And all the host of heaven.
For favors so divine
We'll praise him for his grace
Because he leads his pilgrims home
To heaven that happy place.

3. And when we there arrive
Our parting will be o'er.
We'll join the saints above the skies
And shout forever more,
"All glory to the Lamb."
'Til then let us endure
And help each other on our way
Toward that happy land.

4. But now we all must part
which grieves our hearts full sore.
But let each one his Jesus view
And pray forever more.
And onward move with haste,

The time is coming fast,
When we shall meet to part no more
And view our Jesus' face.

5. Yet while we wait below
Until the summons comes,
Let each of us remember well
Our unconverted friends.
And pray to God for them
For God will answer prayer
And save their souls from harmful hell
And out of deep despair.

6. Lord, save our souls from hell
From endless pain and woe
And give them life and happiness
While they do dwell below.
Then take them up to heaven,
Lord, hear our earnest cries
And give us all to live with thee
Above the starry skies.[44]

Lucy Watson speaks of the same anticipatory quality to Methodist fellowship but changes the image somewhat. In her description of a Methodist meeting, she looks over the Jordan River into the promised land, a biblical type for heavenly reunion.

[I] Awakened this morning with these words, "There is too much self-love." I begin to think I have been too indulgent to the flesh, [and] that I ought to have visited the sick and laid myself over more for doing to my fellow creations. Lord, give me strength and grace to double my diligence. Last night I had a melting time[45] at the Old Church.[46] [I] was permitted to look over Jordan and [to] see

---

44. Henry Bradford, Hymnbook, 3-4.
45. A standard Methodist phrase for a moving experience in worship.
46. Meaning the older of the Methodist meeting houses where Watson lived.

the goodly land and to rejoice in the anticipation of shortly meeting my friends on the happy banks of deliverance.[47]

Itinerant preacher Seely Bunn uses a similar image to describe his desire to meet British Methodists in heaven.

We have reason to adore his wisdom and goodness in so wonderfully keeping such a large body of us together, and that we so sweetly draw in one yoke and feel interested in our Master's cause, more than in all the paltry concerns of this world. We hope God is still owning his word in Europe.[48] It is a joy to us to hear of Zion's prosperity[49] on that side of the great ocean. We feel united to our brethren there in ties of the most endearing nature, and the thought of meeting them on the blissful shore of eternity is animating to our souls. We desire them to pray for us as we hope ever to pray for them.[50]

EXCLUDING FROM THE FELLOWSHIP: TRIALS AND DISCIPLINE

Another important component of creating early Methodist fellowship was excluding "disorderly persons." Methodists used various means for excluding such people, including church trials. In the following quote, bishops Coke and Asbury explain why it was necessary for Methodist preachers to have the authority to hold trials.

Our original design in forming our religious Society renders the existence of this authority in our ministers absolutely necessary. But what was this design? To raise a holy people. Our plan of economy shuts us up from the influence of any other motive in respect to our ministerial labors. It is impossible for us to enrich ourselves by Methodist preaching. Again, we bear a constant testimony against the pleasures of the world, and therefore should be esteemed,

---

47. Lucy Fanning Watson, Experiences, 42.
48. Bunn hopes the preaching and testifying of God's word is going well.
49. "Zion's prosperity" means the good welfare of the church.
50. [Seely Bunn], "From Seely Bunn, to the Rev. Dr. Coke. George-Town and City Washington, March 6, 1805," *Methodist Magazine* (London) 28 (1805): 475.

esteemed, even by our own people, as the greatest of hypocrites, if we indulged ourselves in them and would soon be excluded the connection by the various means of trial to which all of us are subject. And as to honor, we are almost the only despised people in Christendom as a religious body. The secondary rank of mankind and the poor are the only persons (with a few exceptions) who receive the Gospel. The rich and great, in general, even those who have not embraced the favorite doctrines of the times, will not submit to the way of the cross, but, on the contrary, look down on the preachers of it as the greatest enthusiasts.[51] And shall we thus sacrifice all that the world holds dear and at the same time lose the only aim of all our public labors, by false complaisance? No. We will have a holy people, or none. In every part of our economy, as well as doctrine, we aim at crucifixion to the world and love to God.[52]

Early Methodists exhibited some variety in working out the disciplining of persons who threatened Methodist fellowship and witness. In 1810, for example, the administrative meeting for the Berkley circuit in Maryland recommended creating an oversight committee in every local congregation.

1st) We the members of the quarterly meeting conference for Berkley Circuit do recommend to the preachers and leaders[53] to appoint committees in every society where it is practicable for the purpose of preserving peace and order among the members.

2nd) The duties of the said committees shall be as follows, namely, they shall meet once a month and examine the state of the Church. And, if they find any disorderly persons among them, they shall make immediate arrangements to wait on them privately, or call on them to attend the committees that they may be talked to by two or three persons as the Gospel and discipline directs.[54] And, if in private or public they can give satisfaction, [it is] well. If not,

---

51. A commonly used derision aimed at the Methodists in the eighteenth century, referring to their sense of having received direct assurance of their doctrines and experiences of salvation. See chapter 6 for more information.

52. *Doctrines and Discipline of the Methodist Episcopal Church* (1798), 167.

53. Meaning local preachers and class leaders.

54. Compare Matthew 18:16. By "discipline," this quarterly meeting conference means the organizational manual for the church.

then they shall cite them before the preachers and the Church or a selected number of them for a final hearing.

3rd) Whenever it may be prudent and practical, the committee and preacher shall meet and examine the peace and order of the church once a quarter and consult on the best means to carry on the work of God.[55]

Methodist preachers also regulated membership by issuing quarterly tickets to members in good standing. Bishops Coke and Asbury explain how doing so gives the itinerant preachers a regular opportunity to speak to every member and preserve "the purity of our church."

He is to deliver tickets quarterly to each member of the society with a portion of the word of God printed on them. This is of no small moment for the preservation of our discipline and the purity of our church. To admit frequently unawakened[56] persons to our society meetings and love feasts would be to throw a damp on those profitable assemblies, and cramp, if not entirely destroy, that liberty of speech, which is always made a peculiar blessing to earnest believers and sincere seekers of salvation. Besides, this regulation affords the preacher who holds the office now under consideration, an opportunity of speaking closely to every person under his care on the state of their souls.[57]

Some members struggled to maintain a strong witness in their lifestyle. In the following case, the administrative body for one Maryland circuit attempts to help a member be faithful in paying debts. As a later entry shows, this attempt was not successful, resulting ultimately in the dismissal of the member, Robert Shankling.

Robert Shankling restored to membership upon the following conditions: first, the said Shankling shall produce a testimonial declaring his regular standing as a member in Ireland; second, deposit in the hands of two trustees, William Smith and Jesse

---

55. Berkley Circuit Steward's Book 1807–1820, 43-44.
56. The bishops are referring to the frequent admission of those who do not have any spiritual awakening through the gospel.
57. *Doctrines and Discipline of the Methodist Episcopal Church* (1798), 73.

Jarratt, annual sums of money for the discharge of his debts. And the trustees aforesaid shall report to the quarterly meeting conferences at least once a year what money is deposited for the satisfaction of the said Robert Shankling's creditors, which shall be applied to the discharge of his debts or paid to any agent appointed by his creditors by the trustees before mentioned.[58]

[Later the circuit's quarterly meeting conference took stronger action:]

At a quarterly meeting conference held at Fork meeting house in August 1801: Resolved that Robert Shankling shall no longer have the privilege of society until he acts agreeably to the rules of conference held at the Fork meeting on August 10, 1799.[59]

It was not only rank-and-file members who were tried and excluded. The records are full of examples of itinerant and local preachers brought to trial. Local preachers were tried at quarterly meeting conferences, the administrative meetings for circuits. Itinerant preachers were tried at annual conferences. In the following case, John Chalmers, a local preacher in the Baltimore circuit, is stripped of his privilege to preach and, seemingly, expelled from the church for drinking and sexual misconduct.

At a meeting of the undersigned committee of local preachers, called by the Reverend Job Guest, assistant preacher on the Baltimore circuit, to hear and determine on several charges made against John Chalmers, Senior, a local preacher

Present: Reverend Job Guest, Assistant Preacher
Greenberry Ridgley
Abner Neal
Joseph Shane
John Baxley

After hearing the first charge read, made by a colored girl in Annapolis named Charily [Charity?], [we] are of [the] opinion that in the liberties taken with her John Chalmers had no criminal intentions but that his conduct was highly imprudent and derogatory to the character of a Christian and minister.

After hearing the second charge read, made by a colored woman of Annapolis named Forty, [we] are of the same opinion, as above

---

58. Harford Circuit Quarterly Meeting Conference Records 1799–1830, 10 August 1799.
59. Ibid., August 1801.

stated, and that such conduct with a woman professing religion was calculated to excite her to sin and was very reprehensible in him, both as a preacher and a man professing religion, [and it] was criminal or sinful.

The opinion of the committee on the third charge is (that however lawful the use of spirituous liquor may be as a medicine) that J. Chalmers indulged himself too freely in the use of the same, so as to affect him in a moral point of view and to implicate him in the eyes of men.

On the fourth charge, [we] the committee are of [the] opinion that J. Chalmers has been reprehensibly negligent in the management of his business in some instances, but cannot say positively that he is wanting in principle.

And, lastly, [we] the committee are of [the] opinion that, taking into view all of the charges above stated, the aforesaid John Chalmers ought to be suspended from all official services in the Methodist Episcopal Church. Given under our hands this 13th day of January 1813 at the city of Baltimore

> Greenberry Ridgley
> Abner Neal
> Joseph Shane
> John Baxley

This [quarterly meeting] conference proceeded to examine the charges and evidences exhibited to the foregoing committee previous to its award [i.e., determination] and unanimously agreed to first confirm the award, and secondly, to expel the said John Chalmers, Sr., who omitted to appear and make defense.[60]

In the following account, John Jeremiah Jacob, a local preacher in western Maryland, describes the trial of an African American member accused of sexual misconduct. Jacob's description hints at a public nature of these events.

I was this day witness to a scene that I shall long remember. It was calculated to awaken some of the finest feelings of human nature. The case was this: a Black man, a member of our church, was charged by the class leader[61] with an attempt upon the chastity

---

60. Baltimore Circuit Steward's Book 1794–1815, 153-55.
61. A class leader was in charge of the weekly small group meetings required for early Methodists. Much of the ongoing pastoral care also came from class leaders.

of a young black woman, [who was] also a member. The case being stated, the parties were heard. And the young woman gave us such strong proof of her chastity—the soundness of her reasoning with her tempter and yet in language so modest—that I was delighted with her story. I could but express my satisfaction at her conduct. But, when the sentence of excommunication passed on the poor Black man, a scene truly melting followed. A girl about 12 yrs old (I suppose his daughter) ran to him, caught him around the neck, and wept as if her very heart would break.[62]

In a series of journal entries, itinerant preacher George Wells describes a variety of circumstances in which he applies disciplinary standards for membership in 1792.

We went to Brother Marchel's. Brother H. preached. It was a good time. I sifted the class here. I asked them one by one if they still love the Methodist doctrine and discipline. And, as I examined one, I asked the rest if they had anything against the moral conduct of the person. They all stood the test but one.[63]

I went to Brother Barnet's and rested in peace. This man drinks drams [distilled alcohol] and I cannot have that fellowship with him that I want to have. But I intend to have him out of society tomorrow or [have him take] leave of drinking drams. O Lord, help me.[64]

I went to the chapel and preached and met the class. I then gave Brother B[arnet]. his choice either to leave of dram drinking or leave society. He chose to leave society. I should not have given him this choice but [it was necessary] if could not be proved that he was drunk and it could be discerned by his talk as well as breath that he had been drinking. To drink spirituous liquors at all is contrary to our Rules unless in cases of necessity.[65]

---

62. Holmes, "The Life and Diary of the Reverend John Jeremiah Jacob," 152.

63. George Wells, Journal, 18 February 1792.

64. Ibid., 13 March 1792.

65. Ibid., 14 March 1792. Wells is referring to the passage in the foundational membership document called the "General Rules."

I went to Brother P. and preached and met the class. There was a woman wanted to join who is thought to be a witch. I would not join her but allowed her to meet a while with us.[66]

We went up to one Rigleys, a man that I turned out for selling a Negro slave. We preach here now instead of W.[67]

I went to Winchester [Virginia] and preached at 11 o'clock under a great cross. I preached again at 4 and then inquired into the state of the societies. I found 48 Whites. I excommunicated two and joined one. We had a good time. The rules have not been rigorously enough enforced here. Neither has the preacher whom I have succeeded left them in any order. I have not wondered why almost everybody loves some men as preachers when I have found out that they [the indulgent preachers] let them do as they please.[68]

At night I met the Black people. As soon as meeting began, I felt miserable and so continued through the meeting. And then I found out the cause: the Devil had entered one of the greatest professors[69] almost among them and he was the first one I spoke to. He had been guilty of making too free with a woman,[70] who accused him. I heard them both. They had no other witnesses to what each of them said than themselves. I thought they were both guilty in some measure. I suspended them both till I shall see further into the conduct. O Lord, keep me.[71]

Itinerant James Meacham exercises authority to remove disorderly members who had attended balls and barbeques.

In class I found two members who had walked disorderly. I tried to get an acknowledgment from them but I could not. Neither would promise to reform so I told them that they could not be considered members any longer than they continued to evidence their

---

66. Ibid., 29 March 1792.

67. Ibid., 25 April 1792.

68. Ibid., 24 June 1792.

69. A "professor" is one who can profess religion or salvation in Christ. The term does not mean any sort of teacher.

70. Wells seems to mean the man had been flirting too freely with the woman.

71. George Wells, Journal, 4 August 1792.

desire of salvation by coming out from among the wicked and betake [i.e., devote] themselves to the use of all the means of grace,[72] which I presumed they did not do while they would [go to] balls and barbeques and spend whole days & nights in that ungodly devotion.

Wednesday 7 [February 1797]

The young woman who was dismissed yesterday came desiring to be received again, but I told her I could do nothing in that business until I came round again as I would wish to know whether the society could fellowship [with] her or not.[73]

Itinerant William Spencer publicly rebukes a disorderly member in 1790. Although he accepts doing so as a necessary part of his ministry, he finds it difficult to do.

This day I preached at Brother [?] Austin's to a small congregation. I bless God I had liberty in speaking his Word.[74] Sinners were much affected and the dear Christians much comforted. But, alas, after I was done preaching, my poor soul was grieved. One of the members had wounded the cause of God, and I had to deal with the said member in a very severe manner. He was unteachable and not willing to submit to reproof. I was distressed indeed. O! what disagreeable business this is to my poor soul. I love to see professors of religion adorn their profession by their upright walking but poor, miserable backsliders grieve my very soul. I pray the Lord Jesus Christ to direct me how to act in all things to his glory. Dear Lord! I am weak, but thou art strong. I am foolish and ignorant, but thou art wise. O! help me, my blessed Master and be my all in all.[75]

OFFENDING THE HOLINESS OF GOD'S PEOPLE: CHARGEABLE OFFENSES

A variety of offenses resulted in discipline or expulsion. John Early, later a bishop, reports on action taken against itinerant preachers for a variety of reasons.

---

72. Meacham is referring to requirements of the General Rules. See chapter 6 on the means of grace.

73. James Meacham, Journal, 6-7 February 1797.

74. "To have liberty in speaking" means to preach easily and with power.

75. William Spencer, Diary, 26 April 1790.

[Annual] Conference lasted until Tuesday, the first of March [1814]. More of the preachers than usual located.[76] Sixteen were received. Enoch Jones expelled. Erasmus Thomson suspended from his ministerial office and preaching for 12 months for marrying a wicked woman. W. Puckett dropped for getting married and stopping before he traveled 2 years. Surely that was a season of affliction for many camps and particularly in attention to primitive Methodism and discipline.[77]

In one of the strangest scenes from early Methodism, former itinerant preacher Jeremiah Minter describes his expulsion by an annual conference for having received voluntary castration.

I was excommunicated ... and what I had done with the most upright motive was thus, to the view of mankind, turned upside down as a sin. But, although it is now thirteen years since, I have never to this day felt it a sin in my conscience. My viewing and embracing in a literal sense the 12th verse of the 19th chapter of Matthew was the offence.[78] If any thing else was included with it as grounds of excommunication, I am willing and desirous to know what it was for I was sent out of the [annual] conference room thrice, and the sentence was passed and sent to me by an individual, in these words, to the best of my remembrance, "You are excluded from among us, and should you come to any of our love feasts or sacraments, you are to be received as a stranger."[79]

Drunkenness was a constant problem. The Frederick circuit disciplined Peter Storm for this infraction in 1810.

Peter Storm, a local preacher being found guilty of intoxication by a committee, was brought before the above [quarterly meeting] conference agreeable to [church] rule, and was excluded by the majority of the Conference.[80]

---

76. That is, they ceased to itinerate actively.

77. John Early, Journal, 21 February 1814.

78. In Minter's King James Bible, Matthew 19:12 says "For there are some eunuchs, which were so born from their mother's womb: and there are some eunuchs, which were made eunuchs of men: and there be eunuchs, which have made themselves eunuchs for the kingdom of heaven's sake. He that is able to receive it, let him receive it."

79. Jeremiah Minter, ed., *Devout Letters*, 49. See also Minter, *Brief Account*, 13-17.

80. Frederick Circuit, Proceedings of the Quarterly Conferences, 9 June 1810.

Hateful threats could bring a rebuke as Benjamin Bowen, a local preacher, discovered.

We the subscribers appointed by Job Guest, assistant preacher in the Baltimore Circuit, for the time being as a committee to investigate a charge brought against Benjamin Bowen, a local preacher in the Methodist Church in said circuit, for an expression which he made use of in the presence of a number of his fellow jurors at July term last[81] in the city of Baltimore "in saying that he wished, or that it would not have been much matter, if all the persons in the house in Charles Street, or all the Tories[82] that were there had been killed." After hearing the evidences relative to the charge and also the candid acknowledgment of the said Benjamin Bowen, as to the latter part of the said charge. That it was an expression he had hastily made use of, for which he is since sorry for, we are therefore of [the] opinion that his conduct has been highly censurable and also unbecoming a preacher of the Gospel of Jesus Christ, and that for [the] time to come he should be more guarded in his expressions and general deportment.

December 21, 1812   Rob Carnan

Cornelius H. Girt

Laban Welsh[83]

The Frederick circuit disciplines William Patterson, a local preacher, for excessive indebtedness and improper letter writing.

First, a charge was brought against William Patterson for contracting debts and not taking proper steps to pay the same. William Patterson having assured the conference that he had the probable means of shortly discharging the debts complained of, the complaint was dismissed for the present.

Secondly, another charge [was] brought against William Patterson for improper conduct towards William Fichtick in a letter to him. And the [quarterly meeting] conference unanimously voted that he ought no longer to be considered as a preacher in the Methodist Church.[84]

---

81. Referring to the schedule for the civil courts.

82. In light of the war with Britain, Bowen must have been unhappy with those sympathetic to England.

83. Baltimore Circuit Steward's Book 1794–1815, 151-52.

84. Frederick Circuit, Proceedings of the Quarterly Conferences, 22 August 1807.

Another circuit does not renew one local preacher's license after he is discovered to hold theological views that were too Calvinist for Methodist liking. A local preacher's license has to be renewed yearly.

The renewal of Aquella Galloway's license was withheld in consequence of his dissenting from the articles of our religion[85] in the matter of predestination, but [he] was retained as a private member in the church.[86]

Dancing moves Noah Fidler, an itinerant preacher, to remove one woman from membership.

I preached at Luis Pierce's on John 5:39 with considerable liberty. After preaching, I read a young woman out of society for dancing, who afterwards told a lie that she might continue in.[87]

Gossip, seemingly, is the grounds for excommunicating another woman.

There was a tolerable assembly at Best's meeting house. I had some liberty in preaching but had a disagreeable time afterwards. A young woman in society being accused and convicted of false and mischievous talk, I was under the necessity of expelling her from [the] society.[88] She wept when she knew her situation. I feel afraid that is not all the purging necessary for this society.[89]

---

85. Referring to doctrinal statements adopted from the organization of the church in 1784. The Methodist articles were adapted from those of the Church of England.

86. Great Falls Circuit Quarterly Meeting Conference Minutes, 12-13 October 1816.

87. Noah Fidler, Journal, 1 June 1802.

88. Society refers to a local Methodist congregation. Being expelled from the society means having her membership in the Methodist church terminated.

89. Jeremiah Norman, Journal, 31 August 1800.

CHAPTER 9
DEATH

The typical early Methodist's experience of death was different than most today will experience. For one thing, death was essentially a domestic occurrence. Dying at home, surrounded by family and acquaintances (including numerous fellow Methodists), was much more common than dying in a hospital or other institutional setting. Likewise, the deceased's body was prepared at home by family and friends rather than by professionals hired for the job. Moreover, the lack of modern medical care meant that early Methodists were quite familiar with people dying in any station of life, and at any time. Death was not restricted largely to the elderly, as it is now. Early Methodists were accustomed to losing their children, their spouses, and their friends at any age. Death's suddenness was sobering. Who knew what any day might bring? This daily wondering made the expectation of death much more vivid.

Of course, such proximity to death was not unique to early Methodists. They shared it with surrounding Christians. They also shared the general structures of their spirituality of death with those other traditions who embraced the basic perspectives of the "religion of the heart." Even so, how early Methodists dealt with death was in some ways a microcosm of everything they held essential to what it meant to be a Methodist.[1] This was particularly

---

1. A. Gregory Schneider, "The Ritual of Happy Dying among Early American Methodists," *Church History* 56 (1987): 349 and 353-54. Compare the Methodists' attitudes toward death with other Protestants in Jeffrey VanderWilt, "Singing about Death in American Protestant Hymnody," *Wonderful Words of Life: Hymns in American Protestant History & Theology*, ed. Richard J. Mouw and Mark A. Noll (Grand Rapids: Eerdmans, 2004), 179-204.

true of how they approached death. Every Methodist's aspiration was to come to the point of death having so "mortified the flesh" that death was welcomed. In this way they could approach death with no fear but with complete assurance. To expire using one's last breath to shout praises to God, testify to God's mercy in Jesus Christ, and exhort the bystanders to be faithful was the pinnacle of Methodist spirituality. This was a "happy death," a phenomenon so important to them that reporting accounts of happy deaths was an important part of all Methodist spirituality from the earliest phases of the movement in the 1740s.[2]

As the term "happy death" suggests, death was a complex paradox in early Methodist spirituality. In some respects, the time of death was the most important moment in a Methodist's life; from another angle, it was the least. In some respects, contemplating death marked what was most essential in being Methodist; on the other hand, Methodist piety about death was hardly unique. The complexity of the paradox existed at many levels.

One of the most important paradoxes of death for Methodists was that there were both known and unknown qualities to death. The known aspect was death's inevitability, death was something that all people had to face. There was no question: "certain comes the awful hour." But there was a question as to when it would come; it was a "time unknown." Within this tension, room existed for the Methodist message of judgment and grace. The tension also provided the impulse for Methodists to see all living as preparation for dying.

The dual possibility of how one approached one's own death—either in fear or in confidence—highlights another of the fundamental paradoxes in death. To early Methodists death was both punishment and promise. The former was rooted in their understanding of the larger sweep of salvation history. Death entered human experience through the sin of the first person, Adam. In this cosmic understanding death was not just a natural completion to a life cycle. Death was an intrusion into the design of human life as

---

2. John Wesley requested accounts of such "happy deaths" be sent to him by his itinerant preachers starting in this decade. For the broader context of Wesley's understanding of assurance and fear in relation to dying, see Kenneth J. Collins, "John Wesley and the Fear of Death as a Standard of Conversion," in *Conversion in the Wesleyan Tradition*, ed. Kenneth J. Collins and John H. Tyson (Nashville: Abingdon, 2001), 56-68.

a punishment by God for Adam's sin. The punishment continued for all Adam's descendants.[3] Death was a sign of God's righteous judgment upon human sinfulness.

Yet the prospect of death also held out promise. As many of the pieces below put it, the righteous could look forward to death as release from pain and toils. By death all troubles created by the "wicked" would be escaped. And, even better, with death the Christian could begin to anticipate the wonderful joy of heaven, a realm of endless pleasures with God and God's people.

The paradox of punishment and promise had preaching value. As a punishment, the approach of death could be lifted up as a warning to the complacent and the ungodly. As promise, on the other hand, death could be offered as opportunity. In using this dual character of death to confront or to comfort, as the case may be, Methodists connected death's exhortatory value to the paradox of death's known and unknown qualities. Death was coming (the known quality) but one never knew exactly when (the unknown aspect). The result was a vivid concern for one's readiness for death. The Methodists saw this readiness as one of the hallmarks of the distinction between a godly person and a wicked one.

The goal for a Methodist was to live in such a way—faithful to Christ, denying the world and self—that she or he would answer in the face of death, "I am ready." The result for some was even a welcoming or desire for death. Sarah Jones, for example, as she became aware over time of the terminal quality of her illness, began to call for death. Long years of ascetic practices had already loosened her connections to this world. As she began to contemplate death's approach, she started anticipating the "celestial blessings" that awaited. She longed for death, saying, "my struggling soul can hardly stay."

Jones was following a Christian path well worn for the time. Recognizing life's transience along with a promise of greater communion with God after death, Methodists, among other like-minded Christians of the period, used death to develop a spiritual approach that sought a degree of detachment from the world. The

---

3. For the connection with John Wesley's views, see Thomas C. Oden, *John Wesley's Scriptural Christianity: A Plain Exposition of His Teaching on Christian Doctrine* (Grand Rapids: Zondervan Publishing House, 1994), 152 and 168.

refusal to be enamored of the pleasure of this world, along with the rigorous practices that they followed, bore fruit for many Methodists on their deathbeds. To die a "happy death" was, as Cynthia Lyerly has put it, "emblematic of the success of Methodist asceticism." Life's sufferings were training for death as the most important moment of self-denial in a Methodist's life.[4]

The root spiritual issue was the ultimate object of a person's trust. Here, too, there was a fundamental contrast. The fallacy, in Methodist opinion, was to place one's trust in the things of this life. Given how quickly one could face death, this was surely foolish. There is only one who is ultimately dependable and trustworthy. That one is God.

This all-encompassing trust in God extended even to the Methodists' sense that death's coming was God's doing. This was another paradox regarding death: God was the author of life, but in some mysterious way God used death and was even the one who brought it. Contrasting God's steadfastness with life's transience was fundamental to an early Methodist worldview. This world and life in it were not dependable. God was totally dependable, even if not totally predictable.

God was also good. God's activity was likewise good even if not totally understandable. Methodists called such activity God's providence and encouraged all to trust in the character of God that stood behind it. In the middle of their grief, the Methodist use of the term "providence" was a statement of faith. It called for trusting resignation. It assumed that there was something of God behind the calamity of death.

One can see here the piety of a people faced by widespread death and bolstered by a view of God as all-powerful and all-merciful. Death was an ultimate concern over which they had little control, but surely God did. One can also sense their recognition of death's potency and speed in an age where medical options were much more limited than now. To have trusting resignation in God's providence was even more poignant in the death of Methodist children. The backdrop of death provided the relief that made fundamental Christian virtues stand out the clearest. The fundamental qualities of someone who had "true religion" were resignation, trust, readi-

---

4. Lyerly, *Methodism and the Southern Mind*, 42, 44.

ness, detachment from the world, and a confident assurance through God.

These virtues merged in the "happy death." With family and friends gathered round, the dying one felt an overwhelming sense of joy in knowing the graciousness of God. The key qualities of the happy death were assurance and joy, resulting in the dying person's praise of God and exhortation of those around. Since being "happy" was a kind of ecstatic state, shouting and visions were also common.

Happy deaths were a countercultural statement to the world. Methodists saw them as an embodiment of the power of grace in contrast to the false promises of this life's allures. In their understanding, dying "happy" reflected the success of their distinctive ethos.[5] This is why they "trained" for happy deaths by cultivating mortification of the flesh, in quest of holiness and the enjoyment of God's love in Jesus Christ.[6] The deaths that the training made possible provided a witness to those who had not yet been made "happy" by grace. If one was in dread of death, the death of a "happy" Methodist witnessed that such dread was not necessary. Experiencing God's grace provided an alternative to fear. Although death was inevitable, fearing it was not.

Simply put, Methodists desired to live well in grace in order to die well in grace. While such concern for the "art" of dying well did not originate with them, the American Methodist practice of it bore the marks of their time and place. By dying well among their American family and acquaintances, Methodists desired to bear witness to a God whose grace in Jesus Christ had conquered even the dreadful sting of death. To have lived so as to die in such a way as to bear this witness in a sinful world—the world of the early American republic—they considered a fitting climax for a Methodist's spiritual journey.

The selections gathered below represent the breadth of early Methodists, bridging ministerial status, gender, and race. The main group of excerpts deals with their contemplation of death itself, expressing both their fears and hopes of this inevitability. The sheer number of entries mirrors how frequently Methodists contemplated

---

5. Schneider, "Ritual of Happy Dying," 350-53.
6. Cf. Lyerly, *Methodism and the Southern Mind*, 42.

death. These passages give some of the most common explanations of Methodist hope in the face of death as well as some of the more unusual. A specific section on the death of children reinforces how common—and sudden—Methodists understood death to be. The final set of selections, giving examples of "happy" deaths is a fitting conclusion for this whole book. Since early Methodists considered a "happy" death to be confirmation of their heart religion, these selections bring us back to the core of this people's spirituality.

CONTEMPLATING DEATH: FEAR AND HOPE

Before he preached a funeral for a woman in 1799, William Colbert wrote a short poem in his journal rejoicing in her arrival in heaven. Colbert's themes of hope are common ones for early Methodists: the deceased has arrived in heaven; heaven is a place where there is no trouble; we shall be reunited one day and all be joyfully engaged in worshipful fellowship with God.

Thursday 15 [August 1799] This morning retired into a little copse of woods and spent a few moments in composing the following lines on the departure of the unblemished Grace Griffith. (After which I went and preached her funeral on Matthew 25:10[7] and was glad of an opportunity of speaking of what God had done for her to an apparent decent congregation.)

Ah! Lovely Grace and art thou gone,
And art thou numbered with the dead:
Thy spirit up to Jesus flown
  Thy Living head?
There where the weary ever rest,
And wicked cease from troubling,
Thy seat, thou hast, among the blest,
  With Christ thy King.
There in a world of spirits bright,
Where endless pleasures banish pain,
Enrobed thou art in spotless white,

---

7. Probably the sermon focused on this part of the verse: "They that were ready went in with him to the marriage."

With Christ to reign.
Cease, O father, cease to mourn,
Mother, wipe your weeping eyes,
Grace's up to glory gone,
    Above the skies.
You, her brother, sister dear,
Rejoice, thy sister's gone to rest,
Her bright example follow here,
    And you'll be blest.
A few more rolling years at most,
Your Grace on that happy shore,
You'll meet with the celestial host
    To part no more.
For she the paths of virtue trod,
And that, in early stage of life,
And to the palace of her God,
    She's gone from strife.
Thy mournful nights, and days of pain
O happy Grace, now are o'er,
May we thee meet nor part again
    On that blest shore.
Where saints and Angels join the song
Of praise unto redeeming love
May this employ my heart and tongue.
    With Grace above.[8]

Itinerant preacher Ezekiel Cooper writes to comfort Rebecca Ridgely in Maryland at the death of her husband, Captain Charles Ridgely. Cooper's letter is sprinkled with biblical references intending on showing the transitory nature of life and dependability of God.

Annapolis

My dear Sister   July 16 1790

I now sit down to improve this opportunity of writing to you again. Have you yet received my last which I informed you of when I had the pleasure of seeing you in Baltimore? It is a little strange how letters miscarry when they have so little way to go.

---

8. William Colbert, Journal, 3:75-77.

You are now in mourning. Permit me to console with you in the loss of your bosom friend. Oh, sister, let this teach us the uncertainty of all things under the sun. Our life is as a dream or a vapor from passing away. I hear the Captain was taken very suddenly and went off. Be ye also ready, with Christ, for in such an hour as ye think not the Son of man cometh.[9] It is our great concern to be prepared for this inevitable lot. It is appointed once for man to die and after death the judgment.[10] But though your cause of sorrow is great, yet you have matter of rejoicing in a variety of instances, particularly that it is your privilege to have communion with the Father and the Son.[11] There is no friend like unto that heavenly and eternal friend. Unto him we are abundantly obligated as being the author of all our blessings. As we receive all good from his providential hand it is right we should with humble submission resign to any cross providences which he sees cause to send upon us. The Lord gave and the Lord taketh away; blessed be the name of the Lord.[12] It is trying to resign a friend into the hands of death, but why? All must die. Sympathy feels it is true, but still let us say, "Good is thy will, Parent of good."

I hope you enjoy the divine comfort in your soul, and are pressing forward toward your future inheritance. This is a great certainty: "There is no standing still in religion." What a pity it is that all men do not believe and know the joys in religion. True it is darkness has covered the face of the earth and gross darkness the mind of the people. The true light now shineth [and] the Sun of righteousness is dispensing his rays abroad.[13] I hope the time is hastening when vice and disobedience shall be all destroyed, and all from the greatest to the least know the Lord.

I am reasonable in body and mind. We have some encouragement in this place: once in a while a few drop in and walk the way of life. My sister, live near to God, be watchful, keep your soul alive, keep up that union with your Savior which you know [is] your duty and privilege. Pray for me, I am in love your brother in Christ.

[Signed] Ezekiel Cooper[14]

---

9. Matthew 24:44.
10. See Hebrews 9:27.
11. See 1 John 1:3.
12. See Job 1:21.
13. A compilation of biblical allusions: Isaiah 60:2, 1 John 2:8, and Malachi 4:2.
14. Ezekiel Cooper to Rebecca Ridgely, 16 July 1790.

Although Methodists thought death to be inevitable, fearing it was not. As this hymn based on Revelation 14:13 affirms, those who die in the Lord are blessed. What is to be feared, in early Methodist opinion, is not dying itself, but dying apart from Christ.

"For a saint's funeral"
1. Bless'd are the dead who, in the Lord,
Did live in life, and die in death;
For great is their divine reward
While sinners sink in endless wrath.

2. The saints who in their Lord expire,
Are lovely in his glorious sight.
Their fall shall raise them but the higher,
They sink to gain an endless height.

3. By death, from all their toils they rest,
No more in pain, nor pressed with care,
For grief, they lean on Jesus blessed,
For sorrow, dwell in joyous cheer.

4. For woe of absence from their love,
Eternal joy in him they have:
Their souls already are above,
And soon their dust shall leave the grave.

5. Then Christ the glorious light of heav'n,
Shall make their bodies like to his;
And while the proud away are driv'n
The pure shall rest in endless bliss.[15]

Christian comfort, according to this early nineteenth century hymn, is due to Jesus having gone the way of death before us.

1. Why do ye mourn departing friends,
Or shake at death's alarms?

---

15. Minter, *Hymns and Spiritual Songs*, 71.

'Tis but the voice that Jesus sends
To call them to his arms.

2. Why should we tremble to convey,
Their bodies to the tomb?
There the dear flesh of Jesus lay,
And left a long perfume.

3. The graves of all the saints he blest
And softened every bed;
Where should the dying members rest
But with their dying head?

4. Then let the last loud trumpet sound,
And bid his kindred rise;
Awake ye nations under ground,
Ye saints ascend the skies![16]

As Sarah Jones entered a phase of a terminal illness, she penned this poem about her aspirations for death. Jones always longed for a closer sense of fellowship with Christ, and death appeared to offer that prospect. She concludes by seeking such heavenly communion while still living.

Beyond the shores of death I see
Celestial blessings wait for me.
Soft angels beckon me away.
My struggling soul can hardly stay.

My Savior calls, my moments fly,
May every breath prepare to die.
Life's rapid current rolls amain.
I soon shall know to die is gain.[17]

Fluttering my spirit learns to fly
And converse with the troops on high.
I listen to their songs above
And find their music all is love.

---

16. Mead, *Hymns and Spiritual Songs*, 96-97.
17. See Philippians 1:21.

Why not begin my heaven here
Since Jesus Christ is always near?
What more can the first angel say,
"'Tis Jesus' smile makes perfect day."[18]

Lucy Watson draws upon the writings of John Wesley to support her beliefs that departed friends become angels. Watson's beliefs in this regard seem a minor theme in Methodist spirituality.

I am well pleased to find that Mr. Wesley sanctioned my belief, namely, that of the spirits of departed friends being our ministering angels. See vol. 9 [for the] Sermon "On Faith."

O may thine angels while I sleep,
Around my bed their vigils keep!
Their love angelical instill,
Stop all the consequence of ill
May thy celestial joys rehearse
And thought to thought with me converse
Or in my stead, the whole night long
Sing to my God a grateful song.[19]

These lines I adopt as agreeing with my experience.[20]

A solemn part of the routine of an annual conference, the yearly regional meeting of itinerant preachers for administrative purposes, was asking which itinerant preachers had died in the previous year. The names of the deceased are recorded in the minutes, along with a short biographical statement. The following entries are from 1791.

Quest[ion]. 9. Who have died this year?
Ans[wer]. 1. Wyatt Andrews, who died full of faith and the Holy Ghost. As long as he could ride, he traveled. And while he had breath, he praised God.

---

18. Sarah Anderson Jones, Diary, 8 November 1792.

19. John Wesley, Sermon 132, "On Faith," §12, *The Works of John Wesley* (Nashville: Abingdon, 1987), 4:197-98. The poem Wesley quotes is by Bishop Thomas Ken. Wesley adds this concluding thought to the poem: "And may not the Father of spirits allot this office jointly to angels, and human spirits waiting to be made perfect?"

20. Lucy Fanning Watson, "Experiences," 26.

2. Lemuel Andrews, four years a laborer in the vineyard of the Lord, who maintained a steady, upright walk, attentive to the work. His last days were the best to himself and the people he preached to. He died without any expressions of the fear of death.

3. Aaron Hutchinson, a man of clear understanding, gospel simplicity, and godly sincerity; [he was] blameless in his life, acceptable as a preacher, fruitful in his labors, which ended in the short space of four years. He was patient, resigned, and confident in his last moments.

4. Eliphalet Reed, a true Israelite, and not without his usefulness. His feeble system failed after three years labor; [he was] a man of a sweet spirit and humble walk with God.[21]

Framed as a self-reflective question, this hymn invites the singer to think about her or his readiness to die. Assuming that dread of death is a sign of guilt before God, it ends with the hopefulness of closer communion with Christ obtained by the righteous through death.

"Triumph over death."
1. And am I ready, or in dread?
The monster death is stalking round.
And numbers are already dead,
And I may be the next that's found.

2. The dread of death is proof of guilt.
The pure are glad that death will come,
The upright soul would faint and melt
To think this world its endless home.

3. Now then, I know my good estate,
For death has not a dread in me.
My God I love, the world I hate,
Then death would only set me free.

4. O death, thy sting my soul dreads not
Through thy dark valley is the way

---

21. *Minutes of the Methodist Conferences* (1813), 101.

To Christ, and glory in his court,
To Christ, and saints in endless day.[22]

Virginia itinerant William Spencer describes how experiencing a terminal illness can bring someone to spiritual seriousness.

Saturday, May 1 [1790] In the evening I walked about a mile to see a poor sick man, from all appearances just at the point of death. He had been a poor careless sinner all his lifetime, but when he came to see death as it was, staring him in the face, he was very serious and humble and asked me to pray for him. Accordingly, I called the family together and we sang a hymn by his bedside and went to prayer. After we had prayed, I talked a good deal with this poor creature about his soul. He was very penitent indeed. My soul was happy to see him so. O! that God may save his soul.[23]

Not all early Methodist hymns concerning death were intended to comfort. The following funeral hymn is an honest reflection about the inevitability of death and one's readiness for it. It was apparently used as a processional to the place of burial. (See the passage from William Colbert below.)

1. A solemn march we make
Towards the silent grave,
A lodging all must quickly take
And carnal pleasures leave.

2. Oh! What a striking scene
In this cold grave appears,
A mortal turned to dust again
Quite spun out all his years.

3. And we who now attend
Must soon resign our breath.
God will the solemn summons send
By dreadful ghastly death.

22. Minter, *Hymns and Spiritual Songs*, 31-32.
23. William Spencer, Diary, 1 May 1790.

4. If [I] the next should be
That crumbles with the dust,
My soul what then becomes of thee
Has thou a lot in Christ?

5. Now I'll prepare to meet
My Jesus at the bar.
Forever worship at his feet
And sing his praises there.[24]

Preacher William Colbert describes an 1805 funeral in Philadelphia. Colbert, a white preacher, participated in the funeral at Bethel Church, the African American congregation in that city. Some of the hymns Colbert mentions are included elsewhere in this chapter.

...in the afternoon attended the funeral of Charles Boston, a Black man, who was interred between the old and new walls of Bethel Church. A great multitude attended the funeral, which was conducted with a great degree of solemnity. Absalom Jones, Richard Allen, and James Champson walked before; James Smith, Jeffry Bula, and myself followed. The singers followed us, and the bearers them. The hymns sung were "Rejoice for a brother deceased," "Hark from the tombs," and "My God, my heart with love inflame." This was ended in the house. I then delivered a short oration, and we went to the grave singing "A solemn march we take." At the grave Absalom Jones, the African minister of the Episcopal Church, with a very audible voice went through the form of the burial of the dead. We then returned from the grave singing a hymn very applicable to the occasion and left the place.[25]

Methodist preachers used the fear of death to get the attention of their listeners. The following warning comes after three men had died in a small village in the winter of 1805–1806.

Some few days before last Christmas I [was] present at a two days meeting[26] we had in Romney, when, among other things,

---

24. Henry Bradford, Hymnbook, 14.
25. William Colbert, Journal, 5:129.
26. A "two days' meeting" was a kind of abbreviated camp meeting without the camping. It was two days full of preaching and other kinds of worship services.

Brother Ward told the people that they might, if they choose, reject the Gospel but that there was a preacher coming (meaning Death) that would take no denial [and] that they should hear him.[27]

As he compiled his handwritten hymnal, Henry Bradford included this short funeral hymn about the certainty of death. It ends by asking God to help us be prepared for this inevitability.

1. Hark from the tomb a doleful sound,
My ears attend the cry.
Ye living men come view the ground
Where you must shortly lie.

2. Princes, this clay must be your bed
In spite of all your powers.
The tall, the wise, the revered head
Must be as low as ours.

3. Great God, is this our certain doom
And are we still secure,
Still walking downward to the tomb
And yet prepare no more?

4. Grant us the pow'r of quickening grace
To fit our souls to fly.
Then when we drop this dying flesh
We'll rise above the sky.[28]

The following hymn also uses contemplation of death as a call to be spiritually prepared.

1. Death is a warning, known to all
Both old and young: a solemn call.
His time unknown moves on secure.
And certain comes the awful hour.

---

27. Holmes, "Life and Diary of ... John Jeremiah Jacob," 216.
28. Henry Bradford, Hymnbook, 7.

2. Hold, then, thou vanity of thought,
Consider death within, without;
His sway is spacious as the earth.
'Tis wise to be prepared for death.

3. Come, O ye living, view the dead.
Here lies the dust; the soul is fled,
Fled to the joys of saints on high,
Else dies the death that ne'er can die!

4. Remember he, so lately known
Move to and fro, pass up and down;
Now lies, with midnight silence, dead,
The grave his land, his house, his bed.

5. O lay to heart, who yet survive!
Short is the span from birth to grave!
Or do you think you've long to stay?
The more you should prepare the way![29]

THE DEATH OF CHILDREN

In a poem entitled "On the Death of a Child, five years of Age," African American Phillis Wheatley offers confidence to grieving parents about the better state of their deceased child. The poem ends on a note of praise. Wheatley's three offspring all died as children, the last in the same year that Wheatley died at the age of thirty-one. Wheatley's poem was included a few years after her death in the denominational periodical, which typically offered poetry considered edifying.

From dark abodes to fair ethereal light
Th' enraptur'd innocent has wing'd her flight;
On the kind bosom of eternal love
She finds unknown beatitude above.

---

29. Minter, *Hymns and Spiritual Songs*, 17-18.

This know, ye parents, nor her loss deplore,
She feels the iron-hand of pain no more;
The dispensations of unerring grace
Should turn your sorrows into grateful praise;
Let then no tears for her henceforward flow,
No more distres'd in our dark vale below.

Her morning-sun, which rose divinely bright,
Was quickly mantl'd with the gloom of night;
But hear in heaven's blest bowers your Nancy fair,
And learn to imitate her language there.

Thou, Lord, whom I behold with glory crown'd,
By what sweet name, and in what tuneful sound
Wilt thou be prais'd? Seraphic powers are faint
Infinite love and majesty to paint.
To thee let all their grateful voices raise,
And saints and angels join their songs of praise.[30]

A different note is sounded by Thomas Morrell, a preacher. He grieves the loss of his only son and then, a few days later, his father. Seeking an explanation for his son's death, Morrell contemplates several possible reasons. Although Morrell's reasoning might sound harsh to us, he was determined that God intended his son's death for a spiritual good.

On Thursday [September 16, 1805] morning, half after 12 o'clock [i.e., 12:30], departed this life my dear, my only child, my darling son, Francis A. Morrell. I am certain that both his mother and myself gave too much of our hearts and God in mercy took away our idol. From the day of his birth to the day of his death my prayer concerning him was "Lord, if he will be a wicked man to dishonor thee and finally lose his own soul, do take him away in his infancy." He was then, I believe, taken away "either in answer to prayer" or lest he should engage too much the hearts of his parents and thereby draw them away from God. I feel tenderly affected by

---

30. Phillis Wheatley, "On the Death of a Child, five years of Age," *Arminian Magazine* (Philadelphia) 1 (1789): 403.

this stroke of God's providence as a parent and as a man. But [I] am resigned as a Christian. My dear wife mourns much but is striving to be fully resigned to God. We both wish to feel and say "The Lord gave and the Lord hath taken away and blessed be his name."[31] Our prayer is "Lord, sanctify this death to the good of our souls."

Death! upon Death! On Wednesday night September 26, 1805 ten minutes before ten o'clock departed this life for a better world, my aged, my honored father, Jonathan Morrell.... Oh to know, to value and redeem my time in a suitable manner. Lord, sanctify this fresh stroke of thy providence to me and to my wife. May we be all devoted to God, and be ready to follow all those who have gone before us.[32]

The following hymn, "On the death of a child," shows how fragile early Methodists held life to be. It seems to temper the joy of a new birth with cautiousness about how quickly a child's life can end.

1. How near is death to life!
The child but lately born
Is gone and lives no more on earth.
The joy is now a moan!

2. As one seem birth and death,
So near in hourly risk;
And though we're slow to be prepared,
Death is not slow but brisk.

3. Let not the old rejoice,
Nor yet the strong and young,
In aught of earthly friends or wealth
We all to death belong.

4. Ah, let not parents hope,
Nor yet the children more,
That they shall find in earthly friends
A joy that shall endure.

---

31. Job 1:21.

32. Thomas Morrell, *The Journals of the Rev. Thomas Morrell*, ed. Michael J. McKay (Madison, N.J.: Historical Society, Northern New Jersey Conference, The United Methodist Church, 1984), 46-47.

5. Babes are from parents torn,
The parents torn from them,
For death is sure, and ever near,
However life may seem.[33]

ACCOUNTS OF "HAPPY" DEATHS

Jarena Lee describes a vision of the crucified Christ appearing above a dying young man who had not yet been converted. Lee proclaimed the gospel to the man, who apparently then believed.

When the hymn was finished, we all kneeled down to pray for him. While calling on the name of the Lord to have mercy on his soul and to grant him repentance unto life, it came suddenly into my mind never to rise from my knees until God should hear prayer in his behalf, until he should convert and save his soul.

Now, while I thus continued importuning heaven, as I felt I was led, a ray of light, more abundant, broke forth among us. There appeared to my view, though my eyes were closed, the Savior in full stature, nailed to the cross, just over the head of the young man, against the ceiling of the room. I cried out, "Brother, look up, the Savior is come. He will pardon you. Your sins he will forgive." My sorrow for the soul of the young man was gone; I could no longer pray—joy and rapture made it impossible. We rose up from our knees, when lo, his eyes were gazing with ecstasy upwards. Over his face there was an expression of joy. His lips were clothed in a sweet and holy smile but no sound came from his tongue. It was heard in its stillness of bliss; full of hope and immortality. Thus, as I held him by the hand, his happy and purified soul soared away, without a sign or a groan, to its eternal rest.[34]

Early Methodists were enamored of death accounts in which a Christian exhibited great joy in Christ to the point of death. A Maryland Methodist, Susan Wyval, dying in 1810 at the age of thirty, shows the ecstatic closeness to God that Methodists desired.

---

33. Minter, *Hymns and Spiritual Songs*, 80.
34. Jarena Lee, *Life*, 21.

About ten days before her dissolution, I found her filled with that joy which is unspeakable and full of glory: shouting and praising her adorable Lord and Savior, for what he had done for her soul and for the boundless prospects of glory which opened to her transported vision!

When I drew near her bedside, she thus addressed me; "All is well, my brother! Complete victory! No doubt, no fear! O that I could tell you what I feel and what views I have of glory! My tongue cannot express it!

> "Angels assist our mighty joys!
>   Strike all your harps of gold;
> But when you raise your highest notes,
>   His love can ne'er be told."[35]

Go, my flesh, and be refined in the dust, and be prepared to dwell in heaven forever! Praise him! Praise him! O, help me to praise the Lord!" The place was truly awful on account of the Divine presence! Every person in the room was bathed in tears while she was clapping her emaciated hands in token of victory!

The day before her departure I called to see her, and found her, surrounded by female friends, in an ecstasy, pouring out her soul in torrents of praise to God, in language which seemed to be almost more than human! Upon my approaching the bedside, she cried out, "The chariots are waiting! Victory! Complete victory! O, what glory opens to my view! Could I but tell you the sweetness that I feel! Never did I feel any thing like this before. The day is broke! The day is broke! Hail him! Hail him! Hail him!" And repeatedly clapped her dying hands in triumph over the King of Terrors.[36] She then requested us to pray and praise after which she cried out in these beautiful and solemn lines of the poet,

> "Soon shall I feel my heartstrings break!
>   How sweet my minutes roll;
> A mortal paleness on my cheek!
>   And glory in my soul!"[37]

---

35. From a hymn by Isaac Watts, eighteenth-century British hymn writer.
36. The devil.
37. From another hymn by Isaac Watts.

Then she said, "The convoy of angels is waiting—surely I see them! Look! I can almost point to where they are! Surely I see them!" [She was] Raising at the same time her feeble hands, and exerting every power of soul and body, as if she would rise to meet the celestial messengers!

"Glory!" "Praise him!" "Hallelujah!" "Victory!" and "Hail him! Hail him!" were alternately poured forth from her quivering lips and faltering tongue.

About three hours before her spirit returned to God, I saw her again for the last time on this mortal shore. Death had then nearly completed his conquest over all in her that was mortal. She was in the last struggle, just passing through the stream of death, with weeping friends silently viewing the arduous conflict. Her reason still maintained its empire. When I asked her, shall we pray and praise God with you, she could but just articulate "Yes; O yes!" When I asked her if Jesus was still precious with the last effort of expiring nature, she said, "Yes!"

Not long after this, like an expiring lamp, or the setting sun without a cloud, she fell asleep in the arms of Jesus![38]

George White narrates the death of a slave, Mary Henery, on 28 October 1809. Henery is "happy" at her death, shouting to the moment of death.

On my return home, I was informed by my family that sister Mary Henery had been sick for some considerable time and had repeatedly sent for me during my absence to visit her. I went immediately to her master's house (for she was a slave) to see her, and found her extremely weak, and exercised with great bodily pain. On my entering her room she cried out, "Glory to God, brother, have you come?" "Yes," said I, "Sister, for Christ's sake I have come."

I then inquired the state of her soul to which she replied, "I am as happy as I can be in the body." After which she sunk into a state of perfect insensibility to every outward object and to all appearance lay entirely lifeless for some time. But after so far recovering as to be able to speak, she broke out in loud shouts of praise to God

---

38. "A short account of the last illness and death of Susan Wyval; who departed this life, on Thursday, Oct. 25, 1810, in the thirtieth year of her age," *Methodist Magazine* (New York) 1 (1818): 181-83.

and said that while she was in that state she saw the gates of heaven opened and a beautiful company of shining personages arrayed in white robes. And observed that she had often thought how delightful the singing was in the Methodist church, but that was incomparable with the singing of these angels in glory....

Between eleven and twelve o'clock the following evening, she requested her mother to call the family together into her room. When they were come, she told them, that her soul, which was bound for heaven, would shortly quit the mortal body. But said she, "I shall give you the signal for my departure by shouting, being fully assured of dying triumphant in the faith."

As she drew near the moment she had said she should expire, she asked her mother (who was quite feeble) if she would shout with the rest present, when she gave the word, [a mother] who, although in great anguish of soul, on account of the prospect of parting with so excellent a child, told her she would, but not expecting the time was so near. But she soon repeated her request and said, "Mother, help me all you can to praise God. I know you are weak but come around my bed and get ready for the chariot is coming. Are you all ready? Are you all ready? Now! Now! Here it comes. Glory! Glory! Glory! Shout! Shout! Mother, are you shouting? Jane, are you shouting? Are you all shouting?" And thus continued till she expired....

I cannot but here remark, that while we see the souls of the righteous leaving the world, with loud shouts of joy and praise to God; that it is not to be wondered at that individuals or whole assemblies of the people of God, in life and health, being filled with the joys of that hope which is full or immortality, should sometimes "Clap their hand, and shout unto God with the voice of triumph," as says the Psalmist.[39] ... For that the upright in heart should shout for joy, while heavenly glory beams upon their ravished souls, can be nothing astonishing to the sincere Christian, who has "felt the powers of the world to come,"[40] where all the glorified host of God's elect continually cry with voices louder than many waters and mighty thunders, "Glory 'to him that has washed us from our sins in his own blood, and made us kings and priests unto God and the Father; to whom be glory for ever and ever.'"[41]

---

39. Psalm 47:1.
40. See Hebrews 6:5.
41. George White, *Brief Account*, 40-45. The scripture reference is Revelation 1:5-6.

SELECTED BIOGRAPHICAL SKETCHES

The following biographical sketches give some idea of the range of people who authored the material in this book. Not everyone whose material is contained in this book is included.

Abbott, Benjamin (1732–1796) was one of the earliest American-born Methodist preachers. Although he lacked formal education, his preaching was effective. Abbott's family came from Long Island and Pennsylvania. A series of dreams led to his conversion in the early 1770s after being a raucous, nominal Presbyterian for many years. He served as both a local and itinerant preacher. During his years preaching, he was a fervent advocate of sanctification. He is buried in Salem, New Jersey.

Adams, William (1759–1779) was born in Fairfax County, Virginia. Adams was converted in 1775 at the age of sixteen. Showing great spiritual prowess quickly, he was asked to assume spiritual charge of older Methodists living nearby. Soon he was holding class meetings and prayer meetings. He was sanctified in 1777. In 1779 he was received into trial status as an itinerant preacher assigned to the Baltimore circuit. He died that same year.

Allen, Richard (1760–1831) was born in Philadelphia as a slave of a Quaker master. Later he became the property of a Methodist farmer in Delaware. In his late teens he was converted and subsequently purchased his own freedom. By 1786 he returned to Philadelphia. Eventually Allen was instrumental in establishing a separate African American congregation (Bethel). In Philadelphia he served as a preacher, being ordained as a deacon in 1799 by special arrangement. He was the author of several works, including a hymnal published in 1801, the first hymnal for African Americans. In 1816 Bethel became the mother church of the African Methodist Episcopal Church, with Allen as the denomination's first bishop.

Asbury, Francis (1745–1816) was born near Birmingham, England. After serving as a craftsman for six and one-half years, he began a ministry as a Methodist preacher, serving several circuits in England before responding to John Wesley's call for itinerants to serve in America. Arriving in 1771, he never returned to England. In 1784 he became one of the Methodist Episcopal Church's founding bishops. More than anyone else, he guided the fledgling church during its first several decades. He never married, constantly traveling and preaching until the end of his life. His journeys through America were legendary. He died near Fredericksburg, Virginia, and is buried in Baltimore, Maryland.

Bangs, Nathan (1778–1862) was born and spent his early childhood in Connecticut. He spent his teen years in New York. He was ordained in 1804 and served six years as a missionary in Canada. In 1819, along with Freeborn Garrettson, he became one of the organizers of Methodism's Missionary Society. In 1820 he became the book agent of the Methodist Book Concern and served in that position for twenty years. He wrote the four-volume *History of the Methodist Episcopal Church* (published 1838–41).

Boehm, Henry (1775–1875) was born in Lancaster County, Pennsylvania, the youngest of eight children. His father, Martin Boehm, was a cofounder of the United Brethren Church. Henry was converted at the age of twenty-five and became a preacher for the next seventy-five years. He married Sarah Hill in 1818 at the age of forty-three. He was the traveling companion of Francis Asbury during Asbury's final years. During his itinerancy, Boehm preached in English and German, and at the age of ninety-one wrote *Reminiscences*, which tells about his father and numerous Methodist preachers.

Bradford, Henry (?) was a resident of Halifax County, North Carolina and apparently served as a local preacher in that area. Bishop Francis Asbury ordained him a deacon in 1804. Asbury's repeated references in his journal to Bradford suggest that his house was a common stop for the bishop on his journeys.

Bunn, Seely (1765–1834) was a native of Poughkeepsie, New York. During his childhood his family migrated frequently, finally settling in Berkley County, Virginia. He was converted in 1789. He served as an itinerant preacher from 1792 to 1814, when ill health forced him to quit. He was killed by a fall from a gig.

Caldwell, Nancy Woodward (1781–1865) was the daughter of one of the early settlers in part of Maine. She was born in North Yarmouth, Maine on 27 January 1781, and heard Methodist preaching around 1795 from Joel Ketchum. She and her family joined the Methodists shortly before her conversion at age seventeen. She married William Caldwell of Oxford County and had several children.

Coke, Thomas (1747–1814) was educated at the University of Oxford and ordained as a priest in the Church of England. He joined the Methodists and became a valuable assistant to John Wesley. In 1784 Wesley consecrated Coke as the first superintendent of American Methodism and dispatched him to America to ordain and consecrate Francis Asbury as a co-superintendent (bishop) in the newly formed Methodist Episcopal Church. After the Christmas Conference of 1784, he went to the West Indies and other foreign mission fields as an evangelist. He also worked with Asbury to abolish slavery and found the first America Methodist college (appropriately called Cokesbury College). Coke died at sea on his way to begin a Methodist mission in India and Ceylon. During his lifetime, he produced a six-volume commentary on the Bible, a history of the West Indies, and a co-authored biography of John Wesley.

Colbert, William (d. 1833) is somewhat of a mystery, based on the memorial published after his death. Nothing was known of his birth and early life, although his family might have been from the mid-Atlantic states. (When appointed to upper Pennsylvania and New York in 1792, Colbert remarked that he was going quite a distance from his family.) He began itinerant preaching in 1790, serving a range of charges including circuits and city stations. He became a local preacher in 1811 but was readmitted as an itinerant in 1826.

Cooper, Ezekiel (1763–1847) was born in eastern Maryland and started his ministry as an itinerant preacher in 1784 in Maryland. He rode circuits and served as a presiding elder until 1798 when the church elected him book steward of the Methodist Book Concern, the official publishing ministry of the Methodist Church. Under Cooper's leadership, the Book Concern became the largest publishing establishment in America. (Further details can be found in the introduction.)

Dow, Lorenzo (1777–1834) was born in Connecticut and suffered from epilepsy and asthma. He was converted in the 1790s and began preaching at the age of eighteen. His eccentric style of dress and his unconventional, spellbinding way of preaching earned him the nickname "Crazy" Dow. He preached to more people, traveled more miles, and attracted larger crowds to camp meetings than any other preacher of his day.

Dow, Peggy (1780–1820) was born in Granville, Massachusetts. After her mother died when she was five months old, her father remarried. Eventually Peggy went to live with an older married sister in New York state. She married Lorenzo Dow and traveled some with him, including trips to England. She died on 6 January 1820 at the of age thirty-nine.

Dromgoole, Edward (1751–1835) was born in Sligo, Ireland, and immigrated to America. He joined the Methodists in 1770, and began to exhort in 1774. He itinerated from 1774–86 before locating in Brunswick County, Virginia. He continued as a local preacher and was finally ordained as an elder in 1815. During the Revolutionary War he was fined and imprisoned because he refused to join military service.

Elaw, Zilpha (1790–?) was born in Pennsylvania and converted through direct revelation. She joined the Methodists in 1808 and married Joseph Elaw in 1810. She had a successful preaching career in the Northeast and the slave states of the upper South. She also spent six years as a servant in a Quaker family and adopted their simple, neat style of dress.

Garrettson, Catherine Livingston (1752–1849) was a member of the New York Dutch aristocracy. Her father was a prominent judge. She was converted in 1786 and renounced the social privileges of her upbringing, marrying Freeborn Garrettson, a Maryland-born itinerant and antislavery activist, on June 30, 1793 against her family's better judgment. She and her husband opened their home and offered hospitality to itinerant Methodist preachers.

Garrettson, Freeborn (1752–1827) was born in Maryland. He was converted to Christ at age twenty-three in 1775 and became an itinerant preacher that same year. During the Revolutionary War he was persecuted for his pacifist stance. He also opposed slavery. Garrettson became one of the most important presiding elders of the Methodist Episcopal Church, particularly in the New York state area. In 1819 he became one of the founders of Methodism's Missionary Society.

Gatch, Philip (1751–1834) was born on 2 March 1751 in Maryland. He grew up in an Anglican family. In his early twenties he was converted after Methodist preaching had begun in his neighborhood. Sanctification came soon after, triggered by a reading of John Wesley's sermon entitled "Salvation by Faith." Gatch began public preaching in 1773. After several years of itinerant preaching, Gatch married and became a local preacher. In 1798 he moved with family and some friends to southwestern Ohio, where he became an important local preacher and his farm became the site of revival. Eventually he grew in civic rank too, and became a state judge.

Granade, John Adam (1775–1807) was born near Newbern in Jones County, North Carolina. He was teaching school in South Carolina in 1797 when he started attending Methodist class meetings. His conversion took place at a camp meeting in 1799. He was given permission to preach at the next quarterly meeting. Known as a poet and hymn writer, he was also known as the "wild man" because of his intense preaching and exhorting, mainly in western Methodism. After 1803, when he became ill, he was unable to itinerate. He married Polly Wynn in 1805 and died on 6 December 1807.

Jea, John (1773–?) was born in Old Callabar, southern Nigeria, and brought to America as a slave. He worked as a field slave for a New York Dutch family. He was converted at the age of fifteen and gained his freedom when he was miraculously able to read the book of John, though he was illiterate. In the late 1790s he traveled throughout New York and New Jersey as an itinerant preacher. He became a ship's cook and traveled the Atlantic as a sailor and itinerant preacher. He settled in Portsmouth, England, for a while around 1816.

Jessop, William (d. 1795) was originally from Delaware. He became an itinerant preacher in 1784, ministering in Virginia, Maryland, Delaware, Pennsylvania, New York, and Nova Scotia, Canada. He died in Lancaster County, Pennsylvania, in 1795.

Jones, Sarah (1753–1794) was a fervent Methodist in southern Virginia. In a church full of zealous Christians, Jones was one of the most intense and ecstatic. Married with children (one of her sons attended the denomination's first school, Cokesbury) and servants, she was an active correspondent with other Methodists. She was also a prolific poet. She died in Mecklenburg County, Virginia, after a lingering illness. (Further details can be found in the introduction.)

Keith, William (1776–1810) was born in Easton, Massachusetts. A long, up-and-down spiritual pilgrimage reached a new phase with his conversion at a quarterly meeting love feast in 1794. He joined a Methodist society and soon felt the call to preach. He first itinerated the Albany, New York, circuit in 1798. He left both the ministry and Methodism for a time. Seeking to regain his former spiritual vitality, he rejoined the Methodists and eventually served as both a local and itinerant preacher. He died while stationed in New York City in 1810, leaving a wife and three children.

Lee, Jarena (1783–1850) was born in Cape May, New Jersey, and converted under the preaching of Richard Allen. She became the first female preacher in the African Methodist Episcopal Church and preached her first sermon in 1819. In 1835 she traveled over seven hundred miles and preached almost as many sermons. Her journal tells that her exhortations won a great number of men and women to Christ.

Littlejohn, John (1755–1836) was born in Penrith, Cumberland County, England, in December 1755 as one of eight children. He journeyed to the North American colonies in 1767 and apprenticed himself to several merchants. He was converted in 1774 and began his itinerancy in Virginia in 1776. In December 1778 he married Monica Talbott of Fairfax City, Virginia, and settled soon thereafter in Leesburg, Virginia, serving as a local preacher there and later in Kentucky.

Meacham, James (1763–1820) was born in Sussex County, Virginia, on 7 April 1763. A distant relative through his mother was Revolutionary War hero Richard Henry Lee. According to family tradition, Meacham himself served in the war. He was born again in 1787, becoming an itinerant preacher within a year. He served circuits in Virginia and North Carolina before marrying Mary

Seward. Having married, he became a local preacher, a frequent occurrence in early Methodism. He died in 1820 in southern Virginia.

Newell, Fanny Butterfield (1793–1824) was well known in New England as a Methodist female exhorter. She was converted under the preaching of Henry Martin in October 1808 in her hometown of Sidney, Maine. She first exhorted publicly at her baptism. In 1810 she married Ebenezer Newell (an itinerant preacher) and began riding the preaching circuit with her husband.

Ormond, William (1769–1803) was a native of North Carolina. He was convicted of sin on 10 December 1787, converted a day later, and later sanctified on 20 March 1790. He became a traveling preacher in the year 1791, serving circuits in Maryland, Virginia, North and South Carolina, and Georgia. He died in Brunswick County, Virginia, on 30 October 1803.

Ridgely, Rebecca Dorsey (1739–1812) lived in Baltimore and married Captain Charles Ridgely around 1760. He was one of the city's richest merchants, and they became great supporters of Methodist itinerant preachers. Among early Methodists, Rebecca Dorsey Ridgely would have been much wealthier than average.

Spencer, William (1764–?) was born in Buckingham County, Virginia but moved to Prince Edward County while young. Spencer served as a Methodist circuit rider 1789–97 in Virginia and North Carolina. In 1797 he became a local preacher, teaching school in Prince Edward County. He moved to Lunenberg County in 1804.

Watson, Lucy Fanning (1755–?) was born in Gaston, Connecticut, the tenth and youngest child of John Fanning (Baptist merchant) and Abigail Minor (Presbyterian). She was first exposed to Methodism around 1780 when she attended a prayer meeting. She married William Watson, a sea captain and ship owner.

Watters, William (1751–1833) was the first American-born itinerant preacher. He was born in Baltimore County, Maryland, to Church of England parents. First hearing Methodist preaching in 1770, he was converted in 1771. He became an itinerant preacher in 1773. Like many preachers for the time, he spent time as both an itinerant and a local preacher, alternating between the two.

Wheatley, Phillis (1753–1784) was purchased from a slave ship in Boston Harbor in 1761 as a sickly seven-year-old African girl by John Wheatley and his wife. By her teen years Phillis was writing excellent poetry. In 1773 the Wheatleys sent her to England for her health. There she befriended the Countess of Huntingdon, a Methodist sponsor who helped her publish *Poems on Various Subjects, Religious and Moral*, the first published book of poetry by an African American. The Wheatleys eventually freed her. She died at age thirty-one, after watching her three children die before her.

White, George (1764–1836) was born in Accomack, Virginia, and sold at one and one-half years of age to a slave master in Virginia. He gained his freedom from a Maryland planter while in his teens and became a rural laborer in New Jersey after an unsuccessful search for his mother. He traveled to New York City, became a Methodist, and was converted in 1795. At a camp meeting in 1804 White received a call to preach, and in 1807 he received a permit to exhort. It was 1816 before he would receive his deacon's orders. He traveled on Long Island and into New Jersey as an itinerant. In 1820 he joined Richard Allen's Bethel African Methodist Episcopal Church and continued to itinerate until 1829. White died on 12 January 1836 at the age of seventy-two. (More details are given in the introduction.)

Wooster, Hezekiah Calvin (1771–1798) was another itinerant preacher whose death cut short his ministry. Wooster died at the age of twenty-seven after having served as an itinerant minister for five years, mainly in Massachusetts, New York, New Jersey, and, finally, Canada. He died after a half-year illness.

REFERENCE BIBLIOGRAPHY

PRIMARY MATERIALS CITED

Accomack Circuit Quarterly Meeting Conference records, 1804–1825. Ms. Cokesbury United Methodist Church, Onancock, Va.

Allen, Richard. *A Collection of Spiritual Songs and Hymns, selected from various Authors.* Philadelphia: John Ormrod, 1801.

Allen, Richard. *The Life Experience and Gospel Labors of the Rt. Rev. Richard Allen.* Philadelphia: Martin & Boden, 1833; reprint, New York: Abingdon, 1960.

Allen, Richard and Jupiter Gibson. Letter to Ezekiel Cooper, Philadelphia, 22 February 1798. Ezekiel Cooper papers. The United Library at Garrett–Evangelical Theological Seminary and Seabury-Western Theological Seminary, Evanston, Ill.

Andrews, William L., editor. *Sisters of the Spirit: Three Black Women's Autobiographies of the Nineteenth Century.* Bloomington: Indiana University Press, 1986.

Asbury, Francis. *The Journal and Letters of Francis Asbury.* 3 vols. Edited by Elmer T. Clark. Nashville: Abingdon, 1958.

_____. "Letter to Thomas Coke (undated)." *Methodist Magazine* (London) 25 (1802): 218.

Baltimore Circuit Steward's Book, 1794–1815. Ms. Baltimore-Washington Conference Archives, The United Methodist Church, Lovely Lane Museum, Baltimore, Md.

Bangs, Nathan. Journal. Ms. Nathan Bangs papers. United Methodist Archives and History Center, Drew University, Madison, N.J.

Berkley Circuit Steward's Book, 1807–1820. Ms. Baltimore-Washington Conference Archives, The United Methodist Church, Lovely Lane Museum, Baltimore, Md.

Boehm, Henry. Journal. Ms. Henry Boehm Papers, United Methodist Archives and History Center, Drew University, Madison, N.J.

Boyd, William K. "A Journal and Travel of James Meacham." *Annual Publication of Historical Papers of the Historical Society of Trinity College* 10 (1914): 87-102.

Bradford, Henry. Hymnbook. Ms. Southern Historical Collection, Wilson Library, University of North Carolina, Chapel Hill, N.C.

Bruce, Philip. "An extract of a letter from Philip Bruce, elder of the Methodist Episcopal Church, to Bishop Coke, dated Portsmouth, Virginia, March 25, 1788," *Arminian Magazine* (Philadelphia) 2 (1790): 563-64.

Buff, Rachel. "The Experience of Rachel Buff of Talbot County, Maryland." Ms. Garrettson family papers, Box 1, Folder 23. United Methodist Archives and History Center, Drew University, Madison, N.J.

Bunn, Seely. "From Seely Bunn, to the Rev. Dr. Coke. George-Town and City Washington, March 6, 1805." *Methodist Magazine* (London) 28 (1805): 474-75.

Coker, Daniel. *A Dialogue Between a Virginian and an African Minister.* Baltimore: Benjamin Edes, 1810.

Colbert, William. "A Journal of the Travels of William Colbert Methodist Preacher thro' parts of Maryland, Pennsylvania, New York, Delaware, and Virginia in 1790 to 1838." Ts. United Methodist Archives and History Center, Drew University, Madison, N.J.

Colbert, William. Undated Letter to Ezekiel Cooper. Reproduced by Cooper in his "Letter to Thomas Coke. Philadelphia. 7 September 1801." *Methodist Magazine* (London) 25 (1802): 425.

A Collection of Spiritual Songs. Part of Which was never Published Before. Winchester, Ky. Ms. Methodist Episcopal Church Records (Vol. 416), Manuscripts and Archives Division, New York Public Library, Astor, Lenox, and Tilden Foundations, New York, N.Y.

Cooper, Ezekiel. "An Account of the Work of God at Baltimore, in a Letter to ———
———." *Arminian Magazine* (London) 13 (1790): 409.

_____. "His Book, Minutes of various points in religion common place book." Ms. Barratt's Chapel and Museum, Frederica, Del.

_____. Letter to Rebecca Ridgely, 16 July 1790. Ridgely-Pue Papers, 1748–1932, Ms. 693, Box 2. Manuscripts Department. H. Furlony Baldwin Library, Maryland Historical Society Library, Baltimore, Md.

_____. Papers (including Journal). The United Library at Garrett-Evangelical Theological Seminary and Seabury-Western Theological Seminary, Evanston, Ill.

Crowell, Seth. *The Journal of Seth Crowell; containing an Account of His Travels as a Methodist Preacher for Twelve Years.* New York: J. C. Totten, 1813.

Dailey, David. Diary. Ms. St. George's United Methodist Church, Philadelphia, Pa.

The Doctrines and Discipline of the Methodist Episcopal Church, in America. With Explanatory Notes, by Thomas Coke and Francis Asbury. 10th ed. Philadelphia: Henry Tuckniss, 1798; reprint, Nashville: Parthenon Press.

Dow, Lorenzo. *All the Polemical Works of Lorenzo Dow.* New York: J. C. Totten, 1814.

_____. *Vicissitudes in the Wilderness; Exemplified in the Journal of Peggy Dow.* 5th ed. Norwich, Conn.: William Faulkner, 1833.

Dromgoole, Edward. Papers (include a ms. collection of hymns titled "Spiritual Songs"). Southern Historical Collection, Wilson Library, University of North Carolina, Chapel Hill, N.C.

Early, John. "Journal of Bishop John Early who lived Jan. 1, 1786–Nov. 5, 1873." Ts.

Southern Historical Collection, Wilson Library, University of North Carolina, Chapel Hill, N.C.

Elaw, Zilpha. *Memoirs of the Life, Religious Experience, Ministerial Travels and Labours of Mrs. Zilpha Elaw, An American Female of Colour.* London: published by the author, 1846.

Extracts of Letters, Containing some Account of the Work of God Since the Year 1800, written by Preachers and Members of the Methodist Episcopal Church, to their Bishops. New York: J. C. Totten, 1805.

Ffirth, John. *Experience and Gospel Labors of the Rev. Benjamin Abbott; to which is annexed a Narrative of his Life and Death.* New York: Carlton & Phillips, 1853.

Fidler, Daniel. Notebooks 1794. Daniel Fidle Manuscript Collection. Ms. United Methodist Historical Society, Lovely Lane Museum, Baltimore, Md.

Fidler, Noah. Journal. Ts. Transcribed Annie L. Winstead. The Upper Room Devotional Library and Museum, Nashville, Tenn.

Frederick Circuit. "Proceedings of the Quarterly Conferences held in Frederick Circuit Commencing on the 14th Day of December 1805." Ms. photocopy. Wesley Theological Seminary, Washington, D.C.

Frye, Joseph. Letter to Thomas McCormick, 8 July 1813. Ms. Wesley Theological Seminary, Washington, D.C.

Garrettson, Catherine. Garrettson Family Papers. United Methodist Archives and History Center, Drew University, Madison, N.J.

Garrettson, Freeborn. Garrettson Family Papers. United Methodist Archives and History Center, Drew University, Madison, N.J.

Garrettson, R. "An Account of the Revival of the Work of God at Petersburg, in Virginia." *Arminian Magazine* (London) 13 (1790): 303.

Gatch, Philip. Papers. John W. Dickhart Library, The Methodist Theological School in Ohio, Delaware, Ohio.

Great Falls Circuit Quarterly Meeting Conference Minutes and Steward's Records 1809–1830. Ms. Baltimore-Washington Conference Archives, The United Methodist Church, Lovely Lane Museum, Baltimore, Md.

Greene, Myles. Journal. Ms. Rare Book, Manuscript, and Special Collections Library, Duke University Library, Durham, N.C.

Harford Circuit Quarterly Meeting Conference Records 1799–1830. Ms. Baltimore-Washington Conference Archives, The United Methodist Church, Lovely Lane Museum, Baltimore, Md.

Hibbard, Billy. *Memoirs of the Life and Travels of B. Hibbard.* New York, 1825.

Hills, Ebenezer. Hymnal. Ms. Ezekiel Cooper Papers, vol. 24, The United Library at Garrett-Evangelical Theological Seminary and Seabury-Western Theological Seminary, Evanston, Ill.

Hinde, Thomas S., editor. *The Pilgrim Songster.* Chillicothe, Ohio, 1815.

Hockhocking Circuit. Book of Records. Ms. Archives of Ohio United Methodism, Ohio Wesleyan University, Beeghly Library, Delaware, Ohio.

Holmes, Marjorie Moran. "The Life and Diary of the Reverend John Jeremiah Jacob (1757–1839)." Master's thesis, Duke University, 1941.

Horton, James P. *A Narrative of the Early Life, Remarkable Conversion, and Spiritual Labours of James P. Horton, Who has been a Member of the Methodist Episcopal Church Upward of Forty Years.* Printed for the author, 1839.

Humphrey, Richard A., comp. *History and Hymns of John Adam Granade: Holston's Pilgrim-Preacher-Poet.* N.p.: Commission on Archives and History, Holston Annual Conference, The United Methodist Church, 1991.

Jarratt, Devereux. *The Life of the Reverend Devereux Jarratt.* Baltimore: Warner & Hanna, 1806.

Jea, John. *The Life, History, and Unparalleled Sufferings of John Jea, The African Preacher.* Portsea, England, 1811?

Jessop, William. Journal (1788). Ms. United Methodist Archives and History Center, Drew University, Madison, N.J.

———. Journal (1790–1791). Ms. St. George's United Methodist Church, Philadelphia, Pa. [A much later, abbreviated handwritten copy of this journal can be found at the United Library at Garrett-Evangelical Theological Seminary and Seabury-Western Theological Seminary, Evanston, Ill.]

Jones, Sarah Anderson. Diary (1792–1793). Ms. Manuscript and Rare Books Department, Swem Library, College of William and Mary, Williamsburg, Va.

Keith, William. *The Experience of William Keith. [Written by Himself.] Together with Some Observations Conclusive of Divine Influence on the Mind of Man.* Utica: Seward, 1806.

Lakin, Benjamin. Journal. Ms. University of Chicago, Chicago, Ill. Some of Lakin's journal can be found in William Warren Sweet, *The Methodists.* Chicago: University of Chicago Press, 1946.

Lee Jarena. *Life and Religious Experience of Jarena Lee, A Coloured Lady.* Philadelphia: Printed and Published for the Author, 1836.

Littlejohn, John. Journal. Ts. Transcribed by Annie L. Winstead, Kentucky Conference Historical Society, Louisville, Ky. [Available on microfilm from Kentucky Wesleyan College, Owensboro, Ky.]

Madison Circuit Quarterly Meeting Conference records 1810–1825. Ms. Kentucky Wesleyan College Library, Owensboro, Ky.

Mann, Thomas. Journal. Ms. Rare Book, Manuscript, and Special Collections, Duke University, Durham, N.C.

Meacham, James. Journal and Papers. Rare Book, Manuscript, and Special Collections Library, Duke University, Durham, N.C.

Mead, Stith. *A General Selection of the Newest and Most Admired Hymns and Spiritual Songs Now in Use.* 2nd ed. Lynchburg: Jacob Haas, 1811.

———. "Letter to Thomas Coke. Georgia. 11 May 1802." *Methodist Magazine* (London) 25 (November 1802): 522-23.

Mills, Nathaniel. Journal and Papers. Ms. United Methodist Historical Society, Lovely Lane Museum, Baltimore, Md.

M'Lean, John. *Sketch of Rev. Philip Gatch.* Cincinnati: Swormstedt & Poe, 1854.

Minter, Jeremiah. *A Brief Account of the Religious Experience, Travels, Preaching, Persecutions from Evil Men, and God's Special Helps in the Faith and Life, etc.* Washington, 1817.

———, editor. *Devout Letters: or, Letters Spiritual and Friendly. Written by Mrs. Sarah Jones.* Alexandria: Samuel Snowden, 1804.

———. *Hymns and Spiritual Songs, For the Use of All Christians: (Never Before Published).* Baltimore: G. Dobbin and Murphy, 1809.

Minutes of the Methodist Conferences, annually held in America: from 1773–1813, inclusive. New York: D. Hitt and T. Ware, 1813.

Morrell, Thomas. *The Journals of the Rev. Thomas Morrell.* Edited by Michael J. McKay. N.p.: Historical Society, Greater New Jersey Conference, The United Methodist Church, 1984.

Newell, Fanny. *Memoirs of Fanny Newell; Written by Herself, and Published at her Particular Request,* 2nd ed. New York: Francis S. Wiggins, 1833.

Norman, Jeremiah. Journal. Ms. Stephen Beauregard Weeks Papers. Southern Historical Collection, Wilson Library, University of North Carolina, Chapel Hill, N.C.

Ormond, William. Papers. Ms. William Ormond Papers, Rare Book, Manuscript, and Special Collections Library, Duke University, Durham, N.C.

Phoebus, George A., compiler. *Beams of Light on Early Methodism in America.* New York: Phillips & Hunt; Cincinnati: Cranston & Stowe, 1887.

A Pocket Hymn-Book Designed as a Constant Companion for the Pious. Collected from Various Authors. 18th edition. Philadelphia: Parry Hall, 1793; reprint, Nashville: The United Methodist Publishing House, 1992.

Price, John. Sermon Book. Ms. St. George's United Methodist Church, Philadelphia, Pa.

Ridgely, Rebecca. "Reminiscences." Ms. Ridgely-Pue Papers, 1748–1932 (ms. 693, Box 2). Manuscripts Department, H. Furlony Baldwin Library, Maryland Historical Society, Baltimore, Md.

Simpson, Robert Drew, editor. *American Methodist Pioneer: The Life and Journals of The Rev. Freeborn Garrettson.* Rutland, Vt.: Academy Books, 1984.

Smith, Henry. *Recollections and Reflections of an Old Itinerant.* New York: Lane & Tippett, 1848.

Smyrna Circuit and Old Union Church Quarterly Meeting Conference Record Book 1800–1831. Ms. 929.3S9, record group 9551.000. Delaware State Archives, Dover, Del.

Spencer, William. Diary. Ms. on microfilm (m-50). Special Collections, John D. Rockefeller, Jr. Library, Colonial Williamsburg Foundation, Williamsburg, Va.

Tar River Circuit Quarterly Meeting Conference records 6-7 July 1800 (addressed to John Howell, Steward). Ms. William Ormond Papers. Rare Book, Manuscript, and Special Collections Library, Duke University, Durham, N.C.

Thompson, James O., editor. *Walking with God: Leaves from the Journal of Mrs. Nancy Caldwell.* Keyser, W. Va.: For Private Distribution, 1886.

Ward, Francis. *An Account of Three Camp-Meetings held by the Methodists, at Sharon, Litchfield County, Connecticut; at Rhinebeck, in Dutchess County; and at Petersburgh, In Rensselaer County, New-York State.* Brooklyn: Robinson & Little, 1806.

[Watson, John Fanning.] *Methodist Error; Or, Friendly, Christian Advice, To those Methodists, Who indulge in extravagant emotions and bodily exercises.* 2nd ed. Trenton: D. & E. Fenton, 1819.

Watson, Lucy Fanning. "Experiences & Incidences in the Life of Mrs. Lucy Watson, who died at Germantown, Pa. 5 June 1834, aged 79 years." Ms. Watson Family Papers (box 2, folder 4). The Joseph Downs Collection of Manuscripts and Printed Ephemera, Winterthur Museum, Winterthur, Del.

_____. Hymns and Poems (1786). Ms. Watson Family Papers (box 3).The Joseph Downs Collection of Manuscripts and Printed Ephemera, Winterthur Museum, Winterthur, Del.

Watters, William. *A Short Account of the Christian Experience, and Ministereal Labours, of William Watters*. Alexandria: S. Snowden, 1806.

Watts, James. Journal. Ts. United Methodist Historical Society, Lovely Lane Museum, Baltimore, Md. Copy and transcript courtesy of Janet and Jim Yost.

Wells, George. Journal. Ms. George Wells Manuscript Collection, United Methodist Historical Society, Lovely Lane Museum, Baltimore, Md.

Wheatley, Phillis. "On the Death of a Child, five years of Age." *Arminian Magazine* (Philadelphia) 1 (1789): 403.

White, George. *A Brief Account of the Life, Experience, Travels and Gospel Labours of George White, An African*. New York: John C. Totten, 1810.

[Wyval, Susan.] "A short account of the last illness and death of Susan Wyval; who departed this life, on Thursday, Oct. 25, 1810, in the thirtieth year of her age." *Methodist Magazine* (New York) 1 (1818): 181-83.

SELECT SECONDARY STUDIES

Andrews, Dee E. *The Methodists and Revolutionary America, 1760–1800: The Shaping of an Evangelical Culture*. Princeton: Princeton University Press, 2000.

Collins, Kenneth J. *The Scripture Way of Salvation: The Heart of John Wesley's Theology*. Nashville: Abingdon, 1997.

Hatch, Nathan O. and John H. Wigger, editors. *Methodism and the Shaping of American Culture*. Nashville: Kingswood Books, 2001.

Heyrman, Christine Leigh. *Southern Cross: The Beginnings of the Bible Belt*. Chapel Hill, N.C.: University of North Carolina Press, 1997.

Kirby, James E., Russell E. Richey, and Kenneth E. Rowe. *The Methodists*. Westport, Conn.: Greenwood Press, 1996.

Knight, Henry H., III. *The Presence of God in the Christian Life: John Wesley and the Means of Grace*. Metuchen, N.J.: Scarecrow Press, 1992.

Lyerly, Cynthia Lynn. *Methodism and the Southern Mind 1770–1810*. New York: Oxford University Press, 1998.

Maddox, Randy L. *Responsible Grace: John Wesley's Practical Theology*. Nashville: Kingswood Books, 1994.

Richey, Russell E. *Early American Methodism*. Bloomington: Indiana University Press, 1991.

_____. *The Methodist Conference in America: A History*. Nashville: Kingswood Books, 1996.

Richey, Russell E., Kenneth E. Rowe, and Jean Miller Schmidt, editors. *Perspectives on American Methodism: Interpretive Essays*. Nashville: Kingswood Books, 1993.

Richey, Russell E., Kenneth E. Rowe, and Jean Miller Schmidt, editors. *The Methodist Experience in America Volume II: Sourcebook*. Nashville: Abingdon, 2000.

Ruth, Lester. *A Little Heaven Below: Worship at Early Methodist Quarterly Meetings*. Nashville: Kingswood Books, 2000.

Schneider, A. Gregory. *The Way of the Cross Leads Home: The Domestication of American Methodism*. Bloomington: Indiana University Press, 1993.

Scott, Leland Howard. "The Message of Early American Methodism." In *The History of American Methodism*, 1:291-359. Edited by Emory Stevens Bucke. Nashville: Abingdon, 1964.

Taves, Ann. *Fits, Trances, & Visions: Experiencing Religion and Explaining Experience from Wesley to James*. Princeton: Princeton University Press, 1999.

Wigger, John H. *Taking Heaven by Storm: Methodism and the Rise of Popular Christianity in America*. New York: Oxford University Press, 1998.

Index of Names

SUBJECT INDEX

Printed in the United States
42972LVS00006B/109-117